Entrepreneurship

ENTREPRENEURSHIP
Creativity at Work

A Harvard Business Review Paperback

Harvard Business Review paperback No. 90076

ISBN 0-87584-285-2

The *Harvard Business Review* articles in this collection are
available as individual reprints. Discounts apply to quantity
purchases. For information and ordering contact Operations
Department, Harvard Business School Publishing Division,
Boston, MA 02163. Telephone: (617) 495-6192, 9 a.m. to 5
p.m. Eastern Time, Monday through Friday. Fax: (617)
495-6985, 24 hours a day.

Printed in the United States of America by Harvard
University, Office of the University Publisher.
93 92 91   5 4 3 2 1

Contents

Entrepreneurship and Competitiveness

Getting Started

Entrepreneurs aren't afraid to raise money, but are they prepared?

Everything You (Don't) Want to Know About Raising Capital

by Jeffry A. Timmons and Dale A. Sander

Most entrepreneurs understand that if the fundamentals of a business idea – the management team, the market opportunities, the operating systems and controls – are sound, chances are there's money out there. The challenge of landing that capital to grow a company can be exhilarating. But as exciting as the money search may be, it is equally threatening. Built into the process are certain harsh realities that can seriously damage a business. Entrepreneurs can't escape them but, by knowing what they are, can at least prepare for them.

☐ After ten years of hard work and sleepless nights to get the company to $5 million in sales, the founder of Seattle Software (the disguised name of a real company) was convinced he could hit $11 million in the next three years. All he needed was cash. Ten banks refused to extend his credit line and advised him to get more equity. He met a lawyer at a seminar for entrepreneurs who said he'd take the company public in Vancouver or London and raise $2.5 million fast. The founder was tempted to sign him on.

> **It's not enough to make a business plan and hire an adviser.**

☐ Texas Industrial (again, disguised) had grown from an idea to a $50 million-a-year leader in the industrial mowing-equipment business. The company wanted to keep growing and in 1987 decided it was time for an initial public offering. The underwriters agreed. They started the paperwork and scheduled a road show for early November.

The founders of both these companies thought they were prepared for the fund-raising process. They put together business plans and hired advisers. But that isn't enough. Every fund-raising strategy and every source of money implies certain out-of-pocket expenses and commitments of various kinds. Unless the entrepreneur has thought them through and decided how to handle them ahead of time, he or she may end up with a poorly structured deal or an inefficient search for capital.

Entrepreneurs shouldn't be afraid to seek the money they need. Though they may be setting sail on dark waters and will always be at a disadvantage when negotiating with people who make deals every day, they can take steps to ensure that they get the capital they need, when they need it, on terms that don't sacrifice their future options. The first of those steps is knowing the downside of the fund-raising process.

Raising money costs a lot

The lure of money leads founders to grossly underestimate the time, effort, and creative energy required to get the cash in the bank. This is perhaps the least appreciated aspect of raising money. In emerging companies, during the fund-raising cycle, managers commonly devote as much as half their time and most of their creative energy trying to raise outside capital. We've seen founders drop nearly everything else they were working on to find potential money sources and tell their story.

The process is stressful and can drag on for months as interested investors engage in "due diligence" examinations of the founder and the proposed business. Getting a yes can easily take six months; a no can take up to a year. All the while, the emotional and physical drain leaves little

Jeffry A. Timmons is the Frederic C. Hamilton Professor of Free Enterprise Studies at Babson College and the Class of 1954 Visiting Professor at Harvard Business School. Dale A. Sander is senior manager of Ernst & Young's San Diego office, where he consults with entrepreneurs in emerging businesses.

energy for running the business, and cash is flowing out rather than in. Young companies can go broke while the founders are trying to get capital to fund the next growth spurt.

Performance invariably suffers. Customers sense neglect, however subtle and unintended, employees and managers get less attention than they need and are accustomed to, small problems are overlooked. As a result, sales flatten or drop off, cash collections slow, and profits dwindle. And if the fund-raising effort ultimately fails, morale suffers and key

One company spent its seed money trying to find investors.

people may even leave. The effects can cripple a struggling young business.

One startup began its search for venture capital when, after nearly ten years of acquiring the relevant experience and developing a track record in their industry niche, the founders sensed an opportunity to launch a company in a field related to telecommunications. The three partners put up $100,000 of their own hard-earned cash as seed money to develop a business plan, and they set out to raise another $750,000. Eight months later, their seed money was spent, and every possible source of funding they could think of—including more than 25 venture capital firms and some investment bankers —had failed to deliver. The would-be founders had quit their good jobs, invested their nest eggs, and worked night and day for a venture that was failing before it even had a chance to get started.

The entrepreneurs might have spent their time and money differently. We asked them what their sales would have been if they had spent the $100,000 seed money over the previous 12 months to generate their first customers. Their answer? One million dollars. The founders had not been prepared to divert so much of their attention away from

getting the operations up and running. Raising money was actually less important to the company's viability than closing orders and collecting cash.

Even when the search for capital is successful, out-of-pocket costs can be surprisingly high. The costs of going public—fees to lawyers, underwriters, accountants, printers, and regulators—can run 15% to 20% of a smaller offering and can go as high as 35% in some instances. And a public company faces certain incremental costs after the issue, like administration costs and legal fees that increase with the need for more extensive reporting to comply with the SEC. In addition, there are directors' fees and liability insurance premiums that will also probably rise. These expenses often add up to $100,000 a year or more.

Similarly, bank loans over $1 million may require stringent audits and independent reviews to ensure that the values of inventory and receivables are bona fide. The recipient of the funds shoulders all these costs.

The demands on time and money are unavoidable. What entrepreneurs can avoid is the tendency to underestimate these costs and the failure to plan for them.

You have no privacy

Convincing a financial backer to part with money takes a good sales job—and information. When seeking funds, you must be prepared to tell 5, 10, even 50 different people whether you're dependent on one brilliant technician or engineer, what management's capabilities and shortcomings are, how much of the company you own, how you're compensated, and what your marketing and competitive strategies are. And you'll have to hand over your personal and corporate financial statements.

Revealing such guarded secrets makes entrepreneurs uneasy, and understandably so. Although most potential sources respect the venture's confidentiality, information sometimes leaks inadvertently—and with destructive consequences. In one instance, a startup team in Britain had devised a new automatic coin-

counting device for banks and large retailers. The product had a lot of promise, and the business plan was sound. When the lead investor was seeking coinvestors, he shared the business plan with a prospective investor who ultimately declined to participate. The deal came together anyway, but months later the entrepreneurs discovered that the investor, who had decided not to join, had shared the business plan with a competitor.

In another instance, an adviser was helping an entrepreneur sell his business to a Midwestern company. Sitting in the office of a senior bank officer who was considering financing the purchase, the seller asked for more information about the buyer's personal financial position. The bank officer called the buyer's bank a thousand miles away, got a low-level assistant on the line, and listened in amazement as the clerk said, "Yes, I've got his personal balance sheet right here," and proceeded to read it line by line.

The chance that information will get into the wrong hands is an inherent risk in the search for capital— and is one reason to make sure you

"Experts" may contact the sources they know—not the sources you need.

really need the money and are getting it from highly reputable sources. While you can't eliminate the risk, you can minimize it, by discussing the issue with the lead investor, avoiding some sources that are close to competitors, and talking to only reputable sources. You should in effect do your own "due diligence" on the sources by talking with entrepreneurs and reputable professional advisers who have dealt with them.

Experts can blow it

Decisions about how much money to raise, from what sources, in debt or equity, under what terms—all limit management in some way and create commitments that must be fulfilled. These commitments can cripple a growing business, yet managers are quick to delegate their fund-raising strategies to financial advisers. Unfortunately, not all advisers are equally skilled. And of course, it's the entrepreneur—not the outside expert—who must live or die by the consequences.

Opti-Com (the fictitious name of a real company) was a startup spun off from a public company in the fiber optics industry. Though not considered superstars, the startup managers were strong and credible. Their ambition was to take the company to $50 million in sales in five years (the "5-to-50 fantasy"), and they enlisted the help of a large, reputable accounting firm and a law firm to advise them, help prepare their business plan, and forge a fund-raising strategy. The resultant plan proposed to raise $750,000 for about 10% of the common stock.

The adviser urged Opti-Com's founders to submit the business plan to 16 blue-ribbon, mainstream venture capital firms in the Boston area; four months later, they had received 16 rejections. Next they were told to see venture capital firms of the same quality in New York, since—contrary to conventional money-raising wisdom—the others were "too close to home." A year later, the founders were still unsuccessful—and nearly out of money.

Opti-Com's problem was that the entrepreneurs blindly believed that the advisers knew the terrain and would get results. The fact is, the business proposal was not a mainstream venture capital deal, yet the search included none of the smaller, more specialized venture capital funds, private investors, or strategic partners that were more likely to fund that type of business. Furthermore, the deal was overvalued by three to four times, which undoubtedly turned off investors.

Opti-Com eventually changed its adviser. Under different guidance, the company approached a small Massachusetts fund specifically created to provide risk capital to emerging companies not robust enough to attract conventional venture capital but important to the state's economic renewal. This was the right fit. Opti-Com raised the capital it needed and at a valuation more in line with the market for startup deals: about 40% of the company instead of the 10% that the founders had offered.

Choose advisers who have raised money for companies just like yours.

The point is not to avoid using outside advisers but to be selective about them. One rule of thumb is to choose individuals who are actively involved in raising money for companies at your stage of growth, in your industry or area of technology, and with similar capital requirements.

Money isn't all the same

Although money drives your fund-raising effort, it's not the only thing potential financial partners have to offer. If you overlook considerations such as whether the partner has experience in the industry, contacts with potential suppliers or customers, and a good reputation, you may shortchange yourself.

How fast the investor can respond is sometimes another crucial variable. One management group had four weeks to raise $150 million to buy a car phone business before it would be auctioned on the open market. It didn't have enough time to put together a detailed business plan but presented a summary plan to five top venture capital and LBO firms.

One of the firms asked a revealing question: "How do you prevent these phones from being stolen? You can't penetrate the market unless you solve that problem." The founders soon concluded that this source was not worth pursuing. The firm obviously knew little about the business: at that time, car phones weren't stolen like CB radios because they couldn't be used until they'd gone through an authorized installation and activation. The entrepreneurs didn't have time to wait for the investor to get up to speed. They focused their efforts on two investors with experience in telecommunications and got a commitment expediently.

Yet another entrepreneur had a patented, innovative device for use by manufacturers of semiconductors. He was running out of cash from an earlier round of venture capital and needed more to get the product into production. His backers would not invest further since he was nearly two years behind his business plan.

When the well-known venture capital firms turned him down, he sought alternatives. He listed the device's most likely customers and approached the venture capital firms that backed those companies. The theory was that they would be able to recognize the technology's merit and the business opportunity. From a list of 12 active investors in the customer's industry, the entrepreneur landed three offers within three months, and the financing was closed soon thereafter.

The search is endless

After months of hard work and tough negotiations, cash hungry and unwary entrepreneurs are quick to conclude that the deal is closed with the handshake and letter-of-intent or executed-terms sheet. They relax the streetwise caution they've exercised so far and cut off discussions with alternative sources of funds. This can be a big mistake.

An entrepreneur and one of his vice presidents held simultaneous negotiations with several venture capitalists, three or four strategic partners, and the source of a bridge capital loan. After about six months, the company was down to 60 days of cash, and the prospective backer most interested in the deal knew it. It made a take-it-or-leave-it offer of a $10 million loan of 12% with warrants to acquire 10% of the company. The managers felt that while the deal wasn't cheap, it was less expensive than conventional venture capital, and they had few alternatives since none of the other negotiations had gotten that serious.

Yet the entrepreneurs were able to hide their bargaining weakness. Each time a round of negotiations was scheduled, the company founder made sure he scheduled another meeting that same afternoon several hours away. He created the effect of more intense discussion elsewhere than in fact existed. By saying that he had to get to Chicago to continue discussions with venture capitalist XYZ, the founder kept the investors wondering just how strong their position was.

The founder finally struck a deal with the one investor that was interested and on terms he was quite comfortable with. The company has since gone public and is a leader in its industry.

You can't trust your lawyer to read the fine print.

The lead entrepreneur understood what many others don't: you've got to assume the deal will never close and keep looking for investors even when one is seriously interested. While it's tempting to end the hard work of finding money, continuing the search not only saves time if the deal falls through but also strengthens your negotiating position.

Lawyers can't protect you

Why should you have to get involved in the minutiae of legal and accounting documents when you pay professionals big fees to handle them? Because you're the one who has to live with them.

Deals are structured many different ways. The legal documentation spells out the terms, covenants, conditions, responsibilities, and rights of the parties in the transaction. The money sources make deals every day, so naturally they're more comfortable with the process than the entrepreneur who is going through it for the first or second time. Covenants can deprive a company of the flexibility it needs to respond to unexpected situations, and lawyers, however competent and conscientious, can't know for sure what conditions and terms the business is unable to withstand.

Consider a small public company we'll call ComComp. After more than two months of tough negotiations with its bank to convert an unsecured demand bank note of over $1.5 million to a one-year term note, the final documentation arrived. Among the many covenants and conditions was one clause buried deep in the agreement: "Said loan will be due and payable on demand in the event there are any material events of any kind that could affect adversely the performance of the company."

The clause was so open to interpretation that it gave the bank, which was already adversarial, a loaded gun. Any unexpected event could be used to call the loan, thereby throwing an already troubled company into such turmoil that it probably would have been forced into bankruptcy. When the founders read the fine print, they knew instantly that the terms were unacceptable, and the agreement was then revised.

An infusion of capital—be it debt or equity, from private or institutional sources—can drive a company to new heights, or at least carry it through a trying period. Many financing alternatives exist for small enterprises, and entrepreneurs should not be afraid to use them.

They should, however, be prepared to invest the time and money to do a thorough and careful search for capital. The very process of raising money is costly and cumbersome. It cannot be done casually, nor can it be delegated. And it has inherent risks.

Since no deal is perfect and since even the most savvy entrepreneurs are at a disadvantage in negotiating with people who strike deals for a living, there's strong incentive for entrepreneurs to learn as much as they can about the process—including the very things they are probably least interested in knowing.

Reprint 89613

Growing Concerns

Edited by
Edwin Harwood

You *can* negotiate with venture capitalists

*Harold M. Hoffman
and James Blakey*

If you're an entrepreneur looking for venture capital, you're probably well aware of the frustrations in finding loose purse strings in the financial markets. Your business is too new or your product is still too untried to qualify for conventional intermediate- or long-term debt financing. Or, although you know you might qualify for a loan, you don't want to take on the risk of more debt.

You've already used your savings and borrowed from relatives to get the seed capital you need. And you may have reached the point where you're generating healthy sales figures. But you've still got a long way to go before you can think of a public offering, and you can't finance the growth you want from retained earnings alone.

You need equity capital. If your management has a good track record and your business has the potential to generate a very high return on investment—say 30% to 40% per year—professional venture capitalists may be prepared to fork over high-risk capital of $1 million or more to finance your growth. You don't have to have a high-tech company to qualify; venture capitalists will also invest in conventional businesses that offer high ROI potential. We have recently negotiated venture capital deals involving an oil-drilling equipment manufacturer, a movie distributor, and a financial newsletter publisher, among others.

Because you've heard that money talks when a deal gets struc-

tured, you may worry that if you rock the boat by demanding too much, the venture capital firm will lose interest. That's an understandable attitude; venture capital is hard to get and if you've gotten as far as the negotiating process, you're already among the lucky few.

But that doesn't mean you have to roll over and play dead. A venture capital investment is a business deal that you may have to live with for a long time. Although you'll have to give ground on many issues when you come to the bargaining table, there is always a point beyond which the deal no longer makes sense for you. You must draw a line and fight for the points that really count. The extent to which you can stand your ground will depend, of course, on the leverage you have in the negotiations. If your business already shows a profit or if you're selling a highly desirable service or product, you'll have more bargaining power than if your company is burning up cash because sales are still several years down the road.

Structuring the investment

Before you and the venture capitalists agree to a financing package, you have to settle two important issues: the worth of your business before the VCs put their money in and the

type of securities the VCs will receive in exchange for their investment.

Valuation. Although your company's tangible net worth (book value) may be low or negative, the fair market value may be higher because of proprietary technology, sales potential, or other factors. You can more easily defend the value you place on your company if your projections are prepared with the assistance of a reputable accounting firm. It also helps to bring to the negotiations valuation data for comparable business ventures.

It's important to negotiate hard for a reasonable valuation of your company because the amount of equity you give the VCs will depend largely on that calculation. Let's assume, for instance, that you and the venture capitalists agree that your business is now worth $4 million. Based on this valuation and the company's cash needs, you strike a deal whereby the VCs will invest $1 million. The company's worth accordingly rises to $5 million. The VCs' $1 million should therefore buy the equivalent of 20% of the total post-investment equity outstanding.

Capital structure. When it comes to capital structure, VCs like to have their cake and eat it too: they want equity because that will give them a big slice of the profits if your company succeeds, but they also want debt because debt holders get paid before equity holders if the company fails. So VCs usually invest in redeemable preferred stock or debentures. If things go well, the VCs can convert preferred stock or debentures to common stock. If things go badly, however, they will get paid before you and other holders of common stock.

If you have a choice, try to get the VCs to accept a capital structure that consists entirely of common stock, because it's simpler and keeps the balance sheet clean. Chances are, however, that you won't get them to

Messrs. Hoffman and Blakey are partners of Kronish, Lieb, Weiner and Hellman, a New York City law firm. They specialize in negotiating initial public offerings for private corporations as well as private placements and venture capital for both public and private corporations seeking new financing.

agree to this unless your bargaining position is extremely strong.

In some deals, the VCs ask for a debenture together with warrants that allow them to purchase common stock at a nominal price. Under this arrangement, the VCs really do get to eat their cake and have it too because they don't have to convert their debt to equity. They'll regain 100% of their investment when the debt is repaid and still share in the equity appreciation of the company when they exercise their warrants.

Although the documents used to create debentures, preferred stock, and warrants are usually so much boilerplate, they must still be reviewed with care. One consideration is the legal structure of the investment, because the laws that govern what a corporation can do with its securities vary from state to state. Some states, New York for example, do not permit issuance of preferred stock that is redeemable at the holder's option. Antidilution and liquidation provisions, which are discussed in the next section, can have unexpected effects if not carefully crafted. Subordination provisions in debentures are also important, because your trade creditors and institutional lenders will expect clear-cut language placing the VCs' claim to the company's assets behind their own.

Protecting the investment

Many venture capitalists seek to protect their investments by asking for antidilution, performance/forfeiture, and other protective provisions. Their concern over preserving the value of their capital is legitimate. At the same time, you should review these provisions carefully to make sure they are fair to you and any other founders.

Antidilution provisions. The VCs' preferred stock and debentures will be convertible, at their option, into common stock at a specified rate. Obviously, neither you nor the VCs expect the value of your company's stock to drop, but you can't control the value the market places on your business. If your company begins to do poorly and you need more money, you may have

no choice but to sell off new equity more cheaply than in the past. Once they have bought in, the VCs will want to be sure that later stock issuances won't water down the value of their investment.

Don't forget to negotiate for yourself.

Antidilution protection does not mean that an investment must always be convertible into a fixed percentage ownership share of the company, without regard to intervening growth and investment. As long as any new common stock is sold at a price equal to or higher than the rate at which the VCs can convert into common stock, their investment won't be diluted economically. Although their slice of the pie will shrink, the pie itself will grow at least commensurately. But if new common stock is sold for less than that price, the pie won't expand as quickly as the VCs' slice shrinks—and the VCs' investment will consequently be diluted. To guard against this outcome, the VCs' conversion right will usually include an antidilution adjustment, or "ratchet."

There are two kinds of ratchets, full and weighted. With a full ratchet, the rate for converting the VCs' debentures or preferred stock into common is reduced to the lowest price at which any common is subsequently sold—a situation that can have drastic consequences for you and other founders. If the company sells a single share cheaply, *all* the VCs' securities suddenly become convertible into common at that lower rate. The VCs can very quickly end up with the lion's share of the company.

Let's return to the situation in which a VC firm has invested $1 million and received a 20% share of your now $5 million company. On this basis, if your company started out with four million shares outstanding, the VCs' $1 million will be initially convertible at the rate of $1 per share into one million shares of stock (or 20% of the five million shares outstanding after conversion).

Under a full ratchet, if your company sells one share of common stock for 25 cents, the conversion rate of the VCs' securities will drop to that price. The VCs' $1 million will now buy four million common shares. After conversion, the VCs will thus own four million out of eight million shares, or 50% rather than 20% of the company. So even though the sale of this single share would have no material dilutive effect on the VCs' investment, under a full ratchet provision such a sale would severely reduce the value of the equity that you and any other founders hold.

The more common and equitable approach is to negotiate a weighted ratchet whereby the conversion rate for the VCs' shares is adjusted down to the weighted average price per share of all outstanding common after the issuance of cheaper stock. If only a few cheap shares are issued, the downward adjustment will be minor. The usual method is to treat all shares outstanding before the cheaper dilutive issuance as if they were floated at the initial conversion price.

Mechanics aside, negotiating the antidilution adjustment carefully is important because its purpose is to place any dilutive effect of a future stock issuance on you and the other founders, not on the VCs. You can, however, seek to moderate the effect of such a provision. For example, you can ask that any common shares issuable to the VCs on conversion of their preferred stock or debentures be included in the number of outstanding shares used for calculating the adjustment. This will spread the impact of a dilutive issuance over a larger number of shares. You can also request that any common shares sold cheaply to officers, directors, employees, or consultants—a customary practice in start-up situations, and one that benefits all investors—will not trigger the antidilution adjustment.

The risk posed by an antidilution provision, especially one with a full ratchet, is that you and other founders can be squeezed out if the company runs into serious financial problems. If the company's market value falls far enough below the dollar value of the VCs' original investment, an antidilution adjustment will not only wipe out your equity but can actually prevent you from seeking new investors, unless you can get the VCs to waive their antidilution rights.

Performance/forfeiture provisions. As a condition for investment, the VCs may subject your stock—including stock you acquired years earlier—to a performance/forfeiture arrangement. Under this provision, if the company fails to meet certain earnings or other targets, you must forfeit some or all of your stock.

A performance/forfeiture provision serves several purposes. For one, it protects the VCs from paying for an overvalued company. The valuation of unseasoned companies usually relies heavily on speculative sales and earnings projections. If you overestimated operating results by a wide margin, the VCs will have paid too much for their share of the company.

Because sales and earnings forecasts are only projections, not promises, the VCs cannot sue the company if management fails to perform as expected. But if you've agreed to a performance/forfeiture provision, they can compensate themselves by increasing their ownership interest at your expense.

Another reason the VCs may want this provision is that if the company doesn't do well, it will be free to reissue the forfeited stock to any new executives brought in without diluting the VCs' holdings. The performance/forfeiture provision also serves as a golden handcuff: it motivates you and any other founders to work hard and stick with the business.

If your company is in an early stage of development, you may have to place a large portion of your stock at risk of forfeiture because the company's future is still very uncertain. As time passes, your enterprise is more likely to gain in value and enjoy a more predictable future. Then you can legitimately refuse to agree to a forfeiture provision on the grounds that the company's valuation is realistic, based on past performance.

What should you negotiate for? If the VCs insist on including a forfeiture provision, you may be able to persuade them to include stock bonuses for performance that beats your sales and earnings projections. If you're expected to forfeit stock for failing to hit 80% of the sales or earnings targets in your business plan, for example, it stands to reason that you should get an equivalent bonus if you exceed those targets.

Employment contracts. The terms of the founders' employment are always part of the financing arrangement. The VCs will want an agreement covering your salary, bonuses, benefits, and the circumstances under which you can quit or be fired by the board.

It may come as a shock to realize that the VCs are making an investment in the company, not you. As companies grow, they often require professional management skills that you and the other founding entrepreneurs may lack. The time may come when the VCs think you're no longer competent to run the business and decide to terminate your employment.

If the VCs are buying a controlling interest, you should seek an employment contract of reasonable duration—at least two to three years. If your business is well past the start-up stage, you may want to negotiate a longer term of at least five years.

There is, however, one potential drawback: a long-term contract may prevent you from leaving the company to do other things. If the company is doing poorly, the VCs may want you to stay and keep trying after you've decided to move on. Although the VCs can't prevent your departure, they may be able to sue you for breach of contract. Also, your contract may preclude your working in the same industry once you quit.

The grounds on which the board can terminate your employment should be fully spelled out and kept narrow in scope. Good examples of reasonable and narrow grounds include a felony conviction, theft of company property, or chronic failure to carry out reasonable instructions from the board despite repeated requests. If you're fired and you decide to sue for wrongful termination, you'll find it easier to prove your case if specific grounds were written into your contract.

Here are some other provisions to check for in the employment agreement before signing the deal:

☐ Are you assured adequate advance notice of the board's decision not to renew your original contract or its decision to renew but on terms that are less beneficial to you?

☐ Are you getting an adequate severance package, including extended insurance coverage?

☐ If you're obligated not to compete with the company after termination, what is the scope and duration of your obligation? Are you only prohibited from hiring away employees and soliciting business from the company's established customers, or must you leave your line of business altogether?

☐ Is the company required to buy back any or all of your stock if you are terminated, or does it have the option of doing so? How will the price be determined? You should try to negotiate for an option to sell your stock back to the company according to a fixed formula (for instance, a certain multiple of earnings) in the event that you're fired. Many companies resist having to buy back equity, so you may have trouble cashing out unless you include this option in your contract.

You may, of course, persuade the VCs to accept an employment agreement that does not permit the board to terminate you. Moreover, your postemployment rights and obligations may vary depending on whether you quit of your own accord, did something egregiously wrong, or were simply fired because the board was unhappy with your performance.

Control. You will have to let the VCs share in running your company. In all likelihood you'll be required to retain a nationally recognized accounting firm to certify your annual financial statements. You may also have to accept the addition of managers recommended by the VCs to cover areas of the business they think need improvement. The VCs will usually place one of their representatives on your board and possibly more, depending on their ownership interest. Important decisions like whether to merge, liquidate assets, or sell stock will require their consent even if they have only a minority position.

> *If your business shows a profit, you'll have more bargaining power.*

Nevertheless, there is some room for negotiation when it comes to control provisions. If you and other founders agree to a deal that leaves you with a minority interest, ask for no less than the VCs would probably demand: that they guarantee you board representation and obtain your consent before making any major business decisions.

Shareholder agreements. In almost all deals, the VCs will also want the company's founders to enter into a shareholders' agreement. Such an agreement may require the founders to vote for one or more directors of the VCs' choosing. It may also grant the VCs majority control of the board if the business runs into serious trouble, even if they have only a minority interest.

Shareholder agreements can also govern the sale of stock, including newly issued shares. Under most arrangements, the seller is required to offer the stock to the company or other parties to the agreement (insiders) before selling to outsiders. The VCs may also want to include a cosale stipulation that would oblige any selling shareholder to arrange for the other insiders to participate in the sale to an extent proportionate to their holdings.

Usually the company is also bound to the shareholder agreement. Depending on the agreement, the company may have to offer stock to the VCs, to all parties to the agreement, or to all current shareholders (in proportion to their holdings) before issuing any new stock to a third party. Because this preemptive right to purchase additional shares allows investors to maintain an absolute percentage interest in the company, the VCs are almost certain to insist on having it. You should ask for no less for yourself. If the company issues more shares, you should have the same opportunity as the VCs to retain your current percentage of ownership.

Disclosure. Before the VCs hand over the money, they will doubtless want extensive disclosure about your company. You'll be asked to verify that the company is in good standing, has paid its taxes, and is in compliance with all laws. You must also establish that the company's financial statements are correct and that it has no agreements or contingent obligations other than those referred to in an attached disclosure schedule. You should seek, whenever possible, to narrow the scope of these representations and qualify them as being to the best of your knowledge at the time. Inclusion of any matter you think may apply will avoid later argument by the VCs that you failed to disclose relevant information.

It's a good idea to negotiate for a cushion in your favor, so that if there are omissions in your representations that later cost the company no more than, say, $50,000, the omissions won't be considered a breach of the representation. In addition, ask for a time limit on your representations about the company—they should not apply for more than six months to a year after the deal has been closed.

Cashing out the investment

In any venture capital deal, the VCs will be looking ahead to the day when they can liquidate their investment in your company. They'll likely want provisions written into the agreement that will give them the opportunity to cash out on favorable terms at a time of their choosing.

Registration rights. Federal securities laws (and the "blue sky" laws of many states) prohibit you from selling an interest in your company unless you have either filed a registration statement with the SEC or qualified for an exemption from registration. Registration is an expensive process, which most companies avoid by getting a "private placement" exemption. To qualify for this exemption, your company must approach no more than a small number of wealthy and sophisticated investors.

The securities laws also impose legal restrictions that generally will prevent the VCs and other shareholders from reselling any stock acquired under a private placement exemption for at least two years, and may limit the amount that can be sold without a registration even after that period. Accordingly, the VCs will probably want the right to require the company to register their stock at the company's expense.

The VCs' registration rights may include either piggyback rights, which require the company to include the VCs' shares only if the company itself decides to file a registration statement, or demand rights, which allow the VCs to force the company to file a registration statement covering their shares. In granting piggyback rights to the VCs, check to make sure that the provision includes you and the other shareholders on an equal basis and that the company's ability to grant future piggyback rights is not limited.

Demand rights should be negotiated with even greater care. Because of the expense, try to limit the VCs to one request for a demand registration, or they may keep the company in constant registration. Also, try to get them to agree to postpone exercising this right until after the company's first public offering. Without this restriction, the VCs may be able to force the company to go public before it can afford the heavy reporting and other burdens imposed on publicly held companies.

If you agree to registration rights, you should be sure to include yourself. As an insider, you will probably be subject to transfer limitations under the securities laws regardless of how long you have held your stock. If you don't have a contractual right to be included in a registration, you may find yourself squeezed out of a public offering by investors who do. Furthermore, be sure that the company is obliged to pay your registration expenses. If it isn't, you will have to pay a proportionate share of what can be an enormous bill—for lawyers, accountants, printers, state securities filings, and underwriters' expenses. (Certain states will not permit the company to pay insiders' registration expenses; if your underwriter wants to offer stock in those states, you may have to waive your registration rights.)

Liquidation and merger provisions. Provisions governing the liquidation or merger of your business are important, yet they are often overlooked. If you are not careful, you may unwittingly agree to a provision that harms you or creates windfall gains for the VCs in the event of a merger or other corporate combination.

If, for example, preferred shareholders are allowed to treat a merger like a liquidation, they can demand a cash payment at the time of the merger. This kind of provision makes the merger less appealing to a potential partner. It can kill a deal outright, or at least give the preferred shareholders leverage to extract other concessions—usually at your expense.

Clauses relating to liquidation preferences should also get careful scrutiny. Liquidation preferences specify the order in which holders of different classes of securities get paid and how much of the liquidation proceeds they can collect before other investors are repaid. Under some preference provisions, the VCs not only receive 100% of their initial investment back but also have the right to share in any remaining proceeds, as if the investment consisted of common stock.

One risk to you of such a provision is that the VCs may be better off if the company liquidates than if it remains in operation. While the company remains in business, the VCs can only participate as either holders of preferred stock or debt or holders of common stock. On liquidation, they can participate as both. Moreover, liquidation provisions don't apply just in cases of failure, when there is nothing left to distribute; companies are sometimes liquidated even when business is good. And the VCs may control the decision whether to liquidate.

Modifying rights. To avoid a situation in which a right given the VCs can block a transaction crucial to the company's survival, it's important to include a provision that allows the VCs' rights to be changed. The VCs' rights cannot be modified without their consent. Because you may have investments from a number of VCs, and you may therefore not be able to get a unanimous decision, you should try to get the VCs to agree in advance that a majority or two-thirds count of their combined interest can waive the VCs' rights on behalf of all.

The key to weathering the venture capital process is to put the transaction in perspective. When it's all over, your young and not particularly bankable company will have a large sum of cash to put to work. Although some things the VCs demand may seem ridiculous, burdensome, or even insulting, you can't expect to get that amount of money without a lot of strings attached—and some of the things they make you do may even be good for you.

Remember that even though funding risky ventures is their business, venture capitalists will do all they can to avoid losing their capital. Expect them to be tough negotiators.

But this doesn't mean that you don't have the right to protect your interests in the deal. You won't get your way on every provision, but you should be able to persuade the VCs to see matters from your point of view on some. The best strategy is to try to fight any provisions that will keep you from running your company effectively or that are clearly unfair to you, and not wrestle too hard over the others.

Your negotiations should be guided by a spirit of fairness and respect for each other's legitimate interests. Properly handled, these negotiations can build a foundation of trust and cooperation from the very start—giving your business the best possible chance for success. ▽

Reprint 87207

Arthur Rock

Strategy vs. tactics from a venture capitalist

Strategy is easy, but tactics are hard.

As a venture capitalist, I am often asked for my views on why some entrepreneurs succeed and others fail. Obviously, there are no cut-and-dried answers to that question. Still, a few general observations about how I evaluate new businesses should shed some light on what I think it takes to make an entrepreneurial venture thrive and grow.

Over the past 30 years, I estimate that I've looked at an average of one business plan per day, or about 300 a year, in addition to the large numbers of phone calls and business plans that simply are not appropriate. Of the 300 likely plans, I may invest in only one or two a year, and even among those carefully chosen few, I'd say that a good half fail to perform up to expectations. The problem with those companies (and with the ventures I choose *not* to take part in) is rarely one of strategy. Good ideas and good products are a dime a dozen. Good execution and good management—in a word, good *people*—are rare.

To put it another way, strategy is easy, but tactics—the day-to-day and month-to-month decisions required to manage a business—are hard. That's why I generally pay more attention to the people who prepare a business plan than to the proposal itself.

Another venture capitalist I know says, somewhat in jest, that the first thing he looks at in a business plan is the financial projections. Frankly, how anyone can figure out what sales and earnings and returns are going to be five years from now is beyond me. The first place I look is the résumés, usually found at the back. To me, they are the essence of any plan. (Maybe *no one* reads the middle section!)

I see the plan as really an opportunity to evaluate the people. If I like what I see in there, I try to find out more by sitting down and talking with the would-be entrepreneurs. I usually spend a long time on this. (Unless their first question is "How much money am I going to get?" Then the interview is very short.) I don't talk much during these meetings; I'm there to listen. I want to hear what they've got to say and see how they think.

Some of the questions I ask have little to do directly with the particular business under discussion: Whom do they know, and whom do they admire? What's their track record? What mistakes have they made in the past, and what have they learned from them? What is their attitude toward me as a potential investor—do they view me as a partner or as a necessary evil? I also ask specific questions about the kind of company they want to develop—say, whom do they plan to recruit, and how are they going to do it?

I am especially interested in what kind of financial people they intend to recruit. So many entrepreneurial companies make mistakes in the accounting end of the business. Many start shipping products before confirming that the orders are good, or that the customers will take the product, or that the accounts are collectible. Such endeavors are more concerned about making a short-term sales quota than about maximizing the long-term revenue stream.

Granted, the pressure on new businesses to make sales quotas is strong. And that's precisely why the company needs a very, very tough accounting department. Otherwise, it will get into trouble. I always ask what kind of chief financial officer the entrepreneurs plan to bring on board. If they understand the need for

Arthur Rock, principal of Arthur Rock & Company in San Francisco, has provided venture capital to help finance Fairchild Semiconductor, Scientific Data Systems, Teledyne, Intel, Diasonics, and Apple Computer, among other companies, and is presently on the board of directors of the latter four companies.

"Bad news, chief, we're facing a takeover bid by the Easter Bunny."

I get rid of the venture capitalists after they've made their investment?"

I'm looking for entrepreneurs who ask, "How can I make this business a success?"–not "How do I make a fortune?" And I prefer someone who *wants* me to play a role in the enterprise's decision making. Obviously, when they come to me entrepreneurs are interested in getting my money. Many have the attitude, "Uh oh, is this guy going to want to come to staff meetings and open his big mouth?" But they should realize that I can be a resource for them in more ways than one. I've been around for a long time; there just aren't many business problems that I haven't seen before. And most entrepreneurs can use all the help they can get in developing and implementing the tactics that will make them successful in the long run.

someone who will scrutinize the operation closely and impose appropriate controls, they are more likely to be able to translate their strategy into a going concern.

This may go without saying, but I also look at a person's motivation, commitment, and energy. Hard work alone doesn't bring success, of course, but all the effective entrepreneurs I've known have worked long, hard hours. And there's something more than the number of hours: the intensity of the hours. I think of two software entrepreneurs I know who are going at 110 miles per hour, 18 hours per day, 7 days a week. And they have instilled their intensity and their belief in the business in all the people who work for them.

Belief in the business, clearly, is critical. If you're going to succeed, you must have a burning desire to develop your idea; you must believe so firmly in the idea that everything else pales in comparison. I usually can tell the difference between people who have that fire in their stomachs and those who see their ideas primarily as a way to get rich. Far too many people are interested in building a financial empire instead of a great company.

I want to build great companies. That's how I get my kicks. I look for people who want the same thing.

At a presentation I gave recently, the audience's questions were all along the same lines: "What are the secrets to writing a business plan?" "How do I get in touch with venture capitalists?" "What percentage of the equity do I have to give to them?" No one asked me how to build a business! And here's a question that both amused me and bothered me: "How do

There's a thin line between refusing to accept criticism and sticking to your guns.

When I talk to an entrepreneur, I'm evaluating not only his (or her) motivation but also his character, his fiber. And the issue I set the most store by is whether he is honest with himself. It's essential to be totally, brutally honest about how well–or how badly–things are going. It's also very difficult.

Too many businesspeople delude themselves. They want so much to believe that they listen only to what they want to hear and see only what they want to see. A good example is a top executive in the parallel-processing industry; he believed his engineering people when they told him the product would be ready on time, and he believed his marketing people when they told him how much they could sell. So he developed a sales staff and doubled the size of the plant and built up inventories before he had a product to sell. The computer was late because of some last-minute bugs, and he was stuck with it all. The first 98% of designing a computer is easy; the bugs always come up in the last 2%. Fixing the problems took time, which ate up all kinds of overhead. And when he was finally ready, he couldn't meet the company's forecasts–which had been unrealistic from the beginning.

This story illustrates well my thesis that strategy is easy; execution is hard. The company's product was two years ahead of its competition. Execution of the idea, however, was terrible. That the strategy was good is obvious now; several other manufacturers have entered the field and are doing very well. But the company has lost the competitive advantage it would have enjoyed if its management had been better.

I can cite a similar example, also from the computer industry. The three people who started the company were the president, the manager of the software division, and the manager of the hardware division. The two managers kept telling the president that things were going swimmingly, and he wanted to believe what they said. Then one day, faced with an order the company couldn't fill, the software division manager called the president, who was out of town, and let forth a blast that in essence said, "We've been making a lot of mistakes we haven't told you about. We're at least a year behind."

Now, that's a ridiculous situation; the president should have known the status of product development. He had enough background in the field, and he knew the managers well enough that he shouldn't have been caught by surprise. But he didn't look closely enough, and he didn't ask the right questions. In the meantime, the business had a rather large marketing and sales force. Then the question became whether to keep the sales force (which by this time was fully trained but doing nothing) or to let everyone go and wait for the software to be finished. If the latter, they'd have to hire and train a new sales force—a no-win situation either way.

Failure to be honest with yourself is a problem in any business, but it is especially disastrous in an entrepreneurial company, where the risk-reward stakes are so high. As an entrepreneur, you can't afford to make mistakes because you don't have the time and resources needed to recover. Big corporations can live with setbacks and delays in their "skunkworks"; in a start-up situation, you'd better be right the first time.

After being honest with yourself, the next most essential characteristic for the entrepreneur is to know whom to listen to and when to listen, and then which questions to ask. Sometimes a CEO listens only to what he wants to hear beause he's afraid of the truth; in other cases, it's because he's arrogant or has surrounded himself with yes-men. A lot of managers simply will not accept criticism or suggestions from other people; they demand absolute loyalty from their subordinates and call disloyal anybody who tries to tell them something they don't want to hear.

It's usually easy to spot this trait by the way someone talks with outsiders about the organization. If the entrepreneur says, "This guy's lousy and that one doesn't know what he's doing, but I saved the company"—or if he explains how brilliantly he performed at his last job, even though he got fired—I get wary. That kind of attitude is a red flag, like the statement, "I'll be honest with you": you know you're not getting the whole story.

To be sure, there's a thin line between refusing to accept criticism and sticking to your guns. Good entrepreneurs are committed to their ideas. In fact, I knew one company was in trouble when the CEO accepted almost everything I told him without argument or question. But some people have an almost perverse desire to prove to the world that their way is the right way—and the only way. I remember one CEO who had a great strategy—an idea for a unique computer architecture—but who refused to accept any advice on anything from anyone, including potential customers. He ended up with a product that had to be totally re-engineered, and a weak staff. The company is now under new management and may be able to make something out of what is still a good idea, but the CEO's tunnel vision sure stalled it at the starting gate.

A great idea won't make it without great management.

Another important quality—one that also has to do with taking a hard look at oneself and one's situation—is to know when to bring in skills from outside and what kind of skills.

As I see it, a company's growth has three stages. During the start-up, the entrepreneur does everything himself: he's (or she's) involved in engineering the product, he makes sales calls himself, and so on. After a while, the company grows and he has to hire other people to do these things—a vice president of sales, a vice president of engineering—but they report directly to him, and he still knows everything that's going on.

The company reaches the third stage when it hits, say, $100 million to $200 million in sales. At that point, it's just too large for the president to be involved in all the doings. More management layers are in place and a fleet of executive vice presidents, and it now calls for entirely different skills to run the company than it did during its infancy. The president has to work through other people instead of doing it himself, and he has to get his information through two or more organizational layers.

The ideal would be a president who could manage a company at all three stages, starting the business from scratch and staying involved until he retires. Alfred Sloan at General Motors and Tom Watson at IBM were able to do just that, and the leaders of Teledyne and Intel have done it more recently.

But not all entrepreneurs can manage a large company. And many don't want to. Some people who relish business start-ups are simply not interested in running a formal, multitier organization. After Cray Computer grew to a fairly good size, for example, Seymour Cray wanted to get back to designing computers. Similarly, Apple Computer's Steve Wozniak and Steve Jobs (at least in the early stages) recognized that their genius was technical and promotional, not managerial, and that they needed experienced, professional managers to oversee their company's growth.

Other entrepreneurs have been less aware of their own limitations. Consider the experience of Diasonics and Daisy. Both flourished when they were small enough that their founders were able to control all aspects of the business. But they grew too fast, and the managers didn't realize that they now needed a different style of management and control. In both cases, a resounding initial success turned into an ignominious mess. And today, as a result, both enterprises have been reorganized.

Sometimes problems arise because the entrepreneur doesn't grasp the importance of strong management. I know of one young company that has already gone through two CEOs and is looking for a third. On the plus side, the men who founded the business acknowledged that they were engineers, not managers, and they went out and looked for a CEO. They considered their strategy so brilliant, though, that they figured anyone could carry it off. The first man they hired talked a good game but had been a disaster at two other corporations; eventually they had to let him go. He just couldn't manage the company. Then the directors hired another CEO who lasted only a few months. The company's product is still a good one, but without equally good leadership it may die in infancy.

The point of these examples is simple. If entrepreneurs do not have the skills required to manage the company, they should bring in an experienced professional. And they should never settle for someone mediocre by telling themselves that the business is such a winner that it doesn't need the management and controls that other companies do.

An entrepreneur without managerial savvy is just another promoter.

A great idea won't make it without great management. I am sometimes asked whether there is an "entrepreneurial personality." I suppose there are certain common qualities—a high energy level, strong commitment, and so on—but there are as many different personal styles as there are entrepreneurs. Henry Singleton of Teledyne, for example, reminds me of de Gaulle. He has a singleness of purpose, a tenacity that is just overpowering. He gives you absolute confidence in his ability to accomplish whatever he says he is going to do. Yet he's rather aloof, operating more or less by himself and dreaming up ideas in his corner office.

Max Palevsky, formerly at Scientific Data Systems (SDS), is, by contrast, a very warm person. At SDS he'd joke around with his employees and cajole them into doing what needed to be done. His very informal style was evidenced by his open shirt and feet up on the desk.

The CEO's personality is extremely important because it permeates the company, but there's no one style that seems to work better than another. What *is* important is to *have* a style. An "average Joe" won't inspire others and lead a business to success.

I look for an entrepreneur who can manage. A conventional manager isn't risk oriented enough to succeed with a new venture, while an entrepreneur without managerial savvy is just another promoter.

Good entrepreneurs are tough-minded with themselves and with their teams. They can make hard decisions. They have to be able to say, "No, that won't work" to colleagues who come to them with ideas, or to say, "That's a good idea but we can't do it because we have other priorities." To make such professional judgments, managers should ideally be well versed in the technology on which the company is based.

There are exceptions, of course. John Sculley at Apple Computer comes immediately to mind. When Apple was looking for someone to fill the top slot, it instructed the executive recruiter to find a CEO with a technical computer background. But the recruiter asked Apple to consider someone from left field (from the soft-drink industry), and I need not point out that the results have been excellent. It was a lucky fit. In fact, as far as the "secrets of entrepreneurial success" go, it's important to recognize that a little bit of luck helps and a lot of luck is even better.

Another company I know, formed by two young, inexperienced men, benefited from a lucky break. Though very knowledgeable, they seriously underestimated how long it would take to write the 1,500,000 lines of software code they needed to launch their product. Consequently, they were two years late in bringing the product to market. But the market was also slow in developing. If the product had been ready on time, the company probably would have gone bankrupt trying to sell something for which the market wasn't ready. As it turned out, the market and the product were ready at the same time, and the company could exploit the product without competition. Many business success stories are due at least in part to simple good luck.

I emphasize people rather than products, and for good reason. The biggest problem in starting high-tech businesses is the shortage of superior managers. There is too much money chasing too few good managers.

I have always preferred to wait and have entrepreneurs come to me, to approach me because they have a great desire to build a business. Now with all the megafunds available, it's often the venture capitalist who goes out to start a company and looks for people who can head it up.

Those who call us "vulture capitalists" do have a point; some venture capitalists lure away a company's best people, thus hampering its growth. How can an enterprise develop and thrive when its top executives are always being pursued to start new companies? Unfortunately, in the high-tech industries, more and more businesses are being formed simply to make a buck. As for myself, though, I will continue to look for the best people, not the largest untapped market or the highest projected returns or the cleverest business strategy.

After all, a good idea, unless it's executed, remains only a good idea. Good managers, on the other hand, can't lose. If their strategy doesn't work, they can develop another one. If a competitor comes along, they can turn to something else. Great people make great companies, and that's the kind of company I want to be a part of. ▽

Reprint 87612

"The first challenge, of course, will be to get the company back on track."

Growing Concerns

Topics of particular interest to owners and managers of smaller businesses

How to write a winning business plan

Stanley R. Rich and David E. Gumpert

The business plan admits the entrepreneur to the investment process. Without a plan furnished in advance, many investor groups won't even grant an interview. And the plan must be outstanding if it is to win investment funds.

Too many entrepreneurs, though, continue to believe that if they build a better mousetrap, the world will beat a path to their door. A good mousetrap is important, but it's only part of meeting the challenge. Also important is satisfying the needs of marketers and investors. Marketers want to see evidence of customer interest and a viable market. Investors want to know when they can cash out and how good the financial projections are. Drawing on their own experiences and those of the Massachusetts Institute of Technology Enterprise Forum, the authors show entrepreneurs how to write convincing and winning business plans.

Mr. Rich has helped found seven technologically based businesses, the most recent being Advanced Energy Dynamics Inc. of Natick, Massachusetts. He is also a cofounder and has been chairman of the MIT Enterprise Forum, which assists emerging growth companies.

Mr. Gumpert is an associate editor of HBR, where he specializes

in small business and marketing. He has written several HBR articles, the most recent of which was "The Heart of Entrepreneurship," coauthored by Howard H. Stevenson (March-April 1985).

This article is adapted from Business Plans That Win $$$: Lessons from the MIT Enterprise Forum, *by Messrs. Rich and Gumpert (Harper & Row, 1985). The authors are also founders of Venture Resource Associates of Grantham, New Hampshire, which provides planning and strategic services to growing enterprises.*

A comprehensive, carefully thought-out business plan is essential to the success of entrepreneurs and corporate managers. Whether you're starting up a new business, seeking additional capital for existing product lines, or proposing a new activity in a corporate division, you will never face a more challenging writing assignment than the preparation of a business plan.

Only a well-conceived and well-packaged plan can win the necessary investment and support for your idea. It must describe the company or proposed project accurately and attractively. Even though its subject is a moving target, the plan must detail the company or the project's present status, current needs, and expected future. You must present and justify ongoing and changing resource requirements, marketing decisions, financial projections, production demands, and personnel needs in logical and convincing fashion.

Because they struggle so hard to assemble, organize, describe, and document so much, it's not surprising when managers overlook the fundamentals. We have found that the most important one is the accurate reflection of the viewpoints of three constituencies, as follows:

1 The market, including both existing and prospective clients, customers, and users of the planned product or service.

2 The investors, whether of financial or other resources.

3 The producer, whether the entrepreneur or the inventor.

Too many business plans are written from the viewpoint of the third constituency—the producer. They describe the underlying technology or creativity of the proposed product or service in glowing terms and at great length. They neglect the constituencies that give the venture its financial viability—the market and the investor.

Take the case of five executives seeking financing to establish their own engineering consulting firm. In their business plan, they listed a dozen types of specialized engineering services and estimated their annual sales and profit growth at 20%. But the executives did not determine which of the proposed dozen services their potential clients really needed and which would be most profitable. By neglecting to examine these issues closely, they ignored the possibility that the marketplace might want some services not among the dozen listed.

Moreover, they failed to indicate the price of new shares or the percentage available to investors. Dealing with the investor's perspective was important because—for a new venture, at least—backers seek a return of 40% to 60% on their capital, compounded annually. The expected sales and profit growth rates of 20% couldn't provide the necessary return unless the founders gave up a substantial share of the company.

In fact, the executives had only considered their own perspective—including the new company's services, organization, and projected results. Because they hadn't convincingly demonstrated why potential customers would buy the services or how investors would make an adequate return (or when and how they could cash out), their business plan lacked the credibility necessary for raising the investment funds needed.

We have had experience in both evaluating business plans and organizing and observing presentations and investor responses at sessions of the MIT Enterprise Forum over the past seven years (see the insert entitled "The MIT Enterprise Forum"). We believe that business plans must deal convincingly with marketing and investor considerations. This article identifies and evaluates those considerations and explains how business plans can be written to satisfy them.

Emphasize the market

Investors want to put their money into market-driven rather than technology-driven or service-driven companies. The potential of the product's market, sales, and profit is far more important than its attractiveness or technical features.

You can make a convincing case for the existence of a good market by demonstrating user benefit, identifying marketplace interest, and documenting market claims.

Show the user's benefit. It's easy even for experts to overlook this basic notion. At an MIT Enterprise Forum session an entrepreneur spent the bulk of his 20-minute presentation period extolling the virtues of his company's product—an instrument to control certain aspects of the production process in the textile industry. He concluded with some financial projections looking five years down the road.

The first panelist to react to the business plan—a partner in a venture capital firm—was completely

The MIT Enterprise Forum

Organized under the auspices of the Massachusetts Institute of Technology Alumni Association in 1978, the MIT Enterprise Forum offers businesses at a critical stage of development an opportunity to obtain counsel from a panel of experts on steps to take to achieve their goals.

In monthly evening sessions the forum evaluates the business plans of companies accepted for presentation during 60- to 90-minute segments in which no holds are barred. The format allows each presenter 20 minutes to summarize a business plan orally. Each panelist reviews the written business plan in advance of the sessions. Then each of four panelists—who are venture capitalists, bankers, marketing specialists, successful entrepreneurs, MIT professors, or other experts—spends five to ten minutes assessing the strengths and weaknesses of the plan and the enterprise and suggesting improvements.

In some cases, the panelists suggest a completely new direction. In others, they advise more effective implementation of existing policies. Their comments range over the spectrum of business issues.

Sessions are open to the public and usually draw about 300 people, most of them financiers, business executives, accountants, lawyers, consultants, and others with special interest in emerging companies. Following the panelists' evaluations, audience members can ask questions and offer comments.

Presenters have the opportunity to respond to the evaluations and suggestions offered. They also receive written evaluations of the oral presentation from audience members. (The entrepreneur doesn't make the written plan available to the audience.) These monthly sessions are held primarily for companies that have advanced beyond the start-up stage. They tend to be from one to ten years old and in need of expansion capital.

The MIT Enterprise Forum's success at its home base in Cambridge, Massachusetts has led MIT alumni to establish forums in New York, Washington, Houston, Chicago, and Amsterdam, among other cities.

negative about the company's prospects for obtaining investment funds because, he stated, its market was in a depressed industry.

Another panelist asked, "How long does it take your product to pay for itself in decreased production costs?" The presenter immediately responded, "Six months." The second panelist replied, "That's the most important thing you've said tonight."

The venture capitalist quickly reversed his original opinion. He said he would back a company in almost any industry if it could prove such an important user's benefit—and emphasize it in its sales approach. After all, if it paid back the customer's cost in six months, the product would after that time essentially "print money."

The venture capitalist knew that instruments, machinery, and services that pay for themselves in less than one year are mandatory purchases

for many potential customers. If this payback period is less than two years, it's a probable purchase; beyond three years, they don't back the product.

The MIT panel advised the entrepreneur to recast his business plan so that it emphasized the short payback period and played down the self-serving discussion about product innovation. The executive took the advice and rewrote the plan in easily understandable terms. His company is doing very well and has made the transition from a technology-driven to a market-driven company.

Find out the market's interest. Calculating the user's benefit is only the first step. An entrepreneur must also give evidence that customers are intrigued with the user's benefit claims and that they like the product or service. The business plan must reflect clear positive responses of customer prospects to the question "Having heard our pitch, will you buy?'' Without them, an investment usually won't be made.

How can start-up businesses – some of which may have only a prototype product or an idea for a service – appropriately gauge market reaction? One executive of a smaller company had put together a prototype of a device that enables personal computers to handle telephone messages. He needed to demonstrate that customers would buy the product, but the company had exhausted its cash resources and was thus unable to build and sell the item in quantity.

The executives wondered how to get around the problem. The MIT panel offered two possible responses. First, the founders might allow a few customers to use the prototype and obtain written evaluations of the product and the extent of their interest when it became available.

Second, the founders might offer the product to a few potential customers at a substantial price discount if they paid part of the cost – say one-third up front – so that the company could build it. The company could not only find out whether potential buyers existed but also demonstrate the product to potential investors in real-life installations.

In the same way, an entrepreneur might offer a proposed new service at a discount to initial customers as a prototype if the customers agreed to serve as references in marketing the service to others.

For a new product, nothing succeeds as well as letters of support and appreciation from some significant potential customers along with ''reference installations.'' You can use such third-party statements – from would-be customers to whom you've demonstrated the product, initial users, sales representatives, or distributors – to show that you have indeed discovered a sound market that needs your product or service.

You can obtain letters from users even if the product is only in prototype form. You can install it experimentally with a potential user to whom you will sell it at or below cost in return for information on its benefits and an agreement to talk to sales prospects or investors. In an appendix to the business plan or in a separate volume, you can include letters attesting to the val-

ue of the product from experimental customers.

Document your claims.

Having established a market interest, you must use carefully analyzed data to support your assertions about the market and the growth rate of sales and profits. Too often, executives think ''If we're smart, we'll be able to get about 10% of the market'' and ''Even if we only get 1% of such a huge market, we'll be in good shape.''

Investors know that there's no guarantee a new company will get any business, regardless of market size. Even if the company makes such claims based on fact – as borne out, for example, by evidence of customer interest – they can quickly crumble if the company doesn't carefully gather and analyze supporting data.

One example of this danger surfaced in a business plan that came before the MIT Enterprise Forum. An entrepreneur wanted to sell a service to small businesses. He reasoned that he could have 170,000 customers if he penetrated even 1% of the market of 17 million small enterprises in the United States. The panel pointed out that anywhere from 11 million to 14 million of such so-called small businesses were really sole proprietorships or part-time businesses. The total number of full-time small businesses with employees was actually between 3 million and 6 million and represented a real potential market far beneath the company's original projections – and prospects.

Similarly, in a business plan relating to the sale of certain equipment to apple growers, you must have U.S. Department of Agriculture statistics to discover the number of growers who could use the equipment. If your equipment is useful only to growers with 50 acres or more, then you need to determine how many growers have farms of that size, that is, how many are minor producers with only an acre or two of apple trees.

A realistic business plan needs to specify the number of potential customers, the size of their businesses, and which size is most appropriate to the offered products or services. Sometimes bigger is not better. For example, a saving of $10,000 per year in chemical use may be significant to a modest company but unimportant to a Du Pont or a Monsanto.

Such marketing research should also show the nature of the industry. Few industries are more conservative than banking and public utilities. The number of potential customers is relatively small, and industry acceptance of new products or services is painfully slow, no matter how good the products and services have proven to be. Even so, most of the customers are well known and while they may act slowly, they have the buying power that makes the wait worthwhile.

At the other end of the industrial spectrum are extremely fast-growing and fast-changing operations such as franchised weight-loss clinics and computer software companies. Here the problem is reversed. While some companies have achieved multi-million dollar sales in just a few years, they are vulnerable to declines of similar proportions from competitors. These companies must innovate constantly so that potential competitors will be discouraged from entering the marketplace.

You must convincingly project the rate of acceptance for the product or service – and the rate at which it is likely to be sold. From this marketing research data, you can begin assembling a credible sales plan and projecting your plant and staff needs.

Address investors' needs

The marketing issues are tied to the satisfaction of investors. Once executives make a convincing case for their market penetration, they can make the financial projections that help determine whether investors will be interested in evaluating the venture and how much they'll commit and at what price.

Before considering investors' concerns in evaluating business plans, you will find it worth your while to gauge who your potential investors might be. Most of us know that for new and growing private companies, investors may be professional venture capitalists and wealthy individuals. For corporate ventures, they are the corporation itself. When a company offers shares to the public, individuals of all means become investors along with various institutions.

But one part of the investor constituency is often overlooked in the planning process – the founders of new and growing enterprises. By deciding to start and manage a business, they are committed to years of hard work and personal sacrifice. They must try to stand back and evaluate their own businesses in order to decide whether the opportunity for reward some years down the road truly justifies the risk early on.

When an entrepreneur looks at an idea objectively rather than through rose-colored glasses, the decision whether to invest may change. One entrepreneur who believed in the promise of his scientific instruments company faced difficult marketing problems because the product was highly specialized and had, at best, few customers. Because of the entrepreneur's heavy debt, the venture's chance of eventual success and financial return was quite slim.

The panelists concluded that the entrepreneur would earn only as much financial return as he would have had holding a job during the next three to seven years. On the downside, he might wind up with much less in exchange for larger headaches. When he viewed the project in such dispassionate terms, the entrepreneur finally agreed and gave it up.

Investors' primary considerations are:

Cashing out. Entrepreneurs frequently do not understand why investors have a short attention span. Many who see their ventures in terms of a life-time commitment expect that anyone else who gets involved will feel the same. When investors evaluate a business plan, they consider not only whether to get in but also how and when to get out.

Because small, fast-growing companies have little cash available for dividends, the main way investors can profit is from the sale of their holdings, either when the company goes public or is sold to another business. (Large corporations that invest in new enterprises may not sell their holdings if they're committed to integrating the venture into their operations and realizing long-term gains from income.)

Venture capital firms usually wish to liquidate their investments in small companies in three to seven years so as to pay gains while they generate funds for investment in new ventures. The professional investor wants to cash out with a large capital appreciation.

Investors want to know that entrepreneurs have thought about how to comply with this desire. Do they expect to go public, sell the company, or buy the investors out in three to seven years? Will the proceeds provide investors with a return on invested capital commensurate with the investment risk – in the range of 35% to 60%, compounded and adjusted for inflation?

Business plans often do not show when and how investors may liquidate their holdings. For example, one entrepreneur's software company sought $1.5 million to expand. But a panelist calculated that, to satisfy their goals, the investors "would need to own the entire company and then some."

Making sound projections. Five-year forecasts of profitability help lay the groundwork for negotiating the amount investors will receive in return for their money. Investors see such financial forecasts as yardsticks against which to judge future performance.

Too often, entrepreneurs go to extremes with their numbers. In some cases, they don't do enough work on their financials and rely on figures that are so skimpy or overoptimistic that anyone who has read more than a dozen business plans quickly sees through them.

In one MIT Enterprise Forum presentation, a management team proposing to manufacture and market scientific instruments forecast a net income after taxes of 25% of sales during the fourth and fifth years following investment. While a few industries such as computer software average such high profits, the scientific instruments business is so competitive, panelists noted, that expecting such margins is unrealistic.

In fact, the managers had grossly – and carelessly – understated some important costs. The panelists advised them to take their financial estimates back to the drawing board and before approaching investors to consult financial professionals.

Some entrepreneurs think that the financials *are* the business plan. They may cover the plan with a smog of numbers. Such "spreadsheet merchants," with their pages of computer printouts covering every business variation possible and analyzing product sensitivity, completely turn off many investors.

Investors are wary even when financial projections are solidly based on realistic marketing data because fledgling companies nearly always fail to achieve their rosy profit forecasts. Officials of five major venture capital firms we surveyed said they are satisfied when new ventures reach 50% of their financial goals. They agreed that the negotiations that determine the percentage of the company purchased by the investment dollars are affected by this "projection discount factor."

The development stage. All investors wish to reduce their risk. In evaluating the risk of a new and growing venture, they assess the status of the product and the management team. The farther along an enterprise is in each area, the lower the risk.

At one extreme is a single entrepreneur with an unproven idea. Unless the founder has a magnificent track record, such a venture has little chance of obtaining investment funds.

At the more desirable extreme is a venture that has an accepted product in a proven market and a competent and fully staffed management team. This business is most likely to win investment funds at the lowest cost.

Entrepreneurs who become aware of their status with investors and think it inadequate can improve it. Take the case of a young MIT engineering graduate who appeared at an MIT Enterprise Forum session with written schematics for the improvement of semiconductor equipment production. He had documented interest by several producers and was looking for money to complete development and begin production.

The panelists advised him to concentrate first on making a prototype and assembling a management team with marketing and financial know-how to complement his product-development expertise. They explained that because he had never before started a company, he needed to show a great deal of visible progress in building his venture to allay investors' concern about his inexperience.

Packaging is important

A business plan gives financiers their first impressions of a company and its principals.

Potential investors expect the plan to look good, but not too good; to be the right length; to clearly and concisely explain early on all aspects of the company's business; and not to contain bad grammar and typographical or spelling errors.

Investors are looking for evidence that the principals treat their own property with care—and will likewise treat the investment carefully. In other words, form as well as content is important, and investors know that good form reflects good content and vice versa.

Among the format issues we think most important are the following:

Appearance
The binding and printing must not be sloppy; neither should the presentation be too lavish. A stapled compilation of photocopied pages usually looks amateurish, while bookbinding with typeset pages may arouse concern about excessive and inappropriate spending. A plastic spiral binding holding together a pair of cover sheets of a single color provides both a neat appearance and sufficient strength to withstand the handling of a number of people without damage.

Length
A business plan should be no more than 40 pages long. The first draft will likely exceed that, but editing should produce a final version that fits within the 40-page ideal. Adherence to this length forces entrepreneurs to sharpen their ideas and results in a document likely to hold investors' attention.

Background details can be included in an additional volume. Entrepreneurs can make this material available to investors during the investigative period after the initial expression of interest.

The cover and title page
The cover should bear the name of the company, its address and phone number, and the month and year in which the plan is issued. Surprisingly, a large number of business plans are submitted to potential investors without return addresses or phone numbers. An interested investor wants to be able to contact a company easily and to request further information or express an interest, either in the company or in some aspect of the plan.

Inside the front cover should be a well-designed title page on which the cover information is repeated and, in an upper or a lower corner, the legend "Copy number ____" provided. Besides helping entrepreneurs keep track of plans in circulation, holding down the number of copies outstanding—usually to no more than 20—has a psychological advantage. After all, no investor likes to think that the prospective investment is shopworn.

The executive summary
The two pages immediately following the title page should concisely explain the company's current status, its products or services, the benefits to customers, the financial forecasts, the venture's objectives in three to seven years, the amount of financing needed, and how investors will benefit.

This is a tall order for a two-page summary, but it will either sell investors on reading the rest of the plan or convince them to forget the whole thing.

The table of contents
After the executive summary, include a well-designed table of contents. List each of the business plan's sections and mark the pages for each section.

The price. Once investors understand a company qualitatively, they can begin to do some quantitative analysis. One customary way is to calculate the company's value on the basis of the results expected in the fifth year following investment. Because risk and reward are closely related, investors believe companies with fully developed products and proven management teams should yield between 35% and 40% on their investment, while those with incomplete products and management teams are expected to bring in 60% annual compounded returns.

Investors calculate the potential worth of a company after five years to determine what percentage they must own to realize their return. Take the hypothetical case of a well-developed company expected to yield 35% annually. Investors would want to earn 4.5 times their original investment, before inflation, over a five-year period.

After allowing for the projection discount factor, investors may postulate that a company will have $20 million annual revenues after five years and a net profit of $1.5 million. Based on a conventional multiple for acquisitions of ten times earnings, the company would be worth $15 million in five years.

If the company wants $1 million of financing, it should grow to $4.5 million after five years to satisfy investors. To realize that return from a company worth $15 million, the investors would need to own a bit less than one-third. If inflation is expected to average 7.5% a year during the five-year period, however, investors would look for a value of $6.46 million as a reasonable return over five years, or 43% of the company.

For a less mature venture—from which investors would be seeking 60% annually, net of inflation—a $1 million investment would have to bring in close to $15 million in five years, with inflation figured at 7.5% annually. But few businesses can make a convincing case for such a rich return if they don't already have a product in the hands of some representative customers.

The final percentage of the company acquired by the investors is, of course, subject to some negotiation, depending on projected earnings and expected inflation.

Make it happen

The only way to tend to your needs is to satisfy those of the market and the investors—unless you are wealthy enough to furnish your own capital to finance the venture and test out the pet product or service.

Of course, you must confront other issues before you can convince investors that the enterprise will succeed. For example, what proprietary aspects are there to the product or service? How will you provide quality control? Have you focused the venture toward a particular market segment, or are you trying to do too much? If this is answered in the context of the market and investors, the result will be more effective than if you deal with them in terms of your own wishes.

An example helps illustrate the potential conflicts. An entrepreneur at an MIT Enterprise Forum session projected R&D spending of about half of gross sales revenues for his specialty chemical venture. A panelist who had analyzed comparable organic chemical suppliers asked why the company's R&D spending was so much higher than the industry average of 5% of gross revenues.

The entrepreneur explained that he wanted to continually develop new products in his field. While admitting his purpose was admirable, the panel unanimously advised him to bring his spending into line with the industry's. The presenter ignored the advice; he failed to obtain the needed financing and eventually went out of business.

Once you accept the idea that you should satisfy the market and the investors, you face the challenge of organizing your data into a convincing document so that you can sell your venture to investors and customers. We have provided some presentation guidelines in the insert called "Packaging is important."

Even though we might wish it weren't so, writing effective business plans is as much an art as it is a science. The idea of a master document whose blanks executives can merely fill in—much in the way lawyers use sample wills or real estate agreements— is appealing but unrealistic.

Businesses differ in key marketing, production, and financial issues. Their plans must reflect such differences and must emphasize appropriate areas and deemphasize minor issues. Remember that investors view a plan as a distillation of the objectives and character of the business and its executives. A cookie-cutter, fill-in-the-blanks plan or, worse yet, a computer-generated package, will turn them off.

Write your business plans by looking outward to your key constituencies rather than by looking inward at what suits you best. You will save valuable time and energy this way and improve your chances of winning investors and customers. ▽

Reprint 85314

The Case of the Endangered Entrepreneurs

What do you do when you're cash-starved, your distributor wants credit, and your bank starts to squeeze?

by Mary Karr

Fran Conklin, the CEO of First Line Software, could hear it in Charlie Smith's voice—he had not had a nice day at the California headquarters of Microchannels, First Line's major distributor. Smith had gone there to get Microchannels's order for the new line of video games and for MasterGraph, First Line's new product for the business market. He was calling from the airport before flying back to Salt Lake City. He sounded glum.

"Is something wrong, Charlie?" Fran asked.

"Yes, plenty. Micro's game orders are pretty good, but they want to get off credit-hold," Charlie said. "Their order for games comes to about $200,000, and for MasterGraph, about $250,000. But here's the catch: if we don't extend our credit limit, Micro won't order anything."

"I don't get it," Fran interrupted. "Micro owed us $400,000 at the end of the quarter. That's above our limit. Now they want another $450,000 without paying off even part? They

know our bankers won't allow that. Anyway, I can't believe they're out of cash. I thought Cromar Systems would fund Micro until they got back on their feet. Won't Cromar at least guarantee their debts?"

"Bill Clayton says no. Since the acquisition, Cromar has been loud and

> ## Can First Line afford to launch MasterGraph? Can it afford not to?

clear that their subsidiaries have to fend for themselves. And that's not all the bad news. Bill's afraid that video games have peaked, so he wants more concessions—another 5% discount off the new order on games and another 10% off the ones he's still got in stock. He says it's the only way he can sell them. Plus they

want to boost their return rate to 40% on the games and 100% on MasterGraph."

"What? We're talking about the Christmas season. Those orders are crucial to funding MasterGraph. He knows that. Boy, has Bill changed! We go back four years, and that's a long time in this business. If it weren't for Bill, we might still be selling our games out of the back of a car. But this is a whole new ball game. Damn it, I wish we had someone else to take MasterGraph into the business market."

"Well, it's a little late to change horses," Charlie said. "Oh, they're calling my flight. I'll see you later this afternoon. Are you going to speak to Joe?"

"Not yet. At least not if I can help it. I want to get a full report from you. And I think I'll give Bill a ring. I need to get a better feel for this. Try to relax on your flight, but start thinking of alternative strategies. We've got to do something."

Four years earlier Fran Conklin and Joe Wilson had formed First Line Software. Joe, the chairman, was a technical wizard who had been an engineer at a large computer maker for several years. He left to design his own video games, like Underground Warrior and Mind Caravan, two offbeat games that his friends said would go through the roof. Encouraged, he asked Fran, an old friend who had just received an MBA from Wharton, to help set up the corporation. At their first trade show, Bill Clayton, president of Microchannels, a national software and video game distributor, stopped by their booth. He immediately saw potential in Joe's bizarre and complicated games and arranged to become First Line's national distributor. And he helped them get additional financing.

Now First Line's sales topped $10 million, but the company was at a crossroads. The video games market had started to sag and nothing indi-

Mary Karr has been a research consultant at the Harvard Business School and a marketing and communications manager for several high-tech companies. She now heads her own research and writing firm.

cated it would get better soon. Fran and Joe saw the shift earlier than most and made the decision to diversify. They bet the company on the idea of creating a new kind of graphics software that businesses would find easy to use—a product not then

Did Fran drop the ball by not accompanying Charlie to California?

available on the market. Joe was confident that by diverting most of the R&D budget from video games to the graphics project, First Line would come up with a commercial version within a year.

He was right. MasterGraph was everything they had hoped for. It got strong reviews at the May trade show, and now, three months later, MasterGraph was set for launch. Fran and Joe were not dismayed by industry wailings about an oversupply of business software. The product would be a standout, they thought. Even with only moderate sales and MasterGraph's price below $500, First Line would still make back its investment within 18 months.

Microchannels was the obvious choice to distribute MasterGraph. It knew First Line well and accounted for about half of its sales. (The other half was split: 35% by First Line's direct sales to national accounts and 15% by Videolinks, a distributor that handled toy and game retailers.) Microchannels's real forte was business software. Its sales force was especially adept at handling the value-added resellers (VARs) that package hardware and software for business customers. VARs could account for as much as 40% of the market for MasterGraph.

But Microchannels recently had run into problems. It bought a large, midwestern software distributor, and then almost overnight the software market became glutted. Products piled up on shelves, and deep

discounting became routine. Microchannels delayed paying its creditors.

Fran telephoned Bill Clayton. He was as cordial as ever, but he echoed Charlie's report. "Look," Bill said, "I tried to get Cromar to help us. Believe me, it would make *our* situation much easier. But they refused. Maybe they'll change their mind after the market rebounds. But you saw what happened to New York Software last month, and Computer Factors did nothing about it—just let them sink into the mud.

"Anyway," he continued, "we'll put in a strong drive for Master-Graph. I know it's important to your future. Hell, it's important to ours. I've worked up some sexy promotions and a volume discount schedule to lure the chains."

"That's all great, Bill, but this stuff is going to cost us more money, and our bank credit line is close to the limit. We've already spent $500,000 promoting MasterGraph since the Comdex trade show. Remember, it was you who bullied us about retail pull-through. We spent $100,000 alone on mailing demos to retailers and potential customers. We took out ads, and we trained your staff. But we've gone about as far as we can go. You stretch us too far, and we're going to snap."

Fran continued, "Listen, First Fidelity isn't going to go along with more credit unless you pay us something. Those extra discounts would take almost all of our profit. And I especially don't understand the 60% off on MasterGraph. It's set to retail at $395, which is already lower than most business software, and it's gotten great reviews in the trades."

"Fran, the market stinks. You know that. And it's the same at the toy end and at the business end. Retail margins have gone to hell. The VARs say that they're way overstocked in everything too. We're all scrambling just to be able to open our doors tomorrow. I promise we'll do our best, and hopefully, we'll all make a profit."

"And your acquisition of New Horizon last year didn't exactly help, did it?" Fran said with a trace of sarcasm.

"Don't remind me," Bill said. "Buy high, sell low, that's our motto. Yeah, we blew it, but we thought we were buying in a temporary dip in the market and things would turn around fast. We were wrong. It may turn out to be a good buy yet, but you're right. Right now it's bleeding us."

Fran asked, "What if I talk to Cromar's financial people? They might listen to reason."

"No, I really don't think you should go to them directly. Those guys are strange ducks. Between you and me, I think that if it ever did hit the fan they'd bail us out. Did you know they bought two more distributors in the last six weeks? But so far, they're taking a hard, hard line."

"That's not a very good assurance, Bill." Just then, Joe poked his head through her office door. "Look, I'll talk to you later," Fran said and hung up the phone.

Joe was waving the *Wall Street Journal*. "Major market rebound predicted for software," he read excitedly. "Not until the second quarter next year, but hey, compared to those distributor bankruptcy stories we've been hearing...anyway, how did Charlie do in California? Do you want to work his numbers into Friday's board presentation?"

"Oh, I don't know about that," Fran replied. "Anyway, he just gave me the highlights over the phone. I think we should wait until he gets back, later this afternoon."

Fran paused. She didn't want to admit to Joe that they had a problem,

First Line needs a strategy—and the board meets in three days.

especially this one. Joe's stake in First Line was larger than hers—40% versus 30%—and Joe considered First Line his baby. Though he was a better engineer than a businessman, it had taken him two years to loosen the reins. And he still played Monday-morning quarterback. These days Joe spent most of his time down in R&D

with the designers working on MasterGraph II, the follow-on product to MasterGraph, but he kept worrying about how MasterGraph would do in the market.

Fran took a deep breath and plunged in. "Joe, we've got a problem. We're completely in Microchannels's hands on MasterGraph, and now they're shaking us to make the loose change fall out." She related her conversations with Charlie and Bill and watched as Joe's good mood vanished.

"A half-million dollars in orders is OK these days, but we can't handle all those givebacks," Joe said. "No way is the bank going to go along with more credit. And neither will Maury. You know he's been skittish on MasterGraph. He's liable to turn this into a big fight." Maury Flavin was one of three nonemployees on First Line's seven-member board of directors. Each of the three owned 10% of First Line. Maury's strong personality, however, dominated the other two outside directors, and Fran and Joe worried that he'd use the credit issue to divide the board.

"Did you talk to Cromar's financial people?" Joe asked.

Fran shook her head. "Bill didn't want me to, so I thought the better part of valor would be to go along. At least for now."

"You caved in because Bill said not to talk with them?" Joe snapped.

"I wouldn't call it caving in," Fran said. "Bill's important to our success. To go over his head wouldn't make sense."

"Sending Charlie out there alone was a big mistake, Fran. It's our biggest deal yet, and it looks to me like you should have gone along. I just hope we haven't dropped the ball so close to the goal line. Everything's set to launch MasterGraph."

"Dropped the ball? Charlie knows more than we do about marketing and sales. Besides, this trip was just supposed to tie up loose ends plus give us a chance to sell a few chains on MasterGraph. There was no way to know Bill would throw this at us."

Joe thought for a moment. "Look, we've got to think strategy. The bank already thinks we've pumped too much money into MasterGraph, but

if we don't give it more it'll never fly. I know it would cost us, but is there any chance of going with another distributor, like Videolinks or someone like that?"

"Not really. Videolinks is still just videos. They'd be dreadful. Anyway, at this late date, we've got to stick with Microchannels. MasterGraph has to break out fast or it may not move at all. We both know someone is out there right now trying to beat us. Even if we had the money for the training and everything, we would lose the quarter starting over with someone else. Anyway, it's moot. We don't have the money."

"We've got to get funds no matter what we do—that much is clear. Maybe we could find another bank. How much would we need to get us through the next six months, anyway?" Joe asked.

"I don't know how much we'd have to borrow," Fran said. "I guess

we'd need at least $3 million, maybe more with our video games sliding. A lot of the games we sell now will probably be sitting on the shelves come January and then wind up back in our warehouse. And they were supposed to fund MasterGraph for the next three quarters. Even if we get the stuff off the shelves this season, a lot of our retailers won't be enthusiastic next year, unless, of course, MasterGraph goes big fast.

"Look," Fran continued, "the board meeting is Friday. We've got to come up with something. Charlie will be back in a few hours. Let's get Wanda to work up some 'what if' financial scenarios, and the four of us can meet around six o'clock."

"OK. But we should block out the rest of the week to work on this. And let's think positively. I bet we have more options than we know about."

"I hope you're right, because I don't like the ones I can think of."

WHAT WOULD YOU DO?

We asked the following business leaders—people who actually have to deal with such problems—what went wrong at First Line and how they would solve this dilemma. Here are their responses.

Bring in a tough-minded turnaround CEO

The video game business is primarily a fourth-quarter business (Christmas), with the majority of sales coming from new product offerings. First Line made a big mistake in using retained earnings generated from video game profits to fund MasterGraph. Management has used

LELAND B. GOLDBERG, *partner in the Boston office of Coopers & Lybrand, has more than 20 years' experience in assisting financially troubled small and medium-sized companies.*

up its primary source of cash during a period when sales and accounts receivable collections are slow (nine months out of the year). The retained earnings could have been used to develop new products, to cover seasonal cash flow, and to invest in a new graphics-software business.

The company had no real strategy to combat the video game slump. Its "strategy" was to diversify into graphics software, a separate product line catering to the business market. There was no consideration of discounting the video games to reduce inventories and generate more cash flow during the slump.

In making the decision to go into MasterGraph, furthermore, the company should have: (1) attained separate financing for MasterGraph *before* spending money to develop the graphics-software product line; (2) analyzed the cash required to fund the video game business to determine if there was excess cash available for a separate graphics business; and (3) completed a comprehensive market analysis of graphics software prior to making a decision to fund its development.

The company's accounts receivable have aged to the point that, given the questionable value of the existing accounts receivable collateral, the bank is no longer willing to provide additional financing. Since First Line doesn't seem to have other bank financing or outside investors, Fran and Joe must take drastic measures just to stay in business.

They must recognize that regardless of how good a product MasterGraph may be, the company doesn't have the cash to build it. First Line cannot survive by trying to remain in both video games and graphics software. The managers must cut overhead, which will compel the company to get out of graphics software *immediately* by either selling the graphics product to a third party or closing down the graphics business entirely.

Also, First Line must immediately put all of its resources into developing a new video product and generating sufficient cash flow to get it through its current season. In doing so, management must develop a detailed, weekly cash-flow plan. This plan should match expected collection of existing accounts receivable against the cash needed to fund payroll, meet R&D expenses, and carry the minimal overhead to stay in business. To generate cash flow and reduce bank debt, the company must pressure its customers to pay their outstanding balances, even at a discount. Additionally, First Line could stretch trade payables and sell inventory at a discount.

Given the seasonality, market softness, and R&D requirements for new video products, First Line should also put together a 12-month cash forecast to determine how much cash will be required just to stay in the video business (assuming the company is no longer in the graphics business). This cash-flow plan will also predict cash needs during the year. Given a significant cash need, management must hold discussions with its bank and investors to see how much cash can be generated internally, how much receivables collateral is available for additional bank debt, and how much cash is required from outside sources.

The company may not be able to maintain itself as a stand-alone video company. It has used up its cash. Its $2 million to $3 million cash need makes it highly likely that Fran and Joe will have to sell a controlling stock interest in the company to an aggressive investor or sell First Line outright. Potential buyers may include companies that want to expand their present video product offerings or companies with similar distribution channels that would like to expand their existing base to include computer software offerings. Such a purchaser would be able to consolidate First Line's and its own overhead and should have sufficiently deep pockets to fund the seasonal nine-month cash losses.

Whether the company can be a successful turnaround is a function of management's ability to cut costs, maximize cash flow, and buy the time necessary to negotiate with an outside investor or buyer. If outside investors or buyers see that the company is on the verge of bankruptcy, they will attempt to steal the business without providing money to existing stockholders, or they will wait and buy the company out of bankruptcy.

Fran and Joe don't seem to have the management skills needed to pull off a turnaround. Fran is bright but has little experience in this industry. Joe is a good R&D person but is not capable of running this business. The company needs to find a tough-minded CEO who knows the importance of cash flow, who will negotiate hard with the bank, investors, and potential buyers, and who will bring in a CFO experienced in handling troubled situations and maximizing cash flow.

Get quick cash and new distribution

BERT I. HELFINSTEIN *is chairman, president, and CEO of Entré Computer Centers Inc., a McLean, Virginia-based franchiser of computer retail outlets.*

Fran Conklin's critical errors were poor cash-management planning and her heavy reliance on one distributor, Microchannels.

Her apparent loyalty to Bill Clayton got in the way of good longterm business judgment and placed First Line's new product launch in jeopardy. She ignored some important warning signs that should have told her that she might not be able to rely on Bill Clayton even if she had his goodwill. First, his company's acquisition by Cromar Systems transferred important decision-making power away from

Bill to policymakers at Cromar. Fran should have paid a visit to Cromar and Microchannels shortly after the purchase to obtain a new distributor agreement with Cromar and to work out a revised business relationship. Second, payments from Microchannels were falling behind, always a warning sign of potential trouble.

Further, when First Line decided to develop MasterGraph and move from game to business software, management should have reevaluated its distribution strategy as part of the planning for that product. The smart decision to switch from game software to business software is now jeopardized because management didn't take the steps necessary for assured distribution channels and didn't arrange for adequate cash to see the company through the product's introduction.

First Line must take two steps immediately: (1) generate some cash and (2) provide an adequate means of distribution for its products.

First Line could pursue several quick cash-generating scenarios based on the recognition that its game software is the company's current cash cow. First Line has some new games that Bill has offered to push hard. But the trouble with Bill's offer is that he apparently has no cash to pay for the games and wants such high return privileges that he is virtually getting the product on consignment. Not much help when First Line needs cash.

One scenario to raise cash is to go to Videolinks—First Line's other distributor and a games specialist—and offer the new games on an exclusive basis if it will both buy sufficient quantities and pay cash. Videolinks gets an opportunity to gain market share over Microchannels and strengthen its position in its chosen niche of games software. But it only works if Videolinks has the cash. That strategy has the disadvantage of narrowing distribution further for First Line (although in a market segment it's moving away from). The advantage, if it works, is quick cash.

Another approach is for First Line to go to its installed base of game customers, who have presumably mailed in the usual software regis-

tration cards after buying their first First Line games. The company can make a direct mail "special preintroductory offer" of its new games. The advantage is fairly quick cash. The disadvantage is that distributors and dealers don't like manufacturers selling around them.

If First Line's future depends on MasterGraph and the upcoming MasterGraph II, it must find adequate distribution for them. Microchannels is the best short-term choice. Even though it has no cash, it reaches the right market, and its staff is trained on the product. And Cromar could be the solution to its cash problems. Cromar recently bought two more software distributors, and it probably has a strategic interest in the distribution business and a plan that its management is apparently not discussing with Bill. Fran and Joe should call on these other two distributors, both to see if they can learn more about Cromar's plans and to gain through them an alternate entrée to Cromar.

First Line's management should then propose to give Cromar an exclusive on the product for all three of its distributorships (or the single one if its strategy is to combine them) for

a limited time. In exchange, Cromar would pay the receivable owed by Microchannels and provide favorable payment terms for the new product.

An alternative strategy if Cromar is not interested is to have First Line's direct sales force sell this product to the major computer dealer chains and large VARs. In the meantime, Fran and Charlie Smith could find other distributors, sign them up, and train their people. First Line could live off the cash from the accelerated game products strategy and, if necessary, cut costs to survive.

The lessons in this case are clear for any manufacturer who relies on distribution. Be sure you have alternate channels of distribution. This protects against the problems that arise when distributors fail, change direction, or try to put the squeeze on a manufacturer. On the other hand, don't overdistribute your product, because it will become less attractive to all distributors. The other lesson is applicable to almost all businesses. Do careful cash planning and monitoring. If cash is going negative relative to the plan, react early while you have more options.

You need candor with your banker

Bankers despise surprises. Yet the nature of the relationship, or lack of one, between First Line Software and

KAREN N. HORN *is chairman and CEO of Bank One of Cleveland, Ohio. She is also a director of Eli Lilly and Company and Rubbermaid Incorporated.*

its banker guarantees that an unpleasant surprise is imminent. Avoiding this surprise and building and maintaining a positive banking relationship are central elements of this case.

A bank is often a business partner with the corporation to which it lends—after all, the bank often has more money in the corporation than anyone else! First Line's management apparently views its banking relationship as a necessary evil rather than as a resource on which the company can rely for many things besides dollars. This viewpoint leads to a lack of communication and an inability to benefit from what an effective bank can best provide: timely advice. First Line needs candid advice now more than ever.

The implication is that First Line's management should either hide the situation from the banker or find a new bank (a greater fool, perhaps?). All of this would not seem to bode well for an increase in credit.

There are other elements of the situation that are of interest. It would be important to know whether or not First Line's banker is knowledgeable about the software industry, which is rapidly changing. A loan officer unfamiliar with this industry will perhaps be less able to offer helpful service or extend credit than someone who understands software markets and can make some reasoned judgments about First Line's situation.

Apart from an apparent lack of communication and trust, there are some basic business issues that may make the bank reluctant to extend further credit:

1. First Line does not appear to have a financial plan.

2. About 50% of the sales are to one distributor (who is in trouble itself).

3. All of First Line's eggs seem to be in one basket. Both the bank and one of First Line's directors have told management it has spent enough.

4. First Line has spent a large amount of money on R&D and marketing rather than on hard assets that could be used as collateral.

All of this limits the options available to First Line. A year or two ago, there would have been time to find a new distributor, develop a financial plan, and raise new capital. (Note that it is easier to raise money when you don't need it.) Certainly, because of the importance of its distributor, First Line should have taken some action when financial trouble appeared, like requesting financial support from Cromar.

What about now? Cromar should guarantee any new credit extended to Microchannels. First Line needs to start looking for new distributors immediately—they will take some time to find. If First Line's banker is neither knowledgeable nor responsive, the company might try to find a new banker who would extend further credit. However, this seems unlikely. It will probably be necessary to raise additional capital from directors or other individuals or from venture capitalists who are willing to undertake larger risks (and expect larger fees) than banks.

The situation at First Line Software is by no means hopeless. It seems to have some good products that may sell well in the future. However, management will pay for its lack of an adequate financing plan and its reliance on a single distributor. The conversation between Fran and Joe suggests that they wish to hide the situation from both their directors and their bankers. Should this be true, it is really more disturbing than any of the purely business and financial factors. Problems are endemic to business. And a banker (or other manager) should expect to handle the problems that often arise. What is difficult to deal with is the lack of frankness and honesty. Unless Fran and Joe are willing to actively solicit and consider the advice of their directors, bankers, and other creditors, I have severe doubts about the future of First Line.

More power to the board

HARVEY C. KRENTZMAN *is president of Advanced Management Associates, a financial and management consulting firm in Chestnut Hill, Massachusetts. He has been adviser to numerous small companies and serves on the boards of directors of six companies.*

The outside investors positioned themselves poorly when they made their investment. As minority partners, they were not in a position to influence critical policies except by the power of persuasion. Fran and Joe own 70% of the company, which gives them control of the enterprise as long as they work as a team.

The outside investors weakened their position further by agreeing to a seven-person board of directors with management holding control by a four-to-three margin. Such a structure makes it difficult for everyone. Fran is in a delicate position since either of the two employees could exercise the swing vote on critical issues. But it is also very hard for outside directors to criticize the CEO in front of lower level management. Maury Flavin, the de facto leader of the minority, nonmanagement group, cannot seriously influence the direction of the company.

Joe seems to exercise the greatest influence on the company's management, although it's frequently negative. Fran's lack of senior managerial operating experience means she needs all the business assistance she can get from Joe and the directors, not constant criticism. Her fear of facing Microchannels's weak financial position and other new business issues critical to the survival of First Line clearly exhibits her weakness as CEO. Joe was right—Fran should have flown out to Microchannels instead of letting Charlie do it. The account is crucial to First Line's future, and Microchannels is already

$400,000 in arrears. Fran's reluctance to share the problems immediately with Joe also shows a poor operating style.

How Fran and Joe use the board is not clear. It is vital, particularly when forming new enterprises, that board members be selected with the skills and experience that complement those of management. In addition to money, the company's organizers should get a commitment from the investors to be *active* board members who will attend monthly meetings and be on call to assist management when needed. This support process strengthens the company's management in a positive, constructive manner. And it works best when CEOs acknowledge their own limitations and have enough self-confidence to share their company's critical problems with the board instead of concealing them until all hell breaks loose. In this case we have a weak CEO who receives little constructive support from her partners.

Time is of the essence. Fran must bite the bullet on First Line's immediate cash-flow crisis in order to meet product-development and marketing needs. A face-to-face discussion with Bill Clayton is necessary. He helped First Line get going financially and First Line should try to exploit that relationship; at the least, Bill should reveal Cromar's plans for Microchannels, if he knows them. But one way or another, they must resolve the current business problems. Microchannels's credit and buying terms and conditions are unacceptable—no one could run a business with those handcuffs on. A credit guarantee from Cromar is essential, and Fran must insist that Microchannels ease its pricing and return-of-goods policy.

If Fran can't negotiate a satisfactory arrangement with Microchannels, she must develop a "blitz" financial and marketing plan that considers all of First Line's hazards and opportunities. Ideally the plan should reflect the wisdom and experience of Joe, Maury, and First Line's other knowledgeable players—Fran needs their support when she executes the final program.

Fran's survival strategy should consider acquiring Microchannels or selling out to Cromar, depending on what First Line's financial data look like. The company may have to raise more equity immediately. And it should probably accelerate development of MasterGraph II, but the video games are not bringing in enough money to fund it.

The plan may call for introducing new venture capital. The outside directors can play an important role here in tapping into the venture capital network. The funding sources should also have strong relationships to the software market. There are lots of money pools around, and management should look for people who can help grow the company as well as provide financing. The new individuals could acquire stock from any unhappy shareholder or from new company shares.

The tough issue Fran and Joe face is that they may have to give up their majority stake and probably operating control. Sophisticated investors coming into this kind of situation always bargain for power and usually demand seats on the board. Because Fran has been so weak, they may demand to replace her as CEO.

In any event, the board of directors should be restructured. First Line's board clearly has not done its job. A board of directors should act as a disciplinarian to management. Provided with monthly numbers, three-month rolling updates, and the like, the board must urge management to think about where the company is, where it's heading, and where managers thought they were taking it. Joe and Fran didn't have such discipline as they developed and embarked on their alternative strategy to video games. To lend the necessary guidance, First Line's board must have power. For example, it must be able to fire the CEO if necessary. Any newly reconstituted board should have a majority of outside directors and no operating managers at all.

Reprint 88604

People Management in
Small Business

How to conserve cash and still attract the best executives

Compensation and Benefits for Startup Companies

by Joseph S. Tibbetts, Jr. and
Edmund T. Donovan

You've decided to start a company. Your business plan is based on sound strategy and thorough market research. Your background and training have prepared you for the challenge. Now you must assemble the quality management team that venture investors demand. So you begin the search for a topflight engineer to head product development and a seasoned manager to handle marketing, sales, and distribution.

Attracting these executives is easier said than done. You've networked your way to just the marketing candidate you need: a vice president with the right industry experience and an aggressive business outlook. But she makes $100,000 a year in a secure job at a large company. You can't possibly commit that much cash, even if you do raise outside capital. How do you structure a compensation package that will lure her away? How much cash is reasonable? How much and what type of stock should the package include? Is there any way to match the ar-

ray of benefits—retirement plans, child-care assistance, savings programs—her current employer provides? In short, what kind of compensation and benefits program will attract, motivate, and retain this marketing vice president and other

> Be realistic about your limitations. But don't ignore the advantages of being small.

key executives while not jeopardizing the fragile finances of your startup business?

Selecting appropriate compensation and benefits policies is a critical challenge for companies of all sizes. But never are the challenges more difficult—or the stakes higher—than when a company first takes shape. Startups must strike a delicate balance. Unrealistically low levels of

cash compensation weaken their ability to attract quality managers. Unrealistically high levels of cash compensation can turn off potential investors and, in extreme cases, threaten the solvency of the business. How to proceed?

First, be realistic about the limitations. There is simply no way that a company just developing a prototype or shipping product for less than a year or generating its first black ink after several money-losing years of building the business can match the current salaries and benefits offered by established competitors. At the same time, there are real advantages to being small. Without an entrenched personnel bureaucracy and long-standing compensation policies, it is easier to tailor salaries and benefits to individual needs. Creativity and flexibility are at a premium.

Second, be thorough and systematic about analyzing the options. Compensation and benefits plans can be expensive to design, install, administer, and terminate. A program that is inappropriate or badly conceived can be a very costly mistake. Startups should evaluate compensation and benefits alternatives from four distinct perspectives.

How do they affect cash flow? Survival is the first order of business for a new company. Even if you have raised an initial round of equity financing, there is seldom enough working capital to go around. Research and development, facilities and equipment, and marketing costs all make priority claims on resources. Cash compensation must be a lower priority. Despite this awkward tension (the desperate need to attract first-rate talent without having the cash to pay them market rates), marshaling resources for pressing business needs must remain paramount.

What are the tax implications? Compensation and benefits choices

Joseph S. Tibbetts, Jr. is managing partner of the Price Waterhouse Entrepreneurial Services Center in Cambridge, Massachusetts. Edmund T. Donovan, a tax attorney, is manager of employee benefits services at Price Waterhouse in Boston.

have major tax consequences for a startup company and its executives; startups can use the tax code to maximum advantage in compensation decisions. Certain approaches, like setting aside assets to secure deferred compensation liabilities, require that executives declare the income immediately and the company deduct it as a current expense. Other

> **No startup is an island. Factor regional and industry trends into your salary calculations.**

approaches, like leaving deferred compensation liabilities unsecured, allow executives to declare the income later while the company takes a future deduction. Many executives value the option of deferring taxable income more than the security of immediate cash. And since most startups have few, if any, profits to shield from taxes, deferring deductions may appeal to them as well.

What is the accounting impact? Most companies on their way to an initial public offering or a sellout to a larger company must register particular earning patterns. Different compensation programs affect the income statement in very different ways. One service company in the startup stage adopted an insurance-backed salary plan for its key executives. The plan bolstered the company's short-term cash flow by deferring salary payments (it also deferred taxable income for those executives). But it would have meant heavy charges to book earnings over the deferral period—charges that might have interfered with the company's plans to go public. So management backed out of the program at the eleventh hour.

What is the competition doing? No startup is an island, especially when vying for talented executives. Companies must factor regional and industry trends into their compensation and benefits calculations. One

newly established law firm decided not to offer new associates a 401(k) plan. (This program allows employees to contribute pretax dollars into a savings fund that also grows tax-free. Many employers match a portion of their employees' contributions.) The firm quickly discovered that it could not attract top candidates without the plan; it had become a staple of the profession in that geographic market. So it established a 401(k) and assumed the administrative costs, but it saved money by not including a matching provision right away.

Events at a Boston software company illustrate the potential for flexibility in startup compensation. The company's three founders had worked together at a previous employer. They had sufficient personal resources to contribute assets and cash to the new company in exchange for founders' stock. They decided to forgo cash compensation altogether for the first year.

Critical to the company's success were five software engineers who would write code for the first product. It did not make sense for the company to raise venture capital to pay the engineers their market-value salaries. Yet their talents were essential if the company were to deliver the software on time.

The obvious solution: supplement cash compensation with stock. But two problems arose. The five prospects had unreasonably high expectations about how much stock they should receive. Each demanded 5% to 10% of the company, which, if granted, would have meant transferring excessive ownership to them. Moreover, while they were equal in experience and ability and therefore worth equal salaries, each had different cash requirements to meet their obligations and maintain a reasonable life-style. One of the engineers was single and had few debts; he was happy to go cash-poor and bank on the company's growth. One of his colleagues, however, had a wife and young child at home and needed the security of a sizable paycheck.

The founders devised a solution to meet the needs of the company and

its prospective employees. They consulted other software startups and documented that second-tier employees typically received 1% to 3% ownership stakes. After some negotiation, they settled on a maximum of 2% for each of the five engineers. Then they agreed on a formula by which these employees could trade cash for stock during their first three years. For every $1,000 in cash an engineer received over a base figure, he or she forfeited a fixed number of shares. The result: all five engineers signed on, the company stayed within its cash constraints, and the founders gave up a more appropriate 7% of the company's equity.

Cash vs. stock

Equity is the great compensation equalizer in startup companies—the bridge between an executive's market value and the company's cash constraints. And there are endless variations on the equity theme: restricted shares, incentive stock options, nonqualified options, stock appreciation rights (SARs), phantom stock, and the list goes on. This dizzying array of choices notwithstanding, startup companies face three basic questions. Does it make sense to grant key executives an equity interest? If so, should the company use restricted stock, options, or some combination of both? If not, does it make sense to reward executives based on the company's appreciating share value or to devise formulas based on different criteria?

Let's consider these questions one at a time. Some company founders are unwilling to part with much ownership at inception. And with good reason. Venture capitalists or other outside investors will demand a healthy share of equity in return for a capital infusion. Founders rightly worry about diluting their control before obtaining venture funds.

Alternatives in this situation include SARs and phantom shares—programs that allow key employees to benefit from the company's increasing value without transferring voting power to them. No shares actually trade hands; the company compensates its executives to reflect the appreciation of its stock. Many

"Peterson, run down and tell my wife that I'll come out and play as soon as I've wrapped up these contracts and not a minute before."

executives prefer these programs to outright equity ownership because they don't have to invest their own money. They receive the financial benefits of owning stock without the risk of buying shares. In return, of course, they forfeit the rights and privileges of ownership. These programs can get complicated, however, and they require thorough accounting reviews. Reporting rules for artificial stock plans are very restrictive and sometimes create substantial charges against earnings.

Some founders take the other extreme. In the interest of saving cash, they award bits of equity at every turn. This can create real problems. When it comes to issuing stock, startups should always be careful not to sell the store before they fill the shelves. That is, they should award shares to key executives and second-tier employees in a way that protects the long-term company interest. And these awards should

take place only after the company has fully distributed stock to the founders.

The choice of whether to issue actual or phantom shares should also be consistent with the company's strategy. If the goal is to realize the "big payoff" within three to five years through an initial public offering or outright sale of the company, then stock may be the best route. You can motivate employees to work hard and build the company's value since they can readily envision big personal rewards down the road.

The founder of a temporary employment agency used this approach to attract and motivate key executives. He planned from the start to sell the business once it reached critical mass, and let his key executives know his game plan. He also allowed them to buy shares at a discount. When he sold the business a few years later for $10 million, certain executives, each of whom had been

allowed to buy up to 4% of the company, received as much as $400,000. The lure of cashing out quickly was a great motivator for this company's top executives.

For companies that plan to grow more slowly over the first three to five years, resist acquisition offers, and maintain private ownership, the stock alternative may not be optimal. Granting shares in a company that may never be sold or publicly traded is a bit like giving away play money. Worthless paper can actually be a demotivator for employees.

In such cases, it may make sense to create an artificial market for stock. Companies can choose among various book-value plans, under which they offer to buy back shares issued to employees according to a pricing formula. Such plans establish a measurement mechanism based on company performance—like book value, earnings, return on assets or equity—that determines the company's per-share value. As with phantom shares and SARs, book-value plans require a thorough accounting review.

If a company does decide to issue shares, the next question is how to do it. Restricted stock is one alternative. Restricted shares most often require that an executive remain with the company for a specified time period or forfeit the equity, thus creating "golden handcuffs" to promote long-term service. The executive otherwise enjoys all the rights of other shareholders, except for the

> ## Shares in a company that will never go public can actually demotivate your people.

right to sell any stock still subject to restriction.

Stock options are another choice, and they generally come in two forms: incentive stock options (ISOs) and nonqualified stock options (NSOs). As with restricted shares, stock options can create golden handcuffs. Most options, whether ISOs or NSOs, involve a vesting schedule. Executives may receive options on 1,000 shares of stock, but only 25% of the options vest (i.e., executives can exercise them) in any one year. If an executive leaves the company, he or she loses the unexercised options. Startups often prefer ISOs since they give executives a timing advantage with respect to taxes. Executives pay no taxes on any capital gains until they sell or exchange the stock, and then only if they realize a profit over the exercise price. ISOs, however, give the company no tax deductions—which is not a major drawback for startups that don't expect to earn big profits for several years. Of course, if companies generate taxable income before their executives exercise their options, lack of a deduction is a definite negative.

ISOs have other drawbacks. Tax laws impose stiff technical requirements on how much stock can be subject to options, the maximum exercise period, who can receive options, and how long stock must be held before it can be sold. Moreover, the exercise price of an ISO cannot be lower than the fair market value of the stock on the date the option is granted. (Shares need not be publicly traded for them to have a fair market value. Private companies estimate the market value of their stock.)

For these and other reasons, companies usually issue NSOs as well as ISOs. NSOs can be issued at a discount to current market value. They can be issued to directors and consultants (who cannot receive ISOs) as well as to company employees. And they have different tax consequences for the issuing company, which can deduct the spread between the exercise price and the market price of the shares when the options are exercised.

NSOs can also play a role in deferred compensation programs. More and more startups are following the lead of larger companies by allowing executives to defer cash compensation with stock options. They grant NSOs at a below-market exercise price that reflects the amount of sal-ary deferred. Unlike standard deferral plans, where cash is paid out on some unalterable future date (thus triggering automatic tax liabilities), the option approach gives executives control over when and how they will be taxed on their deferred salary. The company, meanwhile, can deduct the spread when its executives exercise their options.

One small but growing high-tech company used a combination of stock techniques to achieve several compensation goals simultaneously. It issued NSOs with an exercise price equal to fair market value (most NSOs are issued at a discount). All the options were exercisable immediately (most options have a vesting schedule). Finally, the company placed restrictions on the resale of stock purchased with options.

This program allowed for maximum flexibility. Executives with excess cash could exercise all their options right away; executives with less cash, or who wanted to wait for signs of the company's progress, could wait months or years to exercise. The plan provided the company with tax deductions on any options exercised in the future (assuming the fair market value at exercise exceeded the stock's fair market value when the company granted the options) and avoided any charges to book earnings in the process. And the resale restrictions created golden handcuffs without forcing executives to wait to buy their shares.

The benefits challenge

No startup can match the cradle-to-grave benefits offered by employers like IBM or General Motors, although young companies may have to attract executives from these giant companies. It is also true, however, that the executives most attracted to startup opportunities may be people for whom standard benefit packages are relatively unimportant. Startup companies have special opportunities for creativity and customization with employee benefits. The goal should not be to come as close to what IBM offers without going broke, but to devise low-cost, innovative programs that meet the needs of a small employee corps.

Of course, certain basic needs must be met. Group life insurance is important, although coverage levels should start small and increase as the company gets stronger. Group medical is also essential, although there are many ways to limit its cost. Setting higher-than-average deductibles lowers employer premiums (the deductibles can be adjusted downward as financial stability improves). Self-insuring smaller claims also conserves cash. One young com-

You'll never match IBM's benefits. So you have to be creative.

pany saved 25% on its health-insurance premiums by self-insuring the first $500 of each claim and paying a third party to administer the coverage.

The list of traditional employee benefits doesn't have to stop here—but it probably should. Most companies should not adopt long-term disability coverage, dental plans, child-care assistance, even retirement plans, until they are well beyond the startup phase. This is a difficult reality for many founders to accept, especially those who have broken from larger companies with generous benefit programs. But any program has costs—and costs of any kind are a critical worry for a new company trying to move from the red into the black. Indeed, one startup in the business of developing and operating progressive child-care centers wisely decided to wait for greater financial stability before offering its own employees child-care benefits.

Many young companies underestimate the money and time it takes just to administer benefit programs, let alone fund them. Employee benefits do not run on automatic pilot. While the vice president of marketing watches marketing, the CFO keeps tabs on finances, and the CEO snuffs out the fires that always threaten to engulf a young company, who is left to mind the personnel store? If a substantial benefits program is in place, someone has to handle the day-to-day administrative details and update the program as the accounting and tax rules change. The best strategy is to keep benefits modest at first and make them more comprehensive as the company moves toward profitability.

Which is not to suggest that the only answer to benefits is setting strict limits. Other creative policies may not only cost less but they also may better suit the interests and needs of executive recruits. Take company-supplied lunches. One startup computer company thought it was important to create a "think-tank" atmosphere. So it set up writing boards in the cafeteria, provided all employees with daily lunches from various ethnic restaurants, and encouraged spirited noontime discussions.

Certainly, Thai food is no substitute for a generous pension. But benefits that promote a creative and energetic office environment may matter more to employees than savings plans whose impact may not be felt for decades. One startup learned this lesson after it polled its employees. It was prepared to offer an attractive—and costly—401(k) program until a survey disclosed that employees preferred a much different benefit: employer-paid membership at a local health club. The company gladly obliged.

Deciding on compensation policies for startup companies means making tough choices. There is an inevitable temptation, as a company shows its first signs of growth and financial stability, to enlarge salaries and benefits toward market levels. You should resist these temptations. As your company heads toward maturity, so can your compensation and benefits programs. But the wisest approach is to go slowly, to make enhancements incrementally, and to be aware at all times of the cash flow, taxation, and accounting implications of the choices you face.

Reprint 89111

First Person

Firsthand lessons from experienced managers.

I wanted employees who would fly like geese. What I had was a company that wallowed like a herd of buffalo.

How I Learned to Let My Workers Lead

by Ralph Stayer

In 1980, I was the head of a successful family business—Johnsonville Sausage—that was in great shape and required radical change.

Our profits were above the average for our industry, and our financial statements showed every sign of health. We were growing at a rate of about 20% annually, with sales that were strong in our home state of Wisconsin and steadily rising in Minnesota, Michigan, and Indiana. Our quality was high. We were respected in the community. I was making a lot of money.

And I had a knot in my stomach that wouldn't go away. For one thing, I was worried about competition. We were a small, regional producer with national competitors who could outpromote, outadvertise, and underprice us any time they chose.

In addition to our big national competitors, we had a host of local and regional producers small enough to provide superior service to customers who were virtually their neighbors. We were too big to have the small-town advantage and too small to have advantages of national scale. Our business was more vulnerable than it looked.

What worried me more than the competition, however, was the gap between potential and performance. Our people didn't seem to care. Every day I came to work and saw people so bored by their jobs that they made thoughtless, dumb mistakes. They mislabeled products or added the wrong seasonings or failed to mix them into the sausage properly. Someone drove the prongs of a forklift right through a newly built wall. Someone else ruined a big batch of fresh sausage by spraying it with water while cleaning the work area. These were accidents. No one was deliberately wasting money, time, and materials; it was just that people took no responsibility for their work. They showed up in the morning, did

halfheartedly what they were told to do, and then went home.

Now, I didn't expect them to be as deeply committed to the company as I was. I owned it, and they didn't. But how could we survive a serious competitive challenge with this low level of attentiveness and involvement?

Getting to Points B and A

In 1980, I began looking for a recipe for change. I started by searching for a book that would tell me how to get people to care about their jobs and their company. Not surprisingly, the search was fruitless. No one could tell me how to wake up my own work force; I would have to figure it out for myself.

And yet, I told myself, why not? I had made the company, so I could fix it. This was an insight filled with pitfalls but it *was* an insight: the fault was not someone else's, the fault was mine.

Of course, I hadn't really built the company all alone, but I had created the management style that kept people from assuming responsibility. Of course, it was counterproductive for me to own all the company's problems by myself, but in 1980 every problem did, in fact, rest squarely on my shoulders, weighing me down and—though I didn't appreciate it at the time—crippling my subordinates and strangling the company. If I was going to fix what I had made, I would have to start by fixing myself. In many ways that was my good luck, or, to put the same thought another way, thank God I was the problem so I could be the solution.

As I thought about what I should do, I first asked myself what I needed to do to achieve the company's goals. But what *were* the company's goals? What did I really want Johnsonville to be? I didn't know.

This realization led me to a second insight: nothing matters more than a goal. The most important question any manager can ask is, "In the best

Ralph Stayer is the CEO of Johnsonville Foods, Inc., of Sheboygan, Wisconsin and the managing partner of Leadership Dynamics, a consulting group that specializes in change.

of all possible worlds, what would I really want to happen?"

I tried to picture what Johnsonville would have to be to sell the most expensive sausage in the industry and still have the biggest market share. What I saw in my mind's eye was definitely not an organization where I made all the decisions and owned all the problems. What I saw was an organization where people took responsibility for their own work, for the product, for the company as a whole. If that happened, our product and service quality would improve, our margins would rise, and we could reduce costs and successfully enter new markets. Johnsonville would be much less vulnerable to competition.

The image that best captured the organizational end state I had in mind for Johnsonville was a flock of geese on the wing. I didn't want an organizational chart with traditional lines and boxes, but a "V" of individuals who knew the common goal, took turns leading, and adjusted their structure to the task at hand. Geese fly in a wedge, for instance, but land in waves. Most important, each individual bird is responsible for its own performance.

With that end state in mind as Point B, the goal, I turned to the question of our starting point, Point A. Johnsonville was financially successful, but I was dissatisfied with employee attitudes. So I conducted an attitude survey to find out what people thought about their jobs and the company and to get an idea of how they perceived the company's attitude toward them. I knew there was less commitment than I wanted, but I was startled all the same to find that Johnsonville attitudes were only average—no better than employee attitudes at big, impersonal companies like General Motors.

At first I didn't want to believe the survey, and I looked for all kinds of excuses. The methodology was faulty. The questions were poorly worded. I didn't want to admit that we had an employee motivation problem because I didn't know how to deal with that. But however strong the temptation, the mistakes and poor performance were too glaring to ignore.

The survey told me that people saw nothing for themselves at Johnsonville. It was a job, a means to some end that lay outside the company. I wanted them to commit themselves to a company goal, but they saw little to commit to. And at that stage, I still couldn't see that the biggest obstacle to changing their point of view was me. Everything I had learned and experienced to that point had convinced me that anything I didn't do myself would not be done right. As I saw it, my job was to create the agenda and then motivate "them" to carry it out.

In fact, I expected my people to follow me the way buffalo follow their leader—blindly. Unfortunately, that kind of leadership model almost led to the buffalo's extinction. Buffalo hunters used to slaughter the herd by finding and killing the leader. Once the leader was dead, the rest of the herd stood around waiting for instructions that never came, and the hunters could (and did) exterminate them one by one.

I realized that I had been focused entirely on the financial side of the business—margins, market share, return on assets—and had seen people as dutiful tools to make the business grow. The business *had* grown—nicely—and that very success was my biggest obstacle to change. I had made all the decisions about purchasing, scheduling, quality, pricing, marketing, sales, hiring, and all the rest of it. Now the very things that had brought me success—my centralized control, my aggressive behavior, my authoritarian business practices—were creating the environment that made me so unhappy. I had been Johnsonville Sausage, assisted by some hired hands who, to my annoyance, lacked commitment. But why should they make a commitment to Johnsonville? They had no stake in the company and no power to make decisions or control their own work. If I wanted to improve results, I had to increase their involvement in the business.

This was an insight that I immediately misused. Acting on instinct, I ordered a change. "From now on," I announced to my management team, "you're all responsible for

JOHNSONVILLE FOODS, INC.
COMPANY PERFORMANCE-SHARE
EVALUATION FORM

Please check one: _____ Self _____ Coach

I. PERFORMANCE

A. Customer Satisfaction
How do I rate the quality of the work I do? Do I contribute my best to producing a product to be proud of—one that I would purchase or encourage someone else to purchase? Score _____

B. Cost-Effectiveness
To what extent do I perform my job in a cost-effective manner? Do I strive to work smarter? To work more productively with fewer errors? To complete my job functions in a timely manner, eliminating overtime when possible? To reduce waste where possible in all departments? Score _____

C. Attitude
To what extent do I have a positive attitude toward my personal, department, and company goals as expressed by my actions, feelings, and thoughts? Do I like to come to work? Am I thoughtful and considerate toward fellow members? Do I work to promote better attitudes? Do I demonstrate company loyalty? Score _____

D. Responsibility
To what extent do I take responsibility for my own job? Do I accept a challenge? Do I willingly take on or look for additional responsibilities? Do I work independently of supervision? Score _____

E. Ideas
To what extent have I offered ideas and suggestions for improvements? Do I suggest better ways of doing things instead of just complaining? Score _____

F. Problem Solver/Preventer
To what extent have I contributed to solving or preventing problems? Do I anticipate problem situations and try to avoid them? Do I push-pull when necessary? Do I keep an open line of communication? Score _____

G. Safety
To what extent do my actions show my concern for safety for myself and others? Do I alert coworkers to unsafe procedures? Do I alert my coach to unsafe conditions in my department? Score _____

H. Quality Image
To what extent have I displayed a high-quality image in my appearance, language, personal hygiene, and working environment? Score _____

making your own decisions." I went from authoritarian control to authoritarian abdication. No one had asked for more responsibility; I forced it down their throats. They were good soldiers, and they did their best, but I had trained them to expect me to solve their problems. I had nurtured their inability by expecting them to be incapable; now they met my expectations with an inability to make decisions unless they knew which decisions I wanted them to make.

After more than two years of working with them, I finally had to replace all three top managers. Worst of all, I now see that in a way they were right. I didn't really *want* them to make independent decisions. I wanted them to make the decisions I would have made. Deep down, I was still in love with my own control; I was just making people guess what I wanted instead of telling them. And yet I had to replace those three managers. I needed people who didn't

guess so well, people who couldn't read my mind, people strong enough to call my bluff and seize ownership of Johnsonville's problems whether I "really" wanted to give it up or not.

I spent those two years pursuing another mirage as well—detailed strategic and tactical plans that would realize my goal of Johnsonville as the world's greatest sausage maker. We tried to plan organizational structure two to three years before it would be needed—who

II. TEAMWORK

A. Contribution to Groups
How would I rate my contribution to my department's performance? Am I aware of department goals? Do I contribute to a team? Do I communicate with team members?   Score _____

B. Communication
To what extent do I keep others informed to prevent problems from occurring? Do I work to promote communication between plants and departments? Do I relay information to the next shift? Do I speak up at meetings and let my opinions and feelings be known?   Score _____

C. Willingness to Work Together
To what extent am I willing to share the responsibility of getting the work done? Do I voluntarily assist others to obtain results? Do I demonstrate a desire to accomplish department goals? Do I complete paperwork accurately and thoroughly and work toward a smooth flow of information throughout the company? Am I willing to share in any overtime?   Score _____

D. Attendance and Timeliness
Do I contribute to the team by being present and on time for work (including after breaks and lunch)? Do I realize the inconvenience and hardship caused by my absence or tardiness?   Score _____

III. PERSONAL DEVELOPMENT

A. To what extent am I actively involved in lifelong learning? Taking classes is not the only way to learn. Other ways include use of our resource center or libraries for reading books, articles, etc.   Score _____

B. Do I improve my job performance by applying what I have learned?   Score _____

C. Do I ask questions pertaining to my job and other jobs too?   Score _____

D. Do I try to better myself not only through work but in all aspects of my life?   Score _____

E. Do I seek information about our industry?   Score _____

TOTAL POINTS: _____

would be responsible for what and who would report to whom, all carefully diagrammed in boxes and lines on charts. Later I realized that these structural changes had to grow from day-to-day working realities; no one could dictate them from above, and certainly not in advance. But at the time, my business training told me this was the way to proceed. The discussions went on at an abstract level for months, the details overwhelmed us, and we got nowhere.

In short, the early 1980s were a disaster. After two years of stewing, it began to dawn on me that my first reactions to most situations were usually dead wrong. After all, my organizational instincts had brought us to Point A to begin with. Pursuing those instincts now would only bring us *back* to Point A. I needed to start thinking before I acted, and the thought I needed to think was, "Will this action help us achieve our new Point B?"

Point B also needed some revision. The early 1980s taught me that I couldn't give responsibility. People had to expect it, want it, even demand it. So my end state needed redefining. The goal was not so much a state of shared responsibility as an environment where people insist on being responsible.

To bring people to that new Point B, I had to learn to be a better coach. It took me additional years to learn the art of coaching, by which, in a nutshell, I mean communicating a vision and then getting people to see their own behavior, harness their own frustrations, and own their own problems.

Early in the change process, for example, I was told that workers in one plant disliked working weekends, which they often had to do to meet deliveries. Suspecting that the weekends weren't really necessary, I pressed plant managers to use the problem as an opportunity. I asked them if they had measured production efficiency, for instance, and if they had tried to get their workers to take responsibility for the overtime problem. The first thing everyone discovered was that machine downtime hovered between 30% and 40%. Then they started coming to terms with the fact that all that downtime had its causes – lateness, absences, sloppy maintenance, slow shift startups. Once the workers began to see that they themselves were the problem, they realized that they could do away with weekend work. In three weeks, they cut downtime to less than 10% and had Saturdays and Sundays off.

Managing the Context

The debacle of ordering change and watching it fail to occur showed me my limitations. I had come to realize that I didn't directly control the performance of the people at Johnsonville, that as a manager I didn't really manage people. They managed themselves. But I did manage the context. I provided and allocated the resources. I designed and implemented the systems. I drew up and executed the organizational structure. The power of any contextual factor lies in its ability to shape the way people think and what they expect. So I worked on two contextual areas: systems and structures.

Systems. I first attacked our quality control system. Quality was central to our business success, one of our key competitive advantages. But even though our quality was better than average, it wasn't yet good enough to be great.

We had the traditional quality control department with the traditional quality control responsibilities – catching errors before they got to the customer. Senior management was a part of the system. Several times a week we evaluated the product – that is to say, we *checked* it – for taste, flavor, color, and texture.

One day it struck me that by checking the product, top management had assumed responsibility for its quality. We were not encouraging people to be responsible for their own performance. We were not helping people commit themselves to making Johnsonville a great company.

> ## Customer letters are answered by the line workers who make the sausage.

This line of reasoning led me to another insight: the first strategic decision I needed to make was who should make decisions. On the theory that those who implement a decision and live with its consequences are the best people to make it, we changed our quality control system. Top management stopped tasting sausage, and the people who made sausage started. We informed line workers that from now on it would be their responsibility to make certain that only top-quality product left the plant. In the future, they would manage quality control.

It surprised me how readily people accepted this ownership. They formed teams of workers to resolve quality problems. For example, one team attacked the problem of leakers – vacuum-packed plastic packages of sausage that leaked air and shortened shelf life. The team gathered data, identified problems, worked with suppliers and with other line workers to develop and implement solutions, even visited retail stores to find out how retailers handled the product so we could make changes that would prevent their problems from occurring. The team took complete responsibility for measuring quality and then used those measurements to improve production processes. They owned and expected to own all the problems of producing top-quality sausage, and they wanted to do the best possible job. The results were amazing. Rejects fell from 5% to less than 0.5%.

Clearly this new quality control system was helping to create the end state we were after. Its success triggered changes in several other systems as well.

Teams of workers in other areas began to taste the product every morning and discuss possible improvements. They asked for information about costs and customer reactions, and we redesigned the information system to give it to them.

We began to forward customer letters directly to line workers. They responded to customer complaints and sent coupons for free Johnsonville sausage when they felt it was warranted. They came to own and expect responsibility for correcting the problems that customers raised in their letters.

People in each section on the shop floor began to collect data about labor costs, efficiency, and yield. They posted the data and discussed it at the daily tasting meeting. Increasingly, people asked for more responsibility, and the information system encouraged them to take it. We were progressing toward our end state, and as we made progress we uncovered deeper and more complex problems.

One of these arose when people on the shop floor began to complain about fellow workers whose performance was still slipshod or indifferent. In fact, they came to senior management and said, "You don't take your own advice. If you did, you wouldn't let these poor performers work here. It's your job to either fix them or fire them."

Our first reaction was to jump in and do something, but by now we had learned to think before acting. We asked ourselves if accepting responsibility for this problem would help us reach Point B. The answer was clearly no. More important, we asked ourselves who was in the best position to own the problem and came to the obvious conclusion that the people on the shop floor knew more about shop-floor performance

How Johnsonville Shares Profits on the Basis of Performance

Every six months, we evaluate the performance of everyone at Johnsonville to help us compute shares in our profit-sharing program. Except "we" is the wrong word. In practice, performance evaluations are done by the employees themselves. For example, 300 wage earners—salaried employees have a separate profit-sharing pool and a different evaluation system—fill out forms in which they rate themselves on a scale of 1 to 9 in 17 specific areas grouped into three categories: performance, teamwork, and personal development.

Scores of 3, 4, or 5—the average range—are simply entered on the proper line. Low scores of 1 or 2 and high scores of 6 to 9 require a sentence or two of explanation.

Each member's coach fills out an identical form, and later both people sit down together and discuss all 17 areas. In cases of disagreement, the rule is only that their overall point totals must agree within nine points, whereupon the two totals are averaged to reach a final score. If they cannot narrow the gap to nine points, an arbitration group is ready to step in and help, but so far mediation has never been needed.

All final scores, names deleted, are then passed to a profit-sharing team that carves out five categories of performance: a small group of superior performers (about 5% of the total), a larger group of better-than-average workers (roughly 20%), an average group amounting to about 50% of the total work force, a below-average group of 20%, and a small group of poor performers who are often in some danger of losing their jobs.

The total pool of profits to be shared is then divided by the number of workers to find an average share—for the purpose of illustration, let's say $1,000. Members of the top group get a check for 125% of that amount or $1,250. Members of the next group get 110% ($1,100), of the large middle group, 100% or $1,000, and so on down to $900 and $750.

Yes, people do complain from time to time, especially if they think they've missed a higher share by only a point or two. The usual way of dealing with such situations is to help the individual improve his or her performance in enough areas to ensure a higher score the next time. But overall satisfaction with the system is very high, partly because fellow workers invented it, administer it, and constantly revise it in an effort to make it more equitable. The person currently in charge of the Johnsonville profit-sharing team is an hourly worker from the shipping department.

Many forms have been used over the years—a new one is under consideration at this moment—but the questions most recently asked, in a slightly edited version, are reprinted in this article.

than we did, so they were the best ones to make these decisions.

We offered to help them set performance standards and to coach them in confronting poor performers, but we insisted that since they were the production-performance experts, it was up to them to deal with the situation. I bit my tongue time and time again, but they took on the responsibility for dealing with performance problems and actually fired individuals who wouldn't perform up to the standards of their teams.

This led to a dramatic change in Johnsonville's human resource system. Convinced that inadequate selection and training of new workers caused performance problems, line workers asked to do the selection and training themselves. Managers helped them set up selection and training procedures, but production workers made them work. Eventually, line workers assumed most of the traditional personnel functions.

The compensation system was another early target for change. We had traditionally given across-the-board annual raises like most other businesses. What mattered was longevity, not performance. That system was also a stumbling block on our way to Point B, so we made two changes.

First, we eliminated the annual across-the-board raise and substituted a pay-for-responsibility system. As people took on new duties—budgeting, for instance, or training—they earned additional base income. Where the old system rewarded people for hanging around, regardless of what they contributed, the new one encouraged people to seek responsibility.

Second, we instituted what we called a "company performance share," a fixed percentage of pre-tax profits to be divided every six months among our employees. We based individual shares on a performance-appraisal system designed and administered by a volunteer team of line production workers from various departments. The system is explained in the insert "How Johnsonville Shares Profits on the Basis of Performance."

These system changes taught me two more valuable lessons. First, just start. Don't wait until you have all the answers. When I set out to make these changes, I had no clear picture of how these new systems would interact with one another or with other company systems and procedures, but if I had waited until I had all the answers, I'd still be waiting. A grand plan was impossible; there were too many variables. I wasn't certain which systems to change; I just knew I had to change something in order to alter expectations and begin moving toward my goal.

Second, start by changing the most visible system you directly control. You want your first effort to succeed. I knew I could control who tasted the product because I was doing the tasting. I also knew it was a highly visible action. Everyone waited to hear my taste-test results. By announcing that I wasn't going to taste the product anymore and that the people who made it were, everyone knew immediately that I was serious about spreading responsibility.

Structures. Along with the system changes, I introduced a number of changes in company structure. Teams gradually took over a number of the functions previously performed by individual managers in the chain of command, with the result that the number of hierarchical layers went from six to three.

Teams had already taken on responsibility for selecting, training, evaluating, and, when necessary, terminating fellow employees. Now they began to make all decisions about schedules, performance standards, assignments, budgets, quality measures, and capital improvements as well. In operations, teams assumed the supervisors' functions, and those jobs disappeared. Those

former supervisors who needed authority in order to function left the company, but most went into other jobs at Johnsonville, some of them into technical positions.

The function of the quality control department was redefined. It stopped checking quality—now done by line workers—and began providing technical support to the production people in a cooperative effort to *improve* quality. The department developed systems for continuous on-line monitoring of fat, moisture, and protein content, for example, and it launched a program of outside taste testing among customers.

The traditional personnel department disappeared and was replaced by a learning and personal development team to help individual employees develop their own Points B and A—their destinations and starting points—and figure out how to use Johnsonville to reach their goals. We set up an educational allowance for each person, to be used however the individual saw fit. In the beginning, some took cooking or sewing classes; a few took flying lessons. Over time, however, more and more of the employees focused on job-related learning. Today more than 65% of all the people at Johnsonville are involved in some type of formal education.

The end state we all now envision for Johnsonville is a company that never stops learning. One part of learning is the acquisition of facts and knowledge—about accounting, machine maintenance, marketing,

even about sky diving and Italian cooking. But the most important kind of learning teaches us to question our own actions and behavior in order to better understand the ways we perform, work, and live.

Helping human beings fulfill their potential is of course a moral responsibility, but it's also good business. Life is aspiration. Learning, striving people are happy people and good workers. They have initiative and imagination, and the companies they work for are rarely caught napping.

Learning is change, and I keep learning and relearning that change is and needs to be continuous. For example, our system and structural changes were reciprocal. The first led to the second, which then in turn led to new versions of the first.

Initially, I had hoped the journey would be as neat and orderly as it now appears on paper. Fortunately—since original mistakes are an important part of learning—it wasn't. There were lots of obstacles and challenges, much backsliding, and myriad false starts and wrong decisions.

For example, team leaders chosen by their team members were supposed to function as communication links, leaving the traditional management functions of planning and scheduling to the group itself. No sooner had the team leaders been appointed, however, than they began to function as supervisors. In other words, they immediately fell into the familiar roles they had always seen.

We had neglected to give them and the plant managers adequate training in the new team model. The structure changed, but mind-sets didn't. It was harder to alter people's expectations than I had realized.

Influencing Expectations

I discovered that change occurs in fits and starts, and that while I could plan individual changes and events, I couldn't plan the whole process. I also learned that expectations have a way of becoming reality, so I tried to use every available means —semantic, symbolic, and behavioral—to send messages that would shape expectations to Johnsonville's advantage.

For example, we wanted to break down the traditional pictures in people's minds of what managers do and how subordinates and employees behave, so we changed the words we used. We dropped the words employee and subordinate. Instead we called everyone a "member" of the organization, and managers became "coordinators" or "coaches."

Our promotion system had always sent a powerful message: to move up the ladder you need to become a manager and solve problems for your people. But this was now the wrong message. I wanted coordinators who could build problem-solving capaci-

> ## The CEO who knows about a problem owns it. My advice: don't ask.

ties in others rather than solve their problems for them. I recast the job requirements for the people whose work I directly coordinated (formerly known as "my management team"), and they, in turn, did the same for the people whose work they coordinated. I took every opportunity to stress the need for coaching skills, and I continually deemphasized technical experience. Whenever someone became a coordinator, I made sure word got around that the promotion was for demon-

strated abilities as a teacher, coach, and facilitator.

This new promotion standard sent a new message: to get ahead at Johnsonville, you need a talent for cultivating and encouraging problem solvers and responsibility takers.

I discovered that people watched my every action to see if it supported or undermined our vision. They wanted to see if I practiced what I preached. From the outset I did simple things to demonstrate my sincerity. I made a sign for my desk that said THE QUESTION IS THE ANSWER, and when people came to me with questions, I asked myself if they were questions I should answer. Invariably, they weren't. Invariably, people were asking me to make decisions for them. Instead of giving answers, I turned the tables and asked the questions myself, trying to make them repossess their own problems. Owning problems was an important part of the end state I'd envisioned. I wasn't about to let people give theirs to me.

I also discovered that in meetings people waited to hear my opinion before offering their own. In the beginning, I insisted they say what they thought, unaware that I showed my own preferences in subtle ways—my tone of voice, the questions I asked—which, nevertheless, anyone could read and interpret expertly. When I realized what was happening, I began to stay silent to avoid giving any clue to where I stood. The result was that people flatly refused to commit themselves to any decision at all. Some of those meetings would have gone on for days if I hadn't forced people to speak out before they'd read my mind.

In the end, I began scheduling myself out of many meetings, forcing others to make their decisions without me. I also stopped collecting data about production problems. I learned that if I had information about daily shortages and yields, I began to ask questions that put me firmly back in possession of the problems.

Eventually, I came to understand that everything I did and said had a symbolic as well as a literal meaning. I had to anticipate the potential impact of every word and act, ask myself again and again if what I was

about to do or say would reinforce the vision or undermine it, bring us closer to Point B or circle us back to Point A, encourage people to own their own problems or palm them off on me. My job, as I had come to see it, was to put myself out of a job.

Watershed

By mid-1985, we had all come a long way. Johnsonville members had started wanting and expecting responsibility for their own performance, and they usually did a good job. Return on assets was up significantly, as were margins and quality. But on the whole, the process of change had been a journey without any major mileposts or station stops.

> ## Palmer's contract offer was close to a bet-the-company decision.

Then Palmer Sausage (not its real name) came along and gave us our watershed—a golden opportunity and a significant threat to our existence.

Palmer is a much larger sausage company that had contracted with us for private-label products during a strike in the early 1980s. Our quality was so high that they kept us on as a supplier after the strike ended. Now Palmer had decided to consolidate several facilities and offered to let us take over part of the production of a plant they were closing. It represented a huge increase in their order, and the additional business was very tempting: it could be very profitable, and it would justify the cost of a new and more efficient plant of our own. The upside was extremely attractive—if we could handle it.

That was what worried me. To handle an expanded Palmer contract, we'd have to hire and train a large group of people quickly and teach our present people new skills, keep quality high on both the Palmer products and our own, work six and seven days a week for more than a year until our new plant was ready, and run the risk if Palmer cancelled – which it could do on 30-days notice – of saddling ourselves with big layoffs and new capacity we no longer had a market for. Maybe it wasn't a bet-the-company decision, but it was as close as I'd like to come.

Before 1982, I would have met for days with my senior team to discuss all these issues, and we would probably have turned down the opportunity in the face of such an overwhelming downside. But by 1985, it was clear to me that the executive group was the wrong group to make this decision. The executives would not be responsible for successfully implementing such a move. The only way we could do Palmer successfully was if everyone at Johnsonville was committed to making it work, so everyone had to decide.

Until that moment, my senior team had always made the strategic decisions. We took advice from people in the operating departments, but the senior staff and I had dealt with the ultimate problems and responsibilities. We needed to move to a new level. This was a problem all of our people had to own.

My senior managers and I called a meeting of the entire plant, presented the problem, and posed three questions. What will it take to make it work? Is it possible to reduce the downside? Do we want to do it?

We asked the teams in each area to discuss these questions among themselves and develop a list of pros and cons. Since the group as a whole was too large to work together effectively, each team chose one member to report its findings to a plantwide representative body to develop a plantwide answer.

The small groups met almost immediately, and within days their representatives met. The discussion moved back and forth several times between the representative body and the smaller groups.

To make it work, the members decided we'd have to operate seven days a week, hire and train people to take new shifts, and increase efficiency to get more from current capacity. They also thought about the downside risk. The biggest danger was that we'd lose the added business after making all the investments and sacrifices needed to handle it. They figured the only way to reduce that downside potential was to achieve quality standards so high that we would actually improve the already first-rate Palmer product and, at the same time, maintain standards on our own products to make sure Johnsonville brands didn't fall by the wayside.

Ralph Stayer's Guide to Improving Performance

Getting better performance from any group or individual, yourself included, means a permanent change in the way you think and run your business. Change of this kind is not a single transaction but a journey, and the journey has a specific starting point and a clear destination.

The journey is based on six observations about human behavior that I didn't fully grasp when I started, though I'd have made faster progress and fewer mistakes if I had.

1. People want to be great. If they aren't, it's because management won't let them be.

2. Performance begins with each individual's expectations. Influence what people expect and you influence how people perform.

3. Expectations are driven partly by goals, vision, symbols, semantics, and partly by the context in which people work, that is, by such things as compensation systems, production practices, and decision-making structures.

4. The actions of managers shape expectations.

5. Learning is a process, not a goal. Each new insight creates a new layer of potential insights.

6. The organization's results reflect me and my performance. If I want to change the results, I have to change myself first. This is particularly true for me, the owner and CEO, but it is equally true for every employee.

So to make the changes that will lead to great performance, I recommend focusing on goals, expectations, contexts, actions, and learning. Lee Thayer, a humanities professor at the University of Wisconsin, has another way of saying pretty much the same thing. He argues that since performance is the key to organizational success, management's job is to establish the conditions under which superb performance serves both the company's and the individual's best interests.

CEOs need to focus first on changing themselves before they try to change the rest of the company. The process resembles an archaeological dig, or at least it did for me. As I uncovered and solved one problem, I almost invariably exposed another, deeper problem. As I gained one insight and mastered one situation, another situation arose that required new insight and more learning. As I approached one goal, a new, more important, but more distant goal always began to take shape.

Two weeks later, the company decided almost unanimously to take the business. It was one of the proudest moments of my life. Left to our traditional executive decision making, we would have turned Palmer down. The Johnsonville people, believing in themselves, rose to the challenge. They really did want to be great.

The results surpassed our best projections. Learning took place faster than anticipated. Quality rose in our own product line as well as for Palmer. The new plant came on line in 1987. Palmer has come back to us several times since to increase the size of its orders even further.

Success – The Greatest Enemy

The pace of change increased after Palmer. Now that all of Johnsonville's people expected and wanted some degree of responsibility for strategic decisions, we had to redefine Point A, our current situation. The new level of involvement also led us to a more ambitious view of what we could ultimately achieve – Point B, our vision and destination.

We made additional changes in our career-tracking system. In our early enthusiasm, we had played down the technical aspects of our business, encouraging everyone to become a coordinator, even those who were far better suited to technical specialties. We also had some excellent salespeople who became coordinators because they saw it as the only path to advancement, though their talents and interests lay much more in selling than in coaching. When they became coordinators, we lost in three ways: we lost good salespeople, we created poor coordinators, and we lost sales from other good salespeople because they worked for these poor coordinators.

A career team recommended that Johnsonville set up dual career tracks – one for specialists and one for coordinators – that would enable both to earn recognition, status, and compensation on the basis of performance alone. The team, not the senior coordinators, agreed to own and fix the compensation problem.

Everyone at Johnsonville discovered they could do considerably better and earn considerably more than they had imagined. Since they had little trouble meeting the accelerated

production goals that they themselves had set, members raised the minimum acceptable performance criteria and began routinely to expect more of themselves and others.

Right now, teams of Johnsonville members are meeting to discuss next year's capital budget, new product ideas, today's production schedule, and yesterday's quality, cost, and yield. More important, these same teams are redesigning their systems and structures to manage their continuing journey toward Point B,

> ▌ For the last five years, my ambition has been to eliminate my job.

which, along with Point A, they are also continually redefining. Most important of all, their general level of commitment is now as high or higher than my own.

In fact, our greatest enemy now is our success. Our sales, margins, quality, and productivity far exceed anything we could have imagined in 1980. We've been studied and written about, and we've spent a lot of time answering questions and giving advice. We've basked in the limelight, telling other people how we did it. All the time we kept telling ourselves, "We can't let this go to our heads." But of course it had already gone to our heads. We had begun to talk and brag about the past instead of about what we wanted for the future. Once we saw what we were doing, we managed to stop and, in the process, learn a lesson about the hazards of self-congratulation.

Author's note: I wish to acknowledge the contribution of my partner, James A. Belasco, to this article.

When I began this process of change ten years ago, I looked forward to the time when it would all be over and I could get back to my real job. But I've learned that change *is* the real job of every effective business leader because change is about the present and the future, not about the past. There is no end to change. This story is only an interim report.

Yet another thing I've learned is that the cause of excitement at Johnsonville Sausage is not change itself but the process used in producing change. Learning and responsibility are invigorating, and aspirations make our hearts beat. For the last five years, my own aspiration has been to eliminate *my* job by creating such a crowd of self-starting, problem-solving, responsibility-grabbing, independent thinkers that Johnsonville would run itself.

Two years ago, I hired a new chief operating officer and told him he should lead the company and think of me as his paid consultant. Earlier this year, he invited me to a management retreat, and I enjoyed myself. Other people owned the problems that had once been mine. My whole job was to generate productive conversations about Johnsonville's goals and to communicate its vision.

On the second evening of the retreat, I was given a message from my COO. There was a special session the next morning, he wrote, and added, "I want you there at 8:15." Instinctively, it made me mad. Johnsonville was my company; I built it; I fixed it; he owed me his job. Who the hell did he think he was giving me orders like a hired consultant?

Then, of course, I laughed. It's not always easy giving up control, even when it's what you've worked toward for ten years. He wanted me there at 8:15? Well, good for him. I'd be there.   ⬒

Reprint 90610

Entrepreneurship in Big Business

Infusing bureaucracy with entrepreneurial energy starts at the top.

Championing Change:
An Interview With Bell Atlantic's CEO Raymond Smith

by Rosabeth Moss Kanter

Competing in the telecommunications industry is increasingly a world game. Rapid scientific advances are increasing communications speed and blurring the distinction between information technologies and communication technologies – computer companies are in the communications business, and telephone companies are selling systems integration. The old-fashioned Phone Company – once a monopoly in the United States and a government ministry elsewhere – is now subject to forces of competition, through changing regulation or privatization.

Few industries as old have been transformed so dramatically in such a short time, and further transformations are on the horizon. The U.S. edge in the telecommunications sector may well depend on the skill with which change – human, organizational, and technological – is managed.

Bell Atlantic Corporation was formed in 1983, in preparation for the breakup of the Bell System telephone monopoly on January 1, 1984. It is one of seven U.S. regional telecommunications holding companies (sometimes called "baby Bells") created when AT&T was required by judicial decree to divest its local telephone operations, ushering in the era of greater competition.

Bell Atlantic began with a charter to provide local telephone service in six mid-Atlantic states and the District of Columbia. By 1990, Bell Atlantic was introducing new products and services at a rapid clip, starting ventures and forming alliances throughout the world, and pursuing leadership in the information technology industry of the future. The corporation reported 1989 earnings of over $1 billion on revenues of $11.4 billion, with 76% of its revenues from its regulated local telephone business.

Bell Atlantic's vision centers around the creation of the "Intelligent Network," a computer-driven network capable of transmitting audio, video, and data signals through speedy fiber-optic lines. Calling itself the world's most efficient telephone company, Bell Atlantic today has the lowest costs among the regional firms. It provides telephone service over 17 million access lines – more lines than any other baby Bell.

Raymond Smith, 53, became Bell Atlantic's CEO in January 1989, adding the responsibilities of chairman of the board in July 1989. Earlier in his career, he managed operations, regulatory affairs, engineering, and finance for AT&T, rising to the presidencies of the Pennsylvania and Delaware companies, positions he held when Bell Atlantic was formed. A year after Bell Atlantic's inception, he moved to the corporate team as vice chairman and chief financial officer (1985 to 1987) and then president and chief operating officer (1988). He worked closely with his predecessor Thomas Bolger to shape the business concept and to eliminate vestiges of the traditionally complacent, monopolistic mind-set known as having "Bell-shaped heads."

Mr. Smith spoke with HBR Editor and Class of 1960 Harvard Business School Professor Rosabeth Moss Kanter about the CEO's role in transforming a monopolistic, bureaucratic corporation into one that is both efficient and entrepreneurial.

HBR: *How did you view the state of your business when you became Bell Atlantic's chief executive?*

Raymond Smith: I saw that the way we had been managing all of these years was going to have to change. The problem was clear. The intrinsic growth of the core business would not sustain the company in the competitive global economy of the twenty-first century.

The difficulty of addressing our basic business problem was complicated by competition on one side and regulation on the other. Even our 3% projected growth rate was subject to considerable, well-financed competition in the most profitable lines. As

> "The intrinsic growth of the core business would not sustain the company in the competitive global economy of the twenty-first century."

a regulated company, we owed a subsidy to the local telephone rate-payers, so we were limited in what we could earn in the core business. And the legislation and judicial decree that broke up the Bell System restricted the kinds of businesses we could enter. For example, the Cable Act of 1984 kept Bell Atlantic from competing in the cable television business in our region.

How did you think the company could increase its rate of growth in revenues and earnings?

We identified five initial strategies. Four of them would sound familiar to many businesses: improved efficiency; substantially improved marketing to protect market share; new products and services; and entirely new businesses operating outside of our territory and outside of the United States.

The fifth strategy was one we had to work on right away. It involved regulatory reform that we called "incentive regulation" to allow us to benefit from our own initiatives while protecting the telephone rate-payers. We worked intensively with regulators and crafted social contracts with consumer groups and those most affected by telephone rates, such as senior citizens and people with disabilities.

With incentive regulation accomplished, we could concentrate on the business growth strategies. But none of our strategies could be achieved with the company culture in place after the breakup. So I had to focus on the culture first.

What was wrong with the culture?

The company had grown out of a long-standing monopoly, with the centralized organizational structure and culture of a monopoly. In the old Bell System culture, no operating company could introduce a product of its own. The way a small work center in a small town in Pennsylvania would operate was mandated by the central staff. There was no strategic planning, no product development, no long-range planning in the operating companies. It was all centralized at AT&T.

What was the consequence of that?

The operating companies had an implementation mentality. They did not understand the initiative, innovation, risks, and accountability necessary to meet our business goals. Managers were held accountable for implementation of a process or practice exactly as it was written, not for the end result. Managers simply could not imagine rewriting a process even if they knew a better one. They were maintenance managers, not business managers.

When I told those same managers that we wanted improved marketing, new products, and new business, it was a mental shock. We had no experience to draw on. And the ways we were accustomed to operating impeded our ability to achieve our goals.

How so?

Cross-departmental competition raised costs and prevented new initiatives. This problem was a consequence of our heritage.

The old Bell System was like a great football team with the best athletes and the best equipment. Every Saturday morning, we'd run up and down the football field and win 100 to 0 because there was no one on the other side of the line of scrimmage; we were a monopoly. Being human, the football players found

> "Cross-departmental competition raised costs and prevented new initiatives."

their competition inside the team. This sometimes resulted in lowest common denominator solutions and substantial inefficiency. Despite dedication and hard work, it often took more resources to get things done than were ever really needed.

The conventions of behavior grew out of cross-departmental competition and were very parochial.

There was no true unifying concept to rally around. I represented my department, you represented your department, and we behaved as if we were opposing lawyers or political opponents.

When did you begin to see that this kind of behavior had to change?

In the early 1980s, when we began to see real competition. Tom Bolger, my predecessor as CEO, and I agreed that we needed a new culture to support our business strategies.

Where did you start?

We started by articulating the values of the corporation. I was personally involved, with another officer, in the design of seminars in which 1,400 managers spent half a week to think through our values and state them clearly. At the seminars, a draft was handed out for discussion. These managers were actively engaged in editing the document word by word. New categories were suggested; eventually, "teamwork" became "respect and trust." I attended virtually every seminar and met with the participants for five or six hours a week.

Ultimately, we agreed on five values: integrity, respect and trust, excellence, individual fulfillment, and profitable growth, with a paragraph of description explaining each.

What happened when the sessions were completed and the statement of values was published?

Not enough! It became very apparent to me and to the managers involved that we needed to move from general statements of values to concrete behaviors and work practices, or what we called the "conventions" of day-to-day business life. So when I became CEO, I announced a ten-year transition to a new way of working together.

Every corporation today is full of rhetoric like "it's time to change" or "we need a new way" or "we want to get rid of bureaucracy." What did you do to show people that you meant it?

One of the first steps I took was to engage the senior officers in a serious examination of our obligations to the corporation. I personally prepared a list of 12 specific guidelines. In a series of day-long meetings, I suggested to each of the top 50 people in Bell Atlantic that they had broad corporate obligations that went beyond their departmental responsibilities. There were arguments and debates about the

The Obligations of Leadership
by Raymond Smith

As Bell Atlantic executives, we have the special obligation to provide an ethical leadership that goes beyond our departmental or subsidiary goals.

We have the obligation to:

☐ Participate in the development of the values, purpose, goals, strategies, and corporate positions of Bell Atlantic and communicate our endorsement to all of our employees.

☐ Provide vigorous input into corporate decisions while maintaining a clear focus on Bell Atlantic's interests.

☐ Work diligently to see that decisions important to Bell Atlantic are made in a timely fashion.

☐ Dissent or escalate problems or decisions when we believe Bell Atlantic's interests are not being served but enthusiastically support the final decision once it has been made.

☐ Obtain the necessary information to communicate Bell Atlantic's values, mission, goals, strategies and corporate positions to all of our constituents.

☐ Define our roles and manage our organizations in a manner that will support the goals of Bell Atlantic while meeting our local obligations to employees, customers, and communities.

☐ Support and encourage local proprietorship, pride, and accountability within the framework of Bell Atlantic's goals and objectives.

☐ Look beyond our groups or companies to encourage teamwork and integration among the Bell Atlantic family of companies.

☐ Encourage innovation within our organizations and share the benefits of that innovation with other Bell Atlantic units.

☐ Find creative solutions to the inevitable disputes that arise from sharing resources among the various Bell Atlantic groups.

☐ Avoid short-term expediencies that will be detrimental to Bell Atlantic's long-term strategies and objectives.

☐ Create an environment for individual initiative, growth, and development.

In brief, Bell Atlantic executives are the role models of the corporation, obliged to demonstrate constructive teamwork and be exemplary representatives. We lead the planners, strategists and implementers of the Bell Atlantic plan. With our employees, we show the Bell Atlantic Way.

obligations, but in the end they stood. It took a year to get the required understanding and commitment.

We made quality a corporate imperative in our 1989 strategic plan, designing a Quality Improvement Process using the Baldrige Award criteria and starting our own Quality Institute. We developed an organized program of internal communications for all employees outlining our obligations to each other, the opportunities ahead, and the need and reasons for change. We called this the Bell Atlantic Way.

What is the Bell Atlantic Way, and why did you think you needed it?

Simply stated, the Bell Atlantic Way is an organized, participative method of working together that allows us to get the most out of our own efforts and maximize our contribution to team goals. The Bell Atlantic Way includes the conventions of daily behavior subscribed to by all of us.

In a large business, the most important determinant of success is the effectiveness of millions of day-to-day interactions between human beings. If those contacts are contentious, turf-oriented, and parochial, the company will flounder, bureaucracies will grow, and internal competition will be rampant. But when employees behave in accountable, team-oriented and collegial ways, it dramatically improves group effectiveness.

The Bell Atlantic Way isn't limited to a list of dos and don'ts, but it does seem to boil down to a few specific behaviors. For example, the plaque on my desk says, "Be Here Now." That just means that it's important that I listen and be totally involved in any discussion we may have. I'm not looking over my shoulder. I'm not taking phone calls. I'm not doodling or having side conversations while you are making a presentation.

In such a large corporation, how do you get people to operate by these codes of behavior?

With the help of consultants, we designed forums to introduce the Bell Atlantic Way to 20,000 managers. The officer group, roughly 50 people, attended first. Then the officers acted as executives-in-residence at forums for the rest of the managers and supervisors. Most of us have been through the sessions two or three times.

We teach the conventions, we don't just talk about them. Each one is impressed on forum participants in experiential exercises that help us examine ourselves and remind us of our obligations to each other. And our responsibilities don't stop at the end of the forum. I'm spending a great deal of my own time in the field meeting with employees and talking about the Bell Atlantic Way. Each of the officers has developed departmental programs of reinforcement and support back on the job.

Why is it important for you and the other officers to spend scarce executive time on this, involving yourselves in a personal way?

We must ourselves model what we are asking others to do. We call this "the shadow of the leader." We

Bell Atlantic Reaches Out: Emerging World Alliances

NORTH AMERICA

California
Sun Microsystems (1990)
  workstation support, Eastern regions

Illinois
RR Donnelley (1988)
  directory graphics joint venture

Massachusetts
Digital Equipment Corporation (1990)
  expert system sales

Connecticut
Deloitte & Touche (1990)
  expert systems development

Virginia
American Management Systems (1989)
  systems integration joint venture

[Bell Atlantic's traditional U.S. telephone district =
New Jersey, Pennsylvania, Delaware, Maryland,
Washington, DC, Virginia, West Virginia]

EUROPE

Belgium
Bell Atlantic-Europe headquarters (1989)

France
CGI Informatique (1990)
  U.S. Local Area Network support with CGI-USA

Spain
Telefonica (1988)
  cooperative marketing, installation of
  operating support system

Germany
Siemans and IBM (1987)
  Intelligent Network product/market study

Czechoslovakia
Czech & Slovak Posts & Telecommunications
Ministry and US West (1990)
  cellular mobile networks and packet data networks

are asking people to change their behavior, to accept a new set of conventions for working together. And I try to provide reinforcement in every way I can. For example, I always wear my Quality button to impress colleagues with my rabid dedication. It serves

> ## "We must ourselves model what we are asking others to do."

to remind us that we have a very special obligation to support those who are supporting the corporation.

It took about a year for top management to internalize the concepts of this change, to recognize it, and to begin to support it fully. Now changes have started to accelerate. We're seeing as much change every three months as we used to see in three years.

What are some tangible signs of change?

The language is changing. The decision process is changing. People are becoming more accountable, more team-oriented, and more effective. For example, our budget process is no longer bitter and contentious. It's still painful and always difficult, but it's much less of a hassle and never personal.

There has been remarkable improvement among the top 400 people of the company who decide on budgets, projects, priorities, and resource allocation.

As corny as it may seem, managers will now open sessions saying, "We've got to break the squares today," referring to one of the Bell Atlantic Way games—meaning we've got to compromise here, break out of thinking about only our own territories. We may know that the corporation has to reduce budgets; so we all must give something up for the good of the whole company.

In the old culture, if I contributed resources for the good of the corporation, I'd lose the support of my own group. Now it is no longer acceptable for someone to say, "I've done my bit. I've met my goal. I'll sit back until you meet yours." It's not acceptable to complain to third parties about the boss or the company or some other department. Someone who does that is likely to be asked, "What did they say when you told them?" One manager said that bitch sessions used to be the social event of the week, but now they're no fun. We expect people to accept accountability for results.

How do you get accountability?

We had to make sure that our reward system encouraged people to focus on results consistent with larger business goals. The first step was to base compensation on corporate and team results as well as individual results. Today the corporate performance award is a much higher percentage of compensation than it was in the past. It used to be zero—or such a tiny percentage that it never meant anything. Now

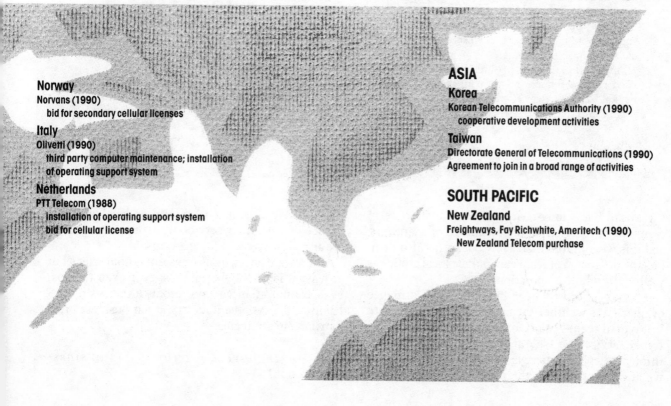

Norway
Norvans (1990)
  bid for secondary cellular licenses

Italy
Olivetti (1990)
  third party computer maintenance; installation
  of operating support system

Netherlands
PTT Telecom (1988)
  installation of operating support system
  bid for cellular license

ASIA
Korea
Korean Telecommunications Authority (1990)
  cooperative development activities

Taiwan
Directorate General of Telecommunications (1990)
  Agreement to join in a broad range of activities

SOUTH PACIFIC
New Zealand
Freightways, Fay Richwhite, Ameritech (1990)
  New Zealand Telecom purchase

Learning the Bell Atlantic Way

The learning sessions begin with a discussion of Bell Atlantic's business situation, but then they depart from tradition. Facilitators guide participants through a set of group exercises that demonstrate the benefits of using the Bell Atlantic principles and help them gain insight into their own attitudes and behaviors.

Exercises such as "breaking the squares" and "finding the blue chips" (originated by the Senn-Delaney Leadership Group) have become the basis for Bell Atlantic symbols and language.

Breaking the Squares

Objective: To demonstrate the importance of compromise and of giving up personal success to help the team achieve a larger goal.

The exercise: Teams of six people are given a variety of puzzle parts and instructed to assemble the parts to make six squares so that each team member has one completed square. The parts can be put together in 57 different ways to make 5 squares, but there is only one way to make 6 squares.

What happens: Some members of the team can quickly assemble a square while others search for a fit. There is a tendency in those who finish early to hang on to their own squares, saying "I've got mine." But in order for the entire team to meet its goal, people must be willing to break up their finished squares, trading parts with the rest of the team until everyone has a full square.

Application on the job: "Breaking the squares" is used as a shorthand expression for the need for each person to break away from advocacy of narrow, parochial interests to see what he or she can contribute to the good of the larger group. To invoke the

need to break the squares is to signal an issue demanding compromise.

Finding the Blue Chips

Objective: To demonstrate the importance of understanding priorities and then focus effort on high-priority tasks.

The exercise: Two teams compete, through a designated representative, to pick up poker chips arranged on a table in front of them. There are white chips close to the participants; red and blue chips farther away. The representatives have one minute to pick up chips – the only instruction they are given. At the end of the minute, the team scores are tabulated: white chips are worth 1, red chips 10, and blue chips 1,000.

What happens: Since white chips are the most accessible, players tend to gather more white chips than others. When the scoring is announced after the round, participants complain that they were tricked. Then they realize that it was their responsibility to ask about any differences between the chips so that they could assess relative value and set priorities.

Application on the job: Blue chips printed with "Bell Atlantic Way" are distributed as reminders. Blue, red, and white are used as shorthand designations of the importance of tasks. If someone is working on a "blue-chip assignment," others are expected to know that such an activity takes precedence. At planning meetings, people might talk about "focusing on the blue chips."

---

the award has a long-term as well as a short-term component for a growing percentage of managers, and it is worth more than a few bucks. It's also flexible; the definition of team can include local groups as well as the whole corporation.

A significant factor in an individual's performance evaluation is whether they have also contributed to the overall team goals. Our team goals include customer service. We look at the customers' attitudes through telephone surveys – whether or not they feel we are conforming to their requirements 100% of

the time. We must reach a minimum level of performance on customer service measures before there are any corporate incentive awards.

Our reward and appraisal system is not perfect, but at least it is getting better. However, even the best evaluation system will not produce the desired behavior unless people understand our business problem and our strategies.

Do your employees get this basic business information?

Now they do, but that was not always the case. As I traveled throughout our company before becoming CEO, I found that very few people really knew what we were trying to do as a company. Sometimes they understood the departmental objectives, and certainly they knew their own objectives, but most people had no idea how to put their day-to-day work life into a corporate context. Actions of the corporation such as the purchase of a new business or the consolidation of an operations center were often a mystery.

How did you clear up the mystery?

My senior officers and I wrote out what we thought was the basic business problem we were trying to solve. We added the specific strategies to solve it, the departmental goals, and finally the individual objectives that were the employees' contributions to the goals. Then we shared it with everyone.

This was somewhat new. The notion of intellectually engaging all of our employees in the solution of the basic business problem was so different from the past that we had to communicate clearly and personally. So we asked the 400 top people in the company, the key managers and communicators, to understand the overall strategy totally and fully, internalize it, and go forth and share it with others. There was a brief hiccup in the company while this idea was absorbed, but then it took off.

You were also giving top managers a big kick in the pants. You were arousing them to action. Shouldn't they have known the strategy and been communicating it all along?

I don't think of it that way. From my first day on the job, I should have made sure that we were all on the same wavelength. I didn't realize that everyone wasn't behaving like a CEO and thinking about the basic corporate problem all day long. When 99% of someone's efforts are engaged in getting a departmental job done, the broad goals of the corporation begin to fade if they are not constantly reinforced. As the head coach and teacher, I hadn't really taught the game plan or the course well enough. So I went on the stump, enlisted the aid of a number of others and spread the word.

Now the top 400 certainly know our business problem. They know our purpose, vision, and strategies, and how they fit together. Because the top 400 talk about this, thousands of other Bell Atlantic employees know it too. They can translate their personal and departmental objectives to those of the company. This makes it easier to deal with the tough realities we face.

What are the tough realities?

We had to eliminate jobs to get our costs in line and reduce wasteful bureaucracy. This is one of the biggest culture shocks we faced. People used to join a Bell System company with the expectation that they'd be taken care of from cradle to grave.

We've tried to do two things to cushion the blow. The first is to level with people. We tell them about the problems in the United States—the troubled companies and the layoffs, plant closings, and ruined careers that come from complacency. We explain that this is the way life is in a competitive world. Wishful thinking won't bring back the old world of no change and total security.

In U.S. business today, the understanding of the real world is vital to survival. In our industry, for example, we have a choice of having a larger number of low-paid employees who will be subject to layoffs, or we can have a smaller group of well-paid, efficient employees with security obtained through hard work and providing customers with more value than they can get elsewhere.

> ## "Almost any organization will succeed if the people feel empowered."

The second thing we do is to try to make stressful changes like downsizing in a participative manner. We eliminated one whole level of management, and we did it by involving the employees in the decision. We had no overall template for the organization, the way the Bell System did in the past. We allowed each organization to eliminate the level it wanted the way it felt was appropriate. After all, almost any organization will succeed if the people feel empowered, are recognized for what they do, and understand the purpose of their jobs.

The idea for this initiative came from New Jersey Bell. The officers thought they could run the business more efficiently if they eliminated a management level, but they wanted to leave the choice of which level to the departments. The departments examined the situation and made the right decision. It worked so well, we made this a Bell Atlantic-wide effort. People in jobs that were about to be eliminated participated in the discussions. Naturally, they were not enthusiastic about cutting their own jobs, so in practice the decision was left to the boss. Still, the "soft" aspects of the organizational change— appreciation, recognition, sharing—were given as much importance as the hard side of reducing the head count.

Was work eliminated along with the level? The criticism of downsizing in many companies is that the people are gone, but the work remains.

Unfortunately, that's true. We saw no way to eliminate all the work first. We reluctantly concluded that we had to reduce the force and then empower the people to eliminate the rest of the work.

On the first day of the new organization, some groups had only eight people to do the work load of ten. But the individual departments were empowered to create the organization they thought would be most efficient. They worked hard to eliminate those activities that were least important. That sort of prioritizing can't be done by some superstaff.

What made you believe that people who had been accustomed to following central mandates would be effective at setting priorities?

People were able to do this because of what they learned from the Bell Atlantic Way. An important part of change is moving from a culture in which people are handed procedures to follow mindlessly to one that helps them make tough choices. This is a difficult process and we're still involved in it. It requires guts and a lot of honest communication.

In the seminars, we play a game with poker chips. The blue chips are valuable; the white chips are practically worthless. Participants learn that it is vital to understand priorities and know what those priorities are based on, such as the goals of the corporation and

> "We are determined to revolutionize staff support, to convert a bureaucratic roadblock into an entrepreneurial force."

not just the goals of the subgroup. The blue chips mean First Things First—priorities. I carry one in my wallet as a reminder.

How do people feel about being involved in a tough restructuring process?

In our regular employee survey, workers cited our downsizing as one reason for improved morale. They told us that although resources are very tight, Bell Atlantic is now a much better place to work. They said since some of the disaffected, cynical people have left, there is much less time for bureaucracy.

What else are you doing to reduce bureaucracy?

We are determined to revolutionize staff support, to convert a bureaucratic roadblock into an entrepreneurial force.

Large staffs that are not subject to bottom-line pressure tend to grow and produce services that may be neither wanted nor required, and their allegiances generally lean toward their professional positions rather than toward their clients. We had to do something to change this.

Three years ago, when I was vice chairman and the staffs reported to me, I decided to place the control of discretionary staff and support expenditures in the hands of those people who were paying for them, that is, the profit centers, the bottom-line groups. We also had to eliminate duplicate staff groups at corporate headquarters and in the operating companies.

Our approach was to create small profit centers within the staff groups, called client service groups or CSGs. For example, the training department became the Training and Educational Services CSG. The accounting department formed the Accounting Operations CSG.

How do the client service groups work?

They sell their services both to the corporate headquarters and to the operating companies. Each year, CSGs develop a budget and an array of products or services based on what Bell Atlantic clients have committed to fund, plus approved amounts for ad hoc or unanticipated business. They have to meet market tests, providing the same value as any outside organization. The CSGs' total annual expenses must equal anticipated revenues (billing credits) from customers. The goal is to break even.

CSGs market their services continuously through items in internal publications, CSG newsletters and brochures, 800-number hotlines, and exhibits at trade shows. The Training and Educational Services CSG publishes a 370-page catalog of offerings. The Information Systems Professional Services CSG heralds new software, programming possibilities, and applications in a regular newsletter.

CSG account managers stay in touch with customers to learn about their needs, answer their questions, facilitate provision of services, and forecast demand. Monthly bills from the CSGs to customers itemize specific services and costs in detail, helping clients to understand and control these costs.

The profit-center customers have to follow a few simple rules. They must give the client service group an opportunity to bid on a project, formally or informally. If the internal organization wins the bid, they use the internal organization. If an outside company wins, they can use the outside firm. But they cannot create their own media group or their own business research group. We want no internal competition.

What happened when you introduced this major structural change?

First of all, it was believed that the client service groups wouldn't work. In some quarters it was considered a dingbat idea that would go away. Still, the first year got off to a pretty good start.

The second year brought a budget crunch and nearly destroyed the process. The budgets of the client service groups were cut by the central financial staffs without the clients' agreement. This is absolutely counter to the rules we devised. It wasn't done surreptitiously, just out of misunderstanding, but it

"Spending for discretionary staff support activities is now controlled by the clients."

happened. The new groups called foul, and we did some damage control to restore their budgets. There were also cases in which individual departments tried to form their own support groups under different labels, under different names.

In the third year, there is no question that the client service groups are working.

What results are you getting?

Market pressures are keeping the client service groups at a reasonable level. Expenditures for discretionary staff services are generally flat, while other corporate expenses have gone up. Because of pent-up demand, some CSGs have seen their budgets increase; for example, internal clients wanted more operations support programming. But the Business Research CSG encountered a substantial decline.

The most important fact is that spending for discretionary staff support activities is now controlled by the clients. That's changed the whole nature of staff groups. Not everyone is totally comfortable with this yet; it is much more fun to set a budget based on your professional opinion and let other people pay for it than to compete for resources. The idea is so different that it is very tender and will require careful cultivation.

I see great progress in attitudes and behavior. We put on one of the largest technical expositions in the United States to let our vendors like AT&T, IBM, and

Siemens show us their stuff. Last year as I was walking through it, I was astonished to see the Medical CSG selling its services. I turned the corner, and there was another client service group hawking its wares. Both were selling back to their own company as vigorously as any vendor.

Because they have to do the work of selling their services to their clients and all the additional accounting, the groups are learning to be business managers. They are slowly becoming more entrepreneurial.

Are other people at Bell Atlantic acquiring entrepreneurial skills?

We are committed to identifying potential corporate entrepreneurs, training them, and developing their ideas into new businesses. We do this primarily through our Champion program.

The Champion program arose from one of our companies, Chesapeake & Potomac Telephone, and we spread it across the whole corporation in 1989. The program provides seed money, guidance, and training to potential entrepreneurs who propose new products and services. People at any level can make proposals. If projects are accepted, their proposers can run them. And they can invest a portion of their wages in the project, in exchange for the prospect of a piece of the action when their product has been marketed.

Are you getting results?

In the first year, 36 Champions were accepted into the program. In 1989, 39 were added. By late 1990, there were about 33 products and services in the pipeline, several of them near the commercialization stage. Projects include *Creative Connections*, a line of designer phone jacks; *Emerg-Alert*, prerecorded emergency messages targeted to latchkey children and the elderly; *CommGuard*, a package of backup phone services in case of a system breakdown; local usage information services for all lines in a Centrex system; and a do-not-disturb service.

Champion's most noteworthy success is *Thinx*, new software so innovative that its creator, Jack Coppley, was one of five finalists for *Discover* magazine's award honoring engineers and scientists making technological breakthroughs. *Thinx* is an intelligent graphics program integrating data with images to help users explore relationships visually and apply data or calculations automatically.

Jack learned about Champion when he attended a meeting introducing it in 1988. At that time, he was a budget manager for the network services staff, but he was intrigued by the opportunity Champion represented. Some of Jack's initial ideas were rejected, but his software idea was warmly received.

After going through the steps to test the idea and develop the business plan, Jack became head of a 20-member team that worked out software glitches, chose the *Thinx* name, and designed packaging. The product was unveiled at Comdex, a large trade show, in November 1989. Jack came home with triple the number of customer leads he had anticipated. In September 1990, *Thinx* hit the market and received rave reviews.

Champion has now become an actual revenue source in our strategic planning process. That's the ultimate testimony of importance in a corporation—a business plan with dollars of investment and targeted returns. In five years, we expect annual revenues of over $100 million from Champion projects. My question when I first saw the 1995 projection was, "Is this hope or smoke?" I was told that the figure was conservatively stated!

There are potentially thousands of great, innovative ideas in a company our size. The Champion program encourages people to take responsibility for acting on them.

How do the internal cultural and operational changes you've described translate into advantage in the marketplace?

We were always an efficient company, but our new approaches are breaking new ground. Our management process provides another major differentiation factor in world markets. When you match our track record of efficiency and quality service with a state-of-the-art understanding of how to manage large, technologically complex organizations, you've got a terrific package.

The most efficient communications networks in the world don't come from just modern switching machines but from computer operating systems and skilled technicians that operate them—all working in an empowered, accountable organization.

This forms an excellent launching pad for new businesses. Our systems-integration business, for ex-

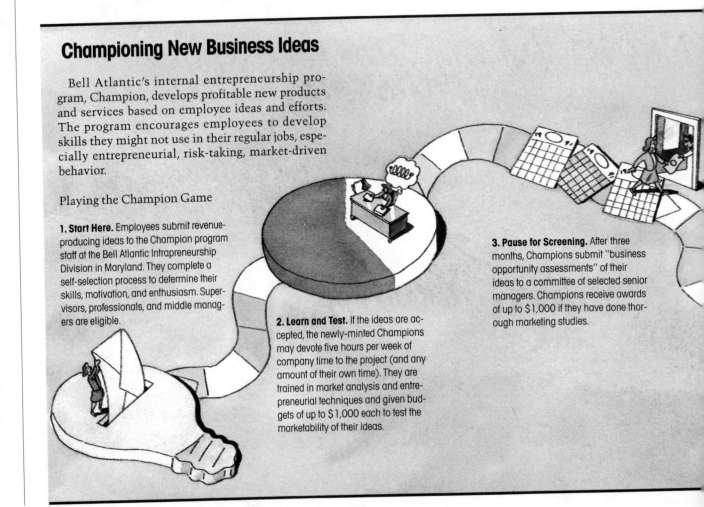

Championing New Business Ideas

Bell Atlantic's internal entrepreneurship program, Champion, develops profitable new products and services based on employee ideas and efforts. The program encourages employees to develop skills they might not use in their regular jobs, especially entrepreneurial, risk-taking, market-driven behavior.

Playing the Champion Game

1. Start Here. Employees submit revenue-producing ideas to the Champion program staff at the Bell Atlantic Intrapreneurship Division in Maryland. They complete a self-selection process to determine their skills, motivation, and enthusiasm. Supervisors, professionals, and middle managers are eligible.

2. Learn and Test. If the ideas are accepted, the newly-minted Champions may devote five hours per week of company time to the project (and any amount of their own time). They are trained in market analysis and entrepreneurial techniques and given budgets of up to $1,000 each to test the marketability of their ideas.

3. Pause for Screening. After three months, Champions submit "business opportunity assessments" of their ideas to a committee of selected senior managers. Champions receive awards of up to $1,000 if they have done thorough marketing studies.

ample, is a natural evolution of that theme. It began as a computer-maintenance business with relatively low margins. But it has evolved into the largest independent field-service business in the country, adding products and services and moving up the value chain to application software, disaster recovery, system operation, consulting, and so on.

You have a very strong vision for what the information system linking the world will be in the future.

It's probably the most important vision in our corporation. I think it is the major contribution that Bell Atlantic will make to the United States. We see the Intelligent Network changing not just our company but changing civilization.

The Intelligent Network means virtually unlimited memory and logic, instantaneous transport to anywhere in the world, providing intellectual linkages between human beings. These links are equivalent, in my mind, to the revolution of the printing press or perhaps even writing or speech. In the near future, a telephone conversation could start in English at one end and be heard in French or Japanese at the other. Information will eventually go to wherever a person is—at home, at work, in a car, or strolling in the park.

What steps are you taking to realize this vision?

We are building the Intelligent Network for the service area in the Bell Atlantic regulated territory. We have introduced 30 new technology-based services, more than any other regional company. We are

> "We have had to develop a culture of tolerance, listening, and intellectual curiosity."

leading in deploying the nervous system of the Intelligent Network, Signaling System 7. We've added massive computer capacity and will have a million

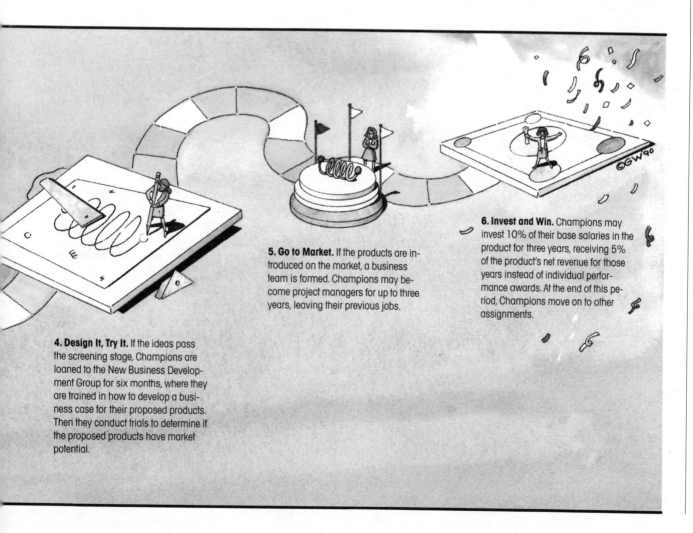

4. Design It, Try It. If the ideas pass the screening stage, Champions are loaned to the New Business Development Group for six months, where they are trained in how to develop a business case for their proposed products. Then they conduct trials to determine if the proposed products have market potential.

5. Go to Market. If the products are introduced on the market, a business team is formed. Champions may become project managers for up to three years, leaving their previous jobs.

6. Invest and Win. Champions may invest 10% of their base salaries in the product for three years, receiving 5% of the product's net revenue for those years instead of individual performance awards. At the end of this period, Champions move on to other assignments.

miles of fiber-optics transport throughout the territory in the next few years. The computers hold extensive database information about customer needs and wants. Fiber optics allow a signal to travel 10,000 times faster than copper wire.

By being focused in the transport and use of information, we realized the capabilities of the Intelligent Network. Our densely populated territory allowed us to visualize and build these kinds of links easily. We concluded, perhaps before others, that this network architecture was a revolutionary way to provide intelligence. We coined the term "Intelligent Network" and began to sell it to our counterparts. The Intelligent Network is a new notion that came out of our search for distinction, our search for a future. The whole world has now accepted it.

How is Bell Atlantic gaining the resources and capability to realize the Intelligent Network vision worldwide?

We recognized very early on that we needed strategic alliances. We've formed partnerships with Siemens, IBM, NTI, and others, including big companies, small companies, and government ministries.

Partnering is a very serious business in Bell Atlantic. Some companies seek strategic alliances because it seems like a good idea in theory or it looks good to be associated with prestigious partners. But often the overall goal of the alliance is lost in the process. Substantial investments are made by large corporations, but little top management attention is given thereafter. Predictably, the local bureaucracy sets up prickly barriers and mousetraps to prove that the new joint venture partner doesn't really understand the business and is an enemy, not a friend.

We can't afford to make that mistake because alliances are too vital for our growth plans, especially outside of the United States. The international field almost always calls for the formation of consortia because of the scale of investment or the preference of governments for local participation. We had to have partners in every one of our investments.

To make sure we are working with our partners effectively and building on their capabilities, we have had to develop a culture of tolerance, listening, and intellectual curiosity, not intellectual arrogance.

How did you develop that culture?

Once again, we turned to the Bell Atlantic Way. A year or so ago, we gathered together 75 people involved in our international business, from lawyers to salespeople to the head of the international business unit. We included all the officers and me.

We went through experiential training, exploring attitudes, and making behavioral commitments. We identified the real purpose of international expansion, which was not to get things "on the board" or "to score" but to produce solutions to the business problem. We wanted long-term investments in our field that would have acceptable risk profiles and higher growth rates than we had in our core business. We worked on how individuals could commit themselves to assist the new effort, to produce real results, not binders, reports, or smoky projections.

"Coaching is not seen as the least bit corny or unusual in our company."

In the past, those kinds of understandings were attempted through a memo or at best a brief meeting. No real interaction, no joint understanding, no commitment, no internalization. New activities were launched without any serious preparation.

In your quest for a more entrepreneurial culture, have you had any personal setbacks?

My biggest personal setback was self-inflicted. In my first year as CEO, I was intensely frustrated because people didn't immediately understand my notions of empowerment, accountability, and teamwork. I finally learned to be less impatient.

How did you come to change your own behavior?

A lot of the impatience was coached out of me. One of the aspects of the Bell Atlantic Way is that everyone has an internal coach; mine is Anton Campanella, our president. Somebody said the reason Campy and I got each other as coaches is that no one else wanted us. There is a certain amount of truth to that.

Coaching is not seen as the least bit corny or unusual in our company. Once a week one of us will ask, "Can I coach you on something?" In the past, I've never been able to do that comfortably. I was never able to do it without it being unnecessarily evasive on the one hand or unnecessarily unpleasant on the other. Now the process is acceptable. It is group sanctioned. It is the way we've decided we're going to work together.

I really know we're doing well when I walk into a room of people and they are discussing a project with tremendous excitement, a project that is going to move our corporation ahead significantly, and I've never heard of it. That is a wonderful feeling.

Reprint 91109

Lessons from a new ventures program

Hollister B. Sykes

In 1970, Exxon Enterprises launched a major new ventures program. I was responsible for initiating that program and for managing it until 1981, when the program's focus shifted to the tasks of consolidation and divestment. At the time I left the program, things had not worked out as I had hoped. In retrospect, I think I have a clear understanding of what went wrong—and of what was needed for success.

Our plan was to make exploratory investments in new ventures operating in emerging markets. We would then accelerate investments that proved to have high potential, spin off the rest, and eventually consolidate ventures with related product lines in promising growth areas. We followed two strategies: the creation of internal ventures and direct investment in venture capital situations.

From 1970 through 1980, we made a total of 37 investments, 19 of which were internal ventures (see *Exhibit I*). Of the 18 venture-capital-funded companies, Exxon later acquired the 6 most promising.

Financially, the venture capital program was very successful. Total investment in the 12 companies that Exxon Enterprises did not ultimately acquire was $12 million. By the end of 1982, they had returned —in cash and the value of securities—$218 million. By contrast, the internal ventures, including those acquired from the venture capital portfolio, though strategically important, did not provide Exxon with a profitable major new business diversification.

My reflections on this experience have taught me some lessons that may be of use to other corporations undertaking an internal ventures program.

Challenges to management

Our internal ventures program was not profitable—in part, because of a heavy R&D orientation and, in part, because of an inability to manage growth.

Present and projected R&D expenditures for these ventures were quite heavy, and that meant an open-ended drag on future profits. Even where the R&D was successful, we often had to make large additional investments before we could bring products to market. When we sold an optical disk memory venture to Storage Technology Corporation, it was still in the R&D stage. STC then spent more than $100 million on the program without completing the development work needed for commercialization.

> *"As Exxon's experience shows, if internal venturing is to work, it must be an important mainstream operation."*

Of our 19 internal ventures, 13 involved entirely new technologies. Inevitably, then, our search for emerging technologies and early entry opportunities meant facing unproven markets—and greater risk. At best, some ventures would not make sales until four or five years down the road. We had to educate potential customers on how to use the products, and we had to try out applications before we could assess their cost-effectiveness.

Where both technology and market were new, as in computerized speech recognition, the risk was doubled. We made our initial investment in Verbex in 1972 and introduced commercial products several years later. Market development costs exceeded revenues, however, and experience showed us that we needed a lower cost, higher performance technology.

Mr. Sykes was senior vice president of Exxon Enterprises, where from 1970 to 1981 he headed up the new ventures program. He is now a private consultant to high-technology start-ups and does research on internal corporate ventures at the New York University Center for Entrepreneurial Studies.

Exhibit I	37 venture investments	
19 internal ventures	Advanced materials, components, and systems	7
	Energy conversion and storage systems	5
	Information systems and system components	7
18 venture capital investments	Air pollution control	1
	Health care	1
	Advanced materials	2
	Energy conversion and storage systems	3
	Information systems	11

Delphi was a venture we began in 1974 to develop a computer with a parallel processor architecture for use in electronic voice mail. It made ground-breaking technical progress. We killed it, though, because the definable market did not justify the huge added costs we faced to complete development. We were there too soon.

Looking back, I compared the relative financial success of all 37 ventures and found an inverse relationship between venture success and the level of market and technical risk at the time of our investment (see *Exhibit II*). As a statistical analysis indicates, market risk (RM) plus technical risk (RT) account for roughly 45% of the variability in venture success.

The real issue, though, was management. The managers of our internal ventures were usually technical people with limited supervisory experience and little or no marketing or sales experience. Those responsible for venture-capital-funded companies were usually more experienced and knew more about their industries and technologies. For example, the six key managers of Intecom Corporation, our successful digital PBX venture, had all held executive positions in their former companies and averaged 15 years of experience apiece.

As shown in *Exhibit III*, which plots relative financial success against the managerial (XM) and the relevant sales and marketing (XS) experience of venture management, differences in experience affected venture success. Surprisingly, the level of technical experience (XT) showed no meaningful correlation with venture success. The correlation here is higher than in *Exhibit II*: levels of sales and managerial experience account for some 65% of the variability in venture success. Taken together with product risk, differences in experience explain a total of 68% of such variance.

Even when initially successful, however, ventures often succumb to the "second-product syndrome." Its primary symptoms are a poor coordination of marketing and R&D and a belief that the first success proves the wisdom of management and ensures success the next time around.

The first product is usually created by a small, closely knit team that communicates well, has a single goal, faces none of the distractions of maintaining an ongoing business, and does not have to worry about making a prior product obsolete or a new product compatible. By the time of the second product, the original team members are usually managing functional departments and spending most of their time supervising others or solving problems on the existing product line. Communications about the new product grow cumbersome, and committees inevitably spring up.

Moreover, the greater the first product's success, the more convinced managers are of their ability to introduce another winner. Often forgetting why that product did so well, they set out to conquer new markets without doing adequate analysis or getting the required capabilities in place. The corollary, of course, is that they fail to build on the success of their initial product by enhancing it or lowering its cost. Apple Computer, with its follow-on products to the Apple II, is a good example here, as is the IBM entry systems division with its PC Jr.

Two of Exxon's most successful initial products were the Vydec word processor and the Zilog Z-80 microprocessor. Vydec led its industry by designing the first CRT text editor with floppy disk memory and daisy wheel printer—features that are still industry standards. Later upgrades did offer more features, but the next major new product introductions aimed at new market niches and fell many months behind the promised dates.

The base product, which had a broad market, was slow to apply new microprocessor technology that would have significantly reduced costs. Competitors entered the market and pushed Vydec out of its leadership position. Indeed, Vydec fell so far behind in the product development race that it had to resort to the purchase of a third-party design to try to catch up.

The Zilog Z-80, still the leading 8-bit microprocessor, was compatible with its competitive forerunner, the Intel 8080, but more powerful. Thus it enjoyed a ready-made market base, without having to make the investment normally required to support a new processor with software and peripheral chips. Riding this success, Zilog tackled the RAM market and then the design of a 16-bit microprocessor (the Z-8000) to compete with the Intel 8086.

Chip yields on the RAMs were too low to provide acceptable margins. The ensuing management turmoil, combined with efforts to achieve profitability, was partly responsible for inadequate allocation of resources to the development and marketing of the 16-bit microprocessor. Consequently, the Z-8000 never reached a significant commercial market share. Meanwhile, the market potential for an upwardly compatible extension of the Z-80 line went unrecognized. When at last development of the Z-800 began, it received inadequate support and so lost the large market opportunity now partly filled by the Intel 8088, which is used in the IBM PC.

Changes in the environment

As our ventures grew and required new levels of investment, corporate involvement expanded. Exxon's management procedures and strategic objectives conflicted with the independent start-up environment of the ventures and pushed them toward a more structured, controls-oriented mode of operation. This was perhaps inevitable, but the way it happened hurt the motivation of key people, slowed decision making, and added to venture managers' work loads.

To Exxon's management, multiple ventures with overlapping sales, manufacturing, and engineering organizations appeared inefficient. To the venture managers, especially in the office systems area, requests to coordinate their product design and sales strategies proved unwelcome and easy to resist. The entrepreneurial factors that had originally made the ventures successful began to hinder their operation as an integrated multiproduct organization. In 1981, we joined six of the ventures to form Exxon Office Systems.

My original venture plan had been to grow successful businesses by allowing only the fittest to survive. This approach would test both venture management capability and the commercial viability of the products. We would then either weed out the weak or merge them into the strongest company, where a single management team that had survived the growth phase would carry out needed integration.

Instead, I bowed to pressures for an early consolidation of the office systems ventures in order to achieve efficiencies in product development, manufacturing, and sales. Since no single venture was strong enough to command the respect of the others, we created a new superstructure to which all six ventures were subordinated.

The new management team members had no history of working together. Commitments to goals set by the previous venture managers were put aside because most of the managers no longer had responsibility for the same activities in the new organi-

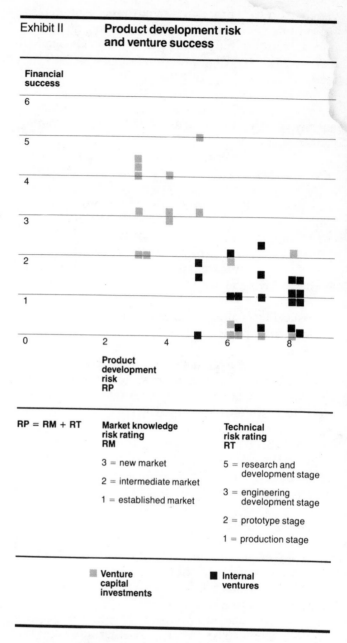

Exhibit II   **Product development risk and venture success**

$RP = RM + RT$

Market knowledge risk rating RM

3 = new market

2 = intermediate market

1 = established market

Technical risk rating RT

5 = research and development stage

3 = engineering development stage

2 = prototype stage

1 = production stage

▨ Venture capital investments

■ Internal ventures

zation. A number eventually resigned, as did talented product development people, who left for greener pastures when development budgets were cut and programs consolidated. The result: overhead increased, sales fell off, and losses widened.

Failure to meet expectations about profitability is bad enough. Coupled with a high profile in the media, it can quickly undermine chances for recovery. Negative publicity turned potential customers away and made it harder for us to recruit the managers we needed. Also, R&D-based ventures are sufficiently risky without throwing a spotlight on them too soon, as happened with a number of ours.

Increased corporate involvement led, in turn, to more complex management procedures and to a shift in the way managers were held accountable – as well as rewarded – for the results they had forecast.

Corporate review procedures removed decision-making authority from the ventures' boards and moved it up to Exxon staff and committees. Venture managers had to spend extra time and effort bringing Exxon's management up to speed. Although justified by the inexperience of some venture managers, these additional reviews slowed the response to a rapidly changing business environment and distracted attention from venture operations.

Corporate concerns about publicity, image, ethics, legal liabilities, and personnel policies required frequent reports to, and reviews by, corporate staff. Exxon's high profile opened it to spurious lawsuits and complaints that would not have come up in connection with a small, independent company. Because of Exxon's high ethical and legal standards, considerable staff effort went to educate venture personnel on these issues and to review venture contracts and agreements. Worries that a venture's advertising might be misleading or affect another venture or an Exxon affiliate led corporate staff to approve all venture advertising.

The proliferation of new ventures led as well to a variety of financial reporting formats and MIS systems. In several cases, a venture's sales outgrew its accounting systems and caused serious control problems. To promote overall efficiency and improved control, the ventures were eventually asked to change over to compatible systems and to install additional procedures and personnel. Corporate financial staffs expanded to assist and monitor these activities.

Ensuring and documenting fairness and consistency in rating systems, termination policies, and salary administration proved a time-consuming challenge. Above certain levels, Exxon management approved all starting salaries, salary increases, and performance bonus plans. At the ventures and at headquarters, staffs grew larger.

Considered separately, each of these procedures made good sense. Taken together, however, they imposed on each venture the superstructure of a larger corporation and the burden of frequent reporting to the parent corporation. The whole amounted to less than the sum of its parts. As Don Valentine, a long-time venture capitalist, describes it, this corporate bear hug amounts to "death by a thousand cuts. A little nick here, a little cut there, a little change here – nothing significant. But at the end of a short period of time the people are so driven by controlling and accounting that the environment of nonconventional solutions is lost."

Exxon's ability to fund rapid growth might seem from the outside to be an enviable advantage. In practice, however, it tended to cushion venture managers from concern about profitability, cost control, focused product development, and competitive realities. Although we stressed that a successful venture

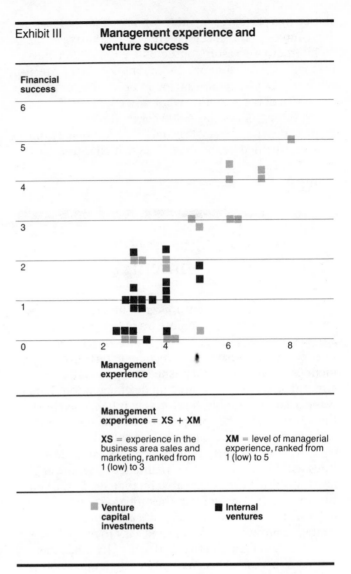

Exhibit III   **Management experience and venture success**

Financial success

Management experience

Management experience = XS + XM

XS = experience in the business area sales and marketing, ranked from 1 (low) to 3

XM = level of managerial experience, ranked from 1 (low) to 5

Venture capital investments

Internal ventures

has to run "lean and mean" – and most started out that way – our internal ventures lost touch with the harsh realities of a cash-thin existence.

Sometimes it took traumatic circumstances to convince managers that their ventures could operate in a leaner fashion. When they grossly missed development schedules or marketing forecasts, they had to justify continuing expenses to a skeptical Exxon management. In marginal cases, when expenses had been cut half-heartedly, the top group often concluded that the venture should be sold or shut down. Only when that threat began to sink in did some venture managers come up with tough-minded proposals to get costs under control. As a former manager of Zilog later learned when managing his own independent venture, "Cash is more important than your mother."

Since most of the new businesses required skills not available within Exxon, we had to look outside for qualified personnel. At lower levels, this was not a problem at first, but we had trouble recruiting key people at the managerial level. Candidates wondered about Exxon's long-term commitment to such small and unfamiliar businesses. Would the company really stay with it?

We could not offer equity participation. Although an equity-like incentive compensation plan did come on stream in 1979 for selected ventures, it was too late and too little. Debate over the valuation of equity when ventures were sold or merged hampered the plan's effectiveness. Any formula that does not rely on a public market to determine value is likely to be controversial.

Further, because we pegged managers' salaries to the size of the activity they ran—and not to future business potential—we could not put experienced senior executives in charge of new internal ventures. If the ventures proved successful, they often outgrew the capabilities of the technical people who started them up.

As the ventures grew, it became apparent that the most important environmental issue was Exxon's inability to provide functional support in the new business areas. For example, the company had no computer-industry-experienced manufacturing or sales executives to fill the holes left when the entrepreneurs departed or proved incapable of managing growth. By contrast, Philip Estridge needed only one month to recruit 150 people from within IBM to staff its new PC small business unit. The first day notices went up about the new unit, 500 IBM employees inquired.

Our Vydec word processor was a preemptive product when it came on the market. During the three years it took us to build a nationwide direct marketing organization, Wang, Lanier, IBM, and others moved in with competitive products.

Lessons learned

Knowing what I know now, here's what I think I would do differently:

1   Acquire an established company in a new business area. Our original "probe and assess" strategy was sound. We made exploratory investments in new areas to determine their potential and to learn about market opportunities. Once we identified these opportunities, however, we should have acquired an established company. Doing so would have given us profits to offset the losses of our R&D ventures, a source of knowledgeable executives, a more attractive career path for new recruits, and a stronger competitive base from which to launch innovative products. We did not follow this course because we were concerned about antitrust objections.

Had we followed this course, we still would have had management problems. In the information systems area, for example, we would have had to give acquired management real autonomy. Even then, we might have lost those key people who valued their complete independence or those for whom we could not work out acceptable compensation and incentive plans.

There is a larger issue here. If a parent company does not provide some added value, then the purchase is no more than a portfolio investment. The alternative is to return the cash to shareholders to invest. The current wave of corporate "restructurings" has the same effect—returning underutilized asset value to the shareholder. We would have to have shown a better return on dollars used to make an acquisition than used to buy back stock. Management is more likely to add value if an acquired company is functionally close to the parent's base business.

2   Start fewer R&D-oriented ventures. The high proportion of R&D ventures in our portfolio greatly increased our risk of failure and stretched out the time from start-up to projected sales. Because most corporations go through cycles in their base businesses, unprofitable operations not in the mainstream are especially vulnerable. Exxon was no exception. The steep slump in the consumption of oil products and natural gas from 1979 to 1982 caused concern. Along with the cutback in Exxon's base business operations, we either sold or liquidated most of our smaller ventures.

The corollary, of course, is to choose new ventures with a short time span between initial investment and profitability. This will cut out most research-based ventures and eliminate the chance of developing another Xerox or Polaroid. But those are pretty long odds anyway.

Because the initial focus of many of our ventures was on developing new technology, we did not bring experienced, high-level marketing managers on board soon enough to shed light on our assumptions about product features and pricing. It is, however, hard to justify full-time marketing executives during a long R&D phase.

3   Use venture capital investments as the primary "probe" strategy. Venture-capital-funded companies are truly independent operations that can attract and hold experienced managers. The incentive for such people to leave solid careers is that they can make a lot of money through capital gains. The drawback, of course, is that successful independent companies usually do not want to be acquired, at least not before the founders and early investors have taken them public. Still, a minority position in a leading growth company can benefit an established corporation—if there is a real fit like that between IBM and Intel in microcomputers.

What are the lessons I have learned?

☐ As Exxon's experience shows, if internal venturing is to work, it must be an important mainstream operation. The corporation should focus new venture activities on those areas where it has (or intends to commit the necessary long-term resources to build) relevant operating capabilities and management experience. The internal venture approach can be a quick and effective way to develop new products and markets. At that point, however, the parent's resources in manufacturing, marketing, and sales are needed to capitalize fully on the venture's promise.

☐ It is impossible to preserve completely an independent entrepreneurial environment within a large, multiproduct corporate setting. The principal problems involve equity compensation, product compatibility and coordination, and corporate liability for what ventures do. Venture personnel should understand from the start that they will eventually have to be integrated back into the larger organization if their venture proves successful.

☐ Politically and strategically, longer term R&D projects are more appropriate to support an established business than to initiate a portfolio of diversified businesses. Unless managers of the base business view the new endeavor as critical to the whole company's future, they are not likely to be tolerant of the high risk of failure and the long period of unprofitability that may precede commercialization.

☐ Successful new ventures usually focus on a single product. Successful mature companies must learn to manage the complexities of multiple products, new product introductions that make older products obsolete, and product compatibility.

☐ Management experience in the relevant industry is a significant factor in determining venture success.

☐ A venture environment that encourages resourcefulness is more important than ample financing. ▽

Reprint 86315

The heart of entrepreneurship

Howard H. Stevenson and David E. Gumpert

An X ray of the entrepreneurial organization reveals these dynamic characteristics: encouragement of individuals' imagination, flexibility, and a willingness to accept risks

"It's much easier and safer for companies to stay with the familiar than to explore the unknown," assert the authors of this article. Staying with the familiar may have its dangers, however, in today's fast-changing world. An injection of entrepreneurship, by which creative people are encouraged to strike out and come up with new products or services, may become important to the financial health of organizations.

Here the reader is offered an anatomy of entrepreneurship. The article describes the entrepreneur's thought pattern in asking and finding answers to these questions: Where is the opportunity? How do I capitalize on it? What resources do I need? How do I gain control over them? What structure is best? The authors combine contrasts of the entrepreneur's state of mind with that of the "administrator," whose object is to husband resources and reduce risks.

Mr. Stevenson is Sarofim-Rock Professor of Business Administration at the Harvard Business School, where he teaches a course in entrepreneurial management. His book, New Business Ventures and the Entrepreneur, *has recently appeared (written with Michael Roberts and Irving Grousbeck; published by Richard D. Irwin). From 1978 to 1982 Stevenson was a vice president at Preco Corporation, a paper manufacturer.*

Mr. Gumpert, associate editor of HBR, conducts its "Growing Concerns" column. He edited a book of articles from HBR, which Wiley published last year, that bore the same title as the column. He is also author, with Stanley R. Rich, of Business Plans That Win $$$, *scheduled by Harper & Row for publication this spring.*

Suddenly entrepreneurship is in vogue. If only our nation's businesses – large and small – could become more entrepreneurial, the thinking goes, we would improve our productivity and compete more effectively in the world marketplace.

But what does entrepreneurial mean? Managers describe entrepreneurship with such terms as innovative, flexible, dynamic, risk taking, creative, and growth oriented. The popular press, on the other hand, often defines the term as starting and operating new ventures. That view is reinforced by the enticing success of such upstarts as Apple Computer, Domino's Pizza, and Lotus Development.

Neither approach to a definition of entrepreneurship is precise or prescriptive enough for managers who wish to be more entrepreneurial. Everybody wants to be innovative, flexible, and creative. But for every Apple, Domino's, and Lotus, there are thousands of new restaurants, clothing stores, and consulting firms that presumably have tried to be innovative, to grow, and to show other characteristics that are entrepreneurial in the dynamic sense – but have failed.

As for the idea of equating the beginning stages of a business with entrepreneurship, note a recent study by McKinsey & Company on behalf of the American Business Conference. It concluded that many mature, medium-sized companies, having annual sales of $25 million to $1 billion, consistently develop new products and markets and also grow at rates far exceeding national averages.[1] Moreover, we're all aware of many of the largest corporations – IBM, 3M, and Hewlett-Packard are just a few of the best known – that make a practice of innovating, taking risks, and showing creativity. And they continue to expand.

1 Richard E. Cavanagh and Donald K. Clifford, Jr., "Lessons from America's Midsized Growth Companies," *McKinsey Quarterly,* Autumn 1983, p. 2.

Exhibit I   **Manager's opportunity matrix**

		Desired future state characterized by growth or change	
		Yes	No
Self-perceived power and ability to realize goals	Yes	Entrepreneur	Satisfied manager
	No	Frustrated potential entrepreneur	Consummate bureaucratic functionary

So the question for the would-be entrepreneur is: How can I make innovation, flexibility, and creativity operational? To help this person discover some answers, we must first look at entrepreneurial behavior.

At the outset we should discard the notion that entrepreneurship is an all-or-none trait that some people or organizations possess and others don't. Rather, we suggest viewing entrepreneurship in the context of a range of behavior. To simplify our analysis, it is useful to view managerial behavior in terms of extremes.

At one extreme is what we might call the *promoter* type of manager, who feels confident of his or her ability to seize opportunity. This manager expects surprises and expects not only to adjust to change but also to capitalize on it and make things happen. At the other extreme is the *trustee* type, who feels threatened by change and the unknown and whose inclination is to rely on the status quo. To the trustee type, predictability fosters effective management of existing resources while unpredictability endangers them.

Most people, of course, fall somewhere between the extremes. But it's safe to say that as managers move closer to the promoter end of the scale they become more entrepreneurial, and as they move toward the trustee end of the scale they become less so (or, perhaps, more "administrative").

When it comes to their own self-interest, the natural tendency of most people is toward the promoter end of our behavior spectrum; they know where their interests lie and pursue them aggressively. A person's most valuable assets are intelligence, energy, and experience – not money or other material things – which are well suited to the promoter role.

A close relationship exists between opportunity and individual needs. To be an entrepreneurial opportunity, a prospect must meet two tests: it must represent a desirable future state, involving growth or at least change; and the individual must believe it is possible to reach that state. This relationship often identifies four groups, which we show in *Exhibit I.*

Companies of all sizes encounter difficulty encouraging entrepreneurship when the individual's interest and the corporate interest don't coincide. Executives may enhance their position or boost their income by serving the status quo through short-term and readily measurable actions such as cost reduction or price cuts, even though such "accomplishments" may not help and may even hurt the company's long-term welfare.

To make the individual's tendency toward entrepreneurship match corporate goals and needs is no easy task for companies. First must come an understanding of the ways in which the promoter and trustee mentalities exert influence within the organization. In these pages we try to further such an understanding and we develop a framework for analyzing the essential aspects of entrepreneurship in companies of all sizes. We then use the framework to offer suggestions for encouraging entrepreneurship.

Entrepreneurial process

Based as they often are on changes in the marketplace, pressures for extension of entrepreneurship tend to be external to the company. Limitations on entrepreneurial behavior tend to come from inside, the result of high-level decisions and the exigencies of hierarchy. In making decisions, administrators and entrepreneurs often proceed with a very different order of questions. The typical administrator asks:

What resources do I control?

What structure determines our organization's relationship to its market?

How can I minimize the impact of others on my ability to perform?

What opportunity is appropriate?

The entrepreneur, at the other end of the spectrum, tends to ask:

Where is the opportunity?

How do I capitalize on it?

What resources do I need?

How do I gain control over them?

What structure is best?

The impact of the difference in approach becomes apparent as we trace the entrepreneurial thought pattern.

Where is the opportunity?

Naturally, the first step is to identify the opportunity, which entails an external (or market) orientation rather than an internal (or resource) orientation. The promoter type is constantly attuned to environmental changes that may suggest a favorable chance, while the trustee type wants to preserve resources and reacts defensively to possible threats to deplete them. (See *Exhibit II*, part A.)

Entrepreneurs are not just opportunistic; they are also creative and innovative. The entrepreneur does not necessarily want to break new ground but perhaps just remix old ideas to make a seemingly new application. Many of today's fledgling microcomputer and software companies, for example, are merely altering existing technology slightly or repackaging it to accommodate newly perceived market segments.

The shakeout now going on in the publications aimed at cable TV subscribers illustrates good and bad reading of opportunity. In 1983 Time Inc. abandoned its *TV-Cable Week* after a pretax loss of $47 million. Still thriving is *The Cable Guide,* which is operated by two entrepreneurs marshaling a fraction of Time Inc.'s resources and working out of a town in Pennsylvania. By listing broadcast programs as well as those available on cable, *TV-Cable Week* aimed its content at viewers and thereby annoyed some cable operators. *The Cable Guide* focuses on cable-transmitted programs only, thereby pleasing the cable operators who distribute it.

Woolworth's recent difficulties demonstrate the challenge posed by changing opportunities. For many years the company thrived because it had the best retail locations in America's cities and towns. That approach worked fine as long as all the best locations remained in the centers of cities and in towns. As the best retail sites shifted to suburban and highway malls, however, Woolworth's was caught off guard and other mass merchandisers grabbed the new top locations. To survive, Woolworth's was forced into a defensive strategy of developing secondary suburban properties while closing old city stores.

Woolworth's is typical of many companies that, preoccupied with the strength of their resource base, are unable or unwilling to perceive momentous environmental changes. These companies turn opportunities into problems for fear of losing strength. For the entrepreneurial mentality, on the other hand, external pressures stimulate opportunity recognition. These pressures include rapid changes in:

1   Technology, which opens new doors and closes others. Advances in producing microcomputer chips helped make possible the personal computer market but at the same time shrank the minicomputer market. This development posed problems for those producers that failed to perceive the change quickly.

2   Consumer economics, which alters both the ability and willingness to pay for new products and services. The sharp rise in energy costs during the mid-1970s made popular the wood-burning stove and chain saw, and spawned the solar energy industry, among others. But these same pressures set back those huge sectors of our industrial economy that thrived on the belief in cheap energy forever.

3   Social values, which define new styles and standards of living. The burgeoning interest in physical fitness has opened up markets for special clothing, "natural" food, workout centers, and other businesses.

4   Political action and regulatory standards, which affect competition. Deregulation of airlines, financial services, and telecommunications has sparked opportunities for assorted new products and services while at the same time disrupting the economics of truckers, airlines, and many concerns in other sectors.

Unfortunately, innovation and the pursuit of opportunity impose a cost that many executives resist—the necessity of change. Like most other people, they tend to take comfort in routine and predictable situations. This is not because they are lazy; they are just more inclined to the administrative end of the organizational spectrum than to the entrepreneurial end. Among the internal pressures that move companies toward the administrative end are the following:

The "social contract." Managers feel a responsibility to employ human, manufacturing, technological, and financial resources once they have been acquired. The American steel industry, which had the best plants in the world during the 1950s but failed to update them in the face of rising foreign competition, is a prominent example of the social contract gone awry.

Performance criteria. Few executives are fired for neglecting to pursue an opportunity compared with the number punished for failing to meet ROI targets. Capacity utilization and sales growth, the typical measures of business success, are almost always based on use of existing resources.

Planning systems and cycles. Opportunities do not show up at the start of a planning cycle and last for the duration of a three- or five-year plan. Better formal planning is often the enemy of organizational adaptability.

How do I capitalize on it?

The ability to identify favorable circumstances is important but isn't enough to qualify a person as an entrepreneur. Many innovative thinkers never get anything done. Promoters, however, move quickly past the identification of opportunity to its pursuit. They are the hawkers with umbrellas who materialize from nowhere on Manhattan street corners at the first rumbles of thunder overhead.

For the trustee, commitment is time consuming and, once made, of long duration. Trustees move so slowly that they may appear to be stationary; once committed, they are tenacious but still very slow moving. Entrepreneurs have gamblers' reputations because of their willingness to get in and out of markets fast. But merely moving quickly does not guarantee success. First, entrepreneurs must know the territory they operate in, then they must be able to recognize patterns as they develop.

Successful risk takers have the confidence to assume that the missing elements of the pattern will take shape as they expect. Thus designers of CAD/CAM equipment feel free to engineer systems around disk drives that have yet to be built. From their knowledge of the industry, the designers feel confident the drives will be built and therefore they can get the right products on the market ahead of competitors. On the other hand, many utilities act like trustees. For example, they resist adoption of digital technology to streamline their operations and stick to electromechanical recording for readings of important data.

The pressures pushing companies toward either the entrepreneurial or administrative end of the spectrum with regard to the timing and duration of their commitment are a mixture of personal, organizational, and environmental forces. They are listed in *Exhibit II*, part B.

Administratively oriented companies approach the question whether to commit to new opportunities more cautiously. Administrators must negotiate with others on what strategy to take and must compromise to achieve necessary approvals. This process produces evolution rather than revolution. The search for perfection is the enemy of the good. Administrators often see the need to change as the result of failure of the planning process.

This disposition helps explain why managers of American electronics concerns sometimes are seen looking on in amazement as their Japanese counterparts consistently bring new electronics products—from videocassette recorders to talking calculators—to market first. These Japanese companies and other successful market-oriented businesses know that change is inevitable and, therefore, keep their organizations learning.

By endlessly studying how to reduce risk, instead of trying to deal with it, administrative companies slow the decision making. The many decision constituencies necessary to satisfy proposals for new products and services lengthen the process. If there's a project that everyone down the line agrees has a three-fourths chance of succeeding, the odds of getting that project through eight approval levels are one in ten. Many executives will justifiably say to themselves, why bother? (The Japanese have learned how to make rapid decisions by consensus without bogging down in layers of bureaucracy.)

What resources do I need?

In grasping opportunities, some institutions with vast resources (such as government agencies, large nonprofit organizations, and big corporations) are tempted to commit resources heavily, to "go first class" all the way. In this way, the rationale goes, you reduce your chances of failure and increase your eventual returns.

From our observation, however, success is unrelated to the size of the resource commitment. More important is the innovativeness with which the institution commits and deploys those resources. The Apple and IBM personal computers were developed and produced by organizations that have little vertical integration. Few successful real estate developers have architects, contractors, or even space salespeople on the payroll. Yet many of these organizations rack up extraordinary ROIs and ROEs.

As necessity is proverbially the mother of invention, people who start businesses often make imaginative use of their limited resources. A computer engineer starting a peripheral equipment company will discover selling skills she never knew she possessed. The owner of a new restaurant quickly adjusts to waiting on tables. Entrepreneurs who are effective make the sparest allotment of resources.

Exhibit II **The entrepreneurial culture vs. the administrative culture**

	Entrepreneurial focus		Administrative focus	
	Characteristics	Pressures	Characteristics	Pressures
A **Strategic orientation**	Driven by perception of opportunity	Diminishing opportunities Rapidly changing technology, consumer economics, social values, and political rules	Driven by controlled resources	Social contracts Performance measurement criteria Planning systems and cycles
B **Commitment to seize opportunities**	Revolutionary, with short duration	Action orientation Narrow decision windows Acceptance of reasonable risks Few decision constituencies	Evolutionary, with long duration	Acknowledgment of multiple constituencies Negotiation about strategic course Risk reduction Coordination with existing resource base
C **Commitment of resources**	Many stages, with minimal exposure at each stage	Lack of predictable resource needs Lack of control over the environment Social demands for appropriate use of resources Foreign competition Demands for more efficient resource use	A single stage, with complete commitment out of decision	Need to reduce risk Incentive compensation Turnover in managers Capital budgeting systems Formal planning systems
D **Control of resources**	Episodic use or rent of required resources	Increased resource specialization Long resource life compared with need Risk of obsolescence Risk inherent in the identified opportunity Inflexibility of permanent commitment to resources	Ownership or employment of required resources	Power, status, and financial rewards Coordination of activity Efficiency measures Inertia and cost of change Industry structures
E **Management structure**	Flat, with multiple informal networks	Coordination of key noncontrolled resources Challenge to hierarchy Employees' desire for independence	Hierarchy	Need for clearly defined authority and responsibility Organizational culture Reward systems Management theory

Besides their reckless invasion of markets, people at the promoter end of our scale have reputations as gamblers because they throw everything they've got at opportunities. But in reality they throw everything they've got simply because they don't have enough. Successful entrepreneurs seek plateaus of success, where they can consolidate their gains before trying to acquire control over additional resources and further pursue the opportunity. They wish they had more to commit, but they do more with less anyway.

What level of resources is required to pursue a given opportunity? Tension prevails between the adequacy of commitment and the potential for return. Handling this tension is part of entrepreneurship's challenge and excitement. (See *Exhibit II*, part C.)

Most of the risk in entrepreneurial management lies in the effort to pursue opportunity with inappropriate resources—either too few or too many. Failures in real estate investing, for example, occur when participants attempt projects larger than their resources can handle. When the investors can't come up with more funds to tide them over unforeseen obstacles or setbacks, they fail. Large corporations tend to make the basic error of overcommitting resources.

Some large companies seem to believe that they can handle all opportunities with the resources they have behind them. But that's not always so: witness Exxon's spectacular entry into the electric motor control business and its subsequent humiliating retreat. A different error made by large corporations is rejection of openings in emerging businesses because they are "too small," thereby allowing new ventures an opportunity to gain footholds that cannot later be dislodged.

Looking beyond the size of the resource commitment, managers must consider its timing. At the administrative end of our spectrum, the tendency is to make a single decision for a total resource commitment. But during times of rapid change, such as we have experienced during the 1970s and 1980s, commitments in stages foster the most effective response to new competitors, markets, and technologies. Familiar by now is the staged entry of IBM into the full range of the microcomputer hardware and software market. Much of the genius of Procter & Gamble's marketing approach rests in trial, test, strategic experiment, and in-stage rollout of new products.

The pressures toward the gradual commitment of resources—toward the entrepreneurial end of our scale—are mostly environmental, and include:

An absence of predictable resource needs. Given the rapid pace of change in today's world, one must assume that in-course corrections will be necessary. The rapid advances have made technology forecasting hazardous, and projecting consumer economics, inflation rates, and market responses has become equally difficult. A multistage commitment allows responsiveness; a one-time commitment creates unnecessary risk.

External control limits. Companies can no longer say they own the forest and will therefore do with it what they want; environmental consideration must be taken into account. Similarly, increasingly strict zoning affects companies' control of real estate. International access to resources is no longer guaranteed, as the mid-1970s oil shortages made very clear. Corporate executives must respond by matching exposure to the terms of control. They have learned the lesson in international operations but seem unwilling to apply the lesson domestically.

Social needs. The "small is beautiful" formulation of E.F. Schumacher and the argument that too large a gulf separates producers and consumers are very persuasive. Gradual commitment of resources allows managers to determine the most appropriate level of investment for a particular task.

In many of our large corporations, however, the pressure is in the opposite direction toward a single, heavy commitment of resources (at the administrative end of the scale) for the following reasons:

The need to reduce risk. Managers limit the risk they face by throwing all the resources they can muster at an opportunity from the outset, even if it means wasting assets. Such a commitment increases the likelihood of early success and reduces the likelihood of eventual failure. This stress on concentrated marshaling of assets fosters the belief that the resources themselves bring power and success.

Fragile tenure of management. At companies in which executives are either promoted every one-and-a-half to two years or exiled to corporate Siberia, they need quick, measurable results. Cash and earnings gains in each period must surpass the last. You must achieve quick, visible success or your job is in danger.

Focus on incentive compensation. Concentration of resources upfront yields quick returns and easily measurable results, which can be readily translated into a manager's bonus compensation. Small-scale strategic experiments, however, often show little in the immediate bottom line and therefore produce no effect on pay tied to ROA or ROE while consuming scarce managerial time.

Single-minded capital allocation systems. They assume that the consequences of future uncertainty can be measured now, or at least that uncertainty a year from now will be no less than that at present. Thus a single decision point seems appropriate. Many capital budget systems make it difficult to get two bites of an apple.

In a typical case, a board of directors gets a request for $1 million next year for a start-up that, if successful, will need $3 million more in the future. The board, thinking in terms of full commitment, inquires into the return on $4 million. It fails to realize that it can buy an option and make a judgment at the $1 million stage without knowing the return on the extra $3 million. Such an approach inhibits the exercise of managerial discretion and skill, which lie in revising plans as needed and doing more with less. Hewlett-Packard and 3M are exceptions to this rule; they encourage multiple budget requests. Approval of a project means that the manager is unlikely to get all that is asked for the first time around.

Bureaucratic planning systems. A project can win the support of 99 people and then get scuttled by just one rejection. An entrepreneur, though, can be rejected 99 times but go ahead if one crucial respondent gives approval.

Once a project has begun, requests for additional resources return executives to a morass of analysis and bureaucratic delays. They try to avoid such problems by making the maximum possible upfront commitment.

An independent entrepreneur can field a salesperson when the need arises, but a corporate manager may put a salesperson in the field before necessary to avoid going through the approval process later. Easy access to small, incremental resources, allocated often on the basis of progress, has great power to motivate employees.

How do I control the resources?

When one thinks of a book publishing company, one imagines large numbers of editors, typesetters, publicists, printing presses, and salespeople. And that's the way most of the nation's largest book publishers are set up. But many of today's young publishing ventures consist of just two or three people who rely heavily on outside professionals and suppliers. When one of these acquires a manuscript, it will often hire a free lance to make editorial improvements. The publisher then contracts with a typesetting company to have the manuscript set in type, a printing and binding concern to produce the volume, and a public relations firm to promote the book. People who are the equivalent of manufacturers' reps sell the book to stores.

Not coincidentally, many large, well-known New York book publishers have struggled financially in recent years, while a number of the small young book publishing ventures have thrived. Although manuscript selection and marketing decisions certainly help determine success, two key factors are the ability to reduce overhead and the acumen to take advantage of cost-lowering technological changes in the printing industry by using outside resources.

Promoter types think that all they need from a resource is the ability to use it; trustee types think that resources are inadequately controlled unless they are owned or on the payroll. Entrepreneurs learn to use other people's resources well while keeping the option open on bringing them in-house. For example: on reaching a certain volume level, the maker of an electronic product decides that it can no longer risk having a particularly valuable component made by an outside supplier who may be subject to severe market or financial pressures. Each such decision pushes the entrepreneur toward the administrative arena. (See *Exhibit II*, part D.)

Because they try to avoid owning equipment or hiring people, entrepreneurs are often viewed as exploitive or even parasitic. But this trait has become valuable in today's fast-changing business environment, for the following reasons:

Greater resource specialization. A VLSI design engineer, a patent attorney, or state-of-the-art circuit-testing equipment may be a necessity for a company, but only occasionally. Using rather than owning enables the company to reduce its risk and its fixed costs.

Risk of obsolescence. Fast-changing technology makes ownership expensive; leasing or renting reduces the risk.

More flexibility. Using instead of owning a resource lowers the cost of pulling out of a project.

Power and status, as expressed in a hierarchy, and financial rewards push organizations toward the administrative end of the spectrum and toward ownership. In many corporations, the extent of resource ownership and control determine the degree of power, the status level, and the amount of direct and indirect compensation. Administrators argue for the ownership of resources for many sound and valid reasons, among them:

Efficiency. Execution is faster because the administrator can order a certain action without negotiation. Moreover, by avoiding having to find or share the right outside resource, companies capture (at least in the short run) all profits associated with an operation.

Stability. Effective managers are supposed to insulate the technical core of production from external shocks. To do this they need buffer inventories, control of raw materials, and control of distribution channels. Ownership also creates familiarity and an identifiable chain of command, which becomes stabilized over time.

Industry custom. If everyone else in an industry owns, it is a competitive risk to buck the tide.

What structure is best?

A strangling organizational structure or a stifling bureaucracy often stirs corporate managers to think about starting or acquiring their own businesses. Rebuffed by "channels" in attempts to get their employer to consider a new product or explore a new market, they long for the freedom inherent in a small and flexible structure.

When it comes to organizing businesses, there is a distinct difference between the promoter and the trustee mentalities. Via contact with the principal actors, the promoter tries to "feel" the way events are unfolding. The trustee views relationships more formally: rights, responsibilities, and authority are conferred on different people and segments of an organization. The trustee is prepared to take action without making contact with those that are affected by the decision.

Also influencing the approach to business organization is the control of resources. To help them coordinate their activities, businesses that use and rent resources by necessity develop informal information networks both internally and externally. But organizations that own and employ resources are easily and naturally organized into hierarchies according to those resources. Because hierarchy inhibits not only the search for and commitment to opportunity but also communication and decision making, networking evolves in most companies. Usually this networking is formalized in matrix and committee structures. (See *Exhibit II*, part E.)

Commentators on organizations often criticize the entrepreneur's antipathy toward formalized structure as a liability stemming from an inability to let go. The entrepreneur is stereotyped as egocentric and unable to manage. In this view, the administrator may not be very spontaneous or innovative, but is a good manager. In reality the entrepreneur isn't necessarily a worse manager than the administrator but has simply chosen different tools to get the task done. Fashioning these tools are the following pressures:

The need to coordinate resources that are not controlled. Entrepreneurs must motivate, handle, and direct outside suppliers, professionals, and others to make sure needed goods and services are available when they're supposed to be.

The need for flexibility. In today's atmosphere of rapid change, the development of much essential operating information outside the company makes communication with external resources even more important. The notion that hierarchy provides stability does not hold true, especially if one considers that in a typical company growing 30% annually, only 40% of the employees three years down the line will have been with the company from the start. A flat and informal structure enhances communication.

Employees' desire for independence. Many of today's managers are still influenced by the antiauthoritarian values of the 1960s and the self-fulfillment values of the 1970s. Furthermore, organizations with little hierarchy breed employees accustomed to authority based on competence and persuasion; they will resist attempts to introduce structure and to rationalize authority based on hierarchy.

Of course, hierarchical organizations arise for rational reasons. According to classic management theory, a formal, well-defined structure ensures attention to all the necessary planning, organizing, and controlling activities. Among the pressures against the entrepreneurial approach and toward the administrative are the following:

The greater complexity of tasks. As planning, coordinating, communicating, and controlling functions become more involved, clearly defined authority and responsibility are needed to ensure adequate differentiation and integration.

Stratified organizational culture. If a desire for routine and order comes to dominate corporate attitudes, a more formal structure is attractive and reassuring.

Control-based reward systems. As we indicated earlier, reward systems are often based on the amount of control executives have, as measured in the organizational structure. Thus incentives reinforce formality.

It's easier, of course, to avoid adding structure than it is to reduce existing structure. Many of the high-technology companies in California's Silicon Valley and along Route 128 in Massachusetts have been notably successful in keeping structure to a minimum by erasing distinctions between upper and lower management and encouraging such group activities as the Friday afternoon beer bust. The fewer the distinctions, the less inhibited lower-level employees will be about approaching top managers with complaints and suggestions about operations. Managers trained to expect an orderly world may feel uncomfortable in such an informal atmosphere, but the dividends in coordination and motivation can be important.

It is possible for companies with extensive structure to reduce it. Sears, Roebuck has trimmed its corporate staff way back and in the process has granted much autonomy to its operating units. Dana Corporation, like many other companies, has found that cutting out the "helping staff" has improved performance.

Stimulating entrepreneurship

Our discussion should have made clear our belief that entrepreneurship is a trait that is confined neither to certain types of individuals nor to organizations. Obviously, it is found more in smaller and younger enterprises than in larger and older ones simply because the conditions favoring its development are more likely to be present.

For many people, the dream of being the boss and being financially self-sufficient is enough to stimulate the pursuit of opportunity. The venturesome are usually forced by capital limitations to commit resources gradually and to rent or use them rather than own them. Similarly, they recoil from the idea of bureaucracy; to them, it's vital to have an organization that can react quickly to new opportunities.

Even so, many of the nation's small businesses inhabit the administrative end of our spectrum. The owners shy from taking risks in pursuit of growth; perhaps they are preoccupied with other financial activities such as investing in real estate or the stock market, paying their children's college expenses, or providing for impending retirement. Perhaps they only want the business to provide a steady living, so they run their businesses in a way to guard what they have.

A society can do much to stimulate or inhibit the development of entrepreneurship. Government policy can do much to create opportunity. Decisions in recent years to lower the capital gains tax and deregulate certain industries have been instrumental in encouraging the establishment of many new businesses that otherwise would probably not exist today. Support of basic research in health, technology, and material science establishes a base on which opportunities are built.

Similarly, the way our colleges and universities teach business management affects approaches to entrepreneurship. Courses and departments in entrepreneurship, set up at many such institutions, will produce increasing numbers of young managers who are attuned to effective ways of pursuing opportunity and managing resources.

While government agencies and educational institutions can create conditions favorable for entrepreneurship to take hold, it's up to individual organizations to foster the conditions that allow it to flourish. That means encouraging the timely pursuit of opportunity, the most appropriate commitment and use of resources, and the breakdown of hierarchy.

Those goals of course are not easy to reach, especially if the organization must be turned around from its habitual administrative approach. We see in corporations the same type of opportunity matrix as we described for individual managers early in this article and in *Exhibit I*. As one can see in *Exhibit III*, movement to the left requires a strategic focus and the instillation of belief throughout the organization that change is acceptable and even desirable. Movement upward presupposes that corporate officers think their organization has the capacity to acquire resources as needed. To foster this belief the leadership of the organization can:

Determine its barriers to entrepreneurship. Is a manager's principal reward found in handling the company's existing resources? Are managers expected to pursue outside opportunities in its behalf

Exhibit III	Corporate opportunity matrix

only when they have extra time? Do management and director committees evaluate opportunities on an all-or-none, one-shot basis? Do superiors have to go through many levels to gain approval for capital budgets and adding personnel?

Seek to minimize risks to the individual for being entrepreneurial. When people are promoted for behaving like trustees while promoter types are shunted aside if not eased out, there's little motive to be venturesome. The leadership can work at reducing the individual's cost of failing in the pursuit of opportunity, especially if the failure is externally caused. To convince skeptical managers that the risks have indeed been reduced, the leadership must not only recognize entrepreneurship as an organizational goal but also eliminate the bottom line as the main determinant of subordinates' success.

Exploit any resource pool. The huge resources that many companies have can be committed intelligently. Indeed, the fact that they are huge can be an important aspect of reducing the perceived risk to managers of pursuing opportunity. After all, resources per se reduce risks associated with exploiting opportunity. Excess resources can also support a thorough search process. And if enough opportunities are pursued, there can be ultimate success even if some fail.

Tailor reward systems to the situation. For some, a primary motivating force is the possibility of becoming wealthy through ownership in a growing enterprise. For a start-up or early-stage venture, then, equity in the company may be the main incentive encouraging entrepreneurial behavior on the part of the initial employees. Large organizations cannot hope to duplicate this lure without creating interest among those who are not offered such rewards. (Managers of these companies are often driven by other objectives anyway, including security and growing responsibility.) The leadership of established corporations, then, must think in terms of fostering team commitment and rewarding successful entrepreneurs with chances to do more of the same on a grander scale.

It's much easier and safer for companies to stay with the familiar than to explore the unknown. Only by encouraging change and experimentation can companies of all sizes adapt and grow in the midst of much uncertainty. ⊖

Reprint 85216

Managing innovation: controlled chaos

James Brian Quinn

Big companies stay innovative by behaving like small entrepreneurial ventures

World technological leadership, some say, is passing from the United States to our international rivals in Europe and the Far East. Critics of corporate America point out that many new products and services originate overseas—especially in Japan—and blame our large bureaucratic organizations for stifling innovation. The innovations that do arise here, according to these observers, come primarily from entrepreneurs and small businesses.

The author of this article, a leading management scholar, takes a different view. Large companies that understand the innovative process have an impressive record of developing new technologies and products. Drawing on a multiyear research project and many case studies, the author analyzes the managerial practices of successful large companies and outlines some common patterns in their approach to technological innovation. These big companies, like many successful small entrepreneurs, accept the essential chaos of development. They pay close attention to their users'

needs and desires, avoid detailed early technical or marketing plans, and allow entrepreneurial teams to pursue competing alternatives within a clearly conceived framework of goals and limits.

Mr. Quinn is William and Josephine Buchanan Professor of Management at the Amos Tuck School of Business Administration at Dartmouth College. He has published widely on strategic management and the management of technological innovation. His most recent book is Strategies for Change: Logical Incrementalism *(Dow Jones-Irwin, 1980).*

Illustrations by Catherine Kanner.

Management observers frequently claim that small organizations are more innovative than large ones. But is this commonplace necessarily true? Some large enterprises are highly innovative. How do they do it? Can lessons from these companies and their smaller counterparts help other companies become more innovative?

This article proposes some answers to these questions based on the initial results of an ongoing 2½ year worldwide study. The research sample includes both well-documented small ventures and large U.S., Japanese, and European companies and programs selected for their innovation records (see insert). More striking than the cultural differences among these companies are the similarities between innovative small and large organizations and among innovative organizations in different countries. Effective management of innovation seems much the same, regardless of national boundaries or scale of operations.

There are, of course, many reasons why small companies appear to produce a disproportionate number of innovations. First, innovation occurs in a probabilistic setting. A company never knows whether a particular technical result can be achieved and whether it will succeed in the marketplace. For every new solution that succeeds, tens to hundreds fail. The sheer number of attempts—most by small-scale entrepreneurs—means that some ventures will survive. The 90% to 99% that fail are distributed widely throughout society and receive little notice.

On the other hand, a big company that wishes to move a concept from invention to the marketplace must absorb all potential failure costs itself. This risk may be socially or managerially intolerable, jeopardizing the many other products, projects, jobs, and communities the company supports. Even if its innovation is successful, a big company may face costs that newcomers do not bear, like converting existing operations and customer bases to the new solution.

By contrast, a new enterprise does not risk losing an existing investment base or cannibalizing customer franchises built at great expense. It does not have to change an internal culture that has successfully supported doing things another way or that has developed intellectual depth and belief in the technologies that led to past successes. Organized groups like labor unions, consumer advocates, and government bureaucracies rarely monitor and resist a small company's moves as they might a big company's. Finally, new companies do not face the psychological pain and the economic costs of laying off employees, shutting down plants and even communities, and displacing supplier relationships built with years of mutual commitment and effort. Such barriers to change in large organizations are real, important, and legitimate.

The complex products and systems that society expects large companies to undertake further compound the risks. Only big companies can develop new ships or locomotives; telecommunication networks; or systems for space, defense, air traffic control, hospital care, mass foods delivery, or nationwide computer interactions. These large-scale projects always carry more risk than single-product introductions. A billion-dollar development aircraft, for example, can fail if one inexpensive part in its 100,000 components fails.

Clearly, a single enterprise cannot by itself develop or produce all the parts needed by such large new systems. And communications among the various groups making design and production decisions on components are always incomplete. The probability of error increases exponentially with complexity, while the system innovator's control over decisions decreases significantly—further escalating potential error costs and risks. Such forces inhibit innovation in large organizations. But proper management can lessen these effects.

Of inventors & entrepreneurs

A close look at innovative small enterprises reveals much about the successful management of innovation. Of course, not all innovations follow a single pattern. But my research—and other studies in combination—suggest that the following factors are crucial to the success of innovative small companies:

Need orientation. Inventor-entrepreneurs tend to be "need or achievement oriented."[1] They believe that if they "do the job better," rewards will follow. They may at first focus on their own view of market needs. But lacking resources, successful small entrepreneurs soon find that it pays to approach potential customers early, test their solutions in users' hands, learn from these interactions, and adapt designs rapidly. Many studies suggest that effective technological innovation develops hand-in-hand with customer demand.[2]

Experts and fanatics. Company founders tend to be pioneers in their technologies and fanatics when it comes to solving problems. They are often described as "possessed" or "obsessed," working toward their objectives to the exclusion even of family or personal relationships. As both experts and fanatics, they perceive probabilities of success as higher than others do. And their commitment allows them to persevere despite the frustrations, ambiguities, and setbacks that always accompany major innovations.

Long time horizons. Their fanaticism may cause inventor-entrepreneurs to underestimate the obstacles and length of time to success. Time horizons for radical innovations make them essentially "irrational" from a present value viewpoint. In my sample, delays between invention and commercial production ranged from 3 to 25 years.[3] In the late 1930s, for example, industrial chemist Russell Marker was working on steroids called sapogenins when he discovered a technique that would degrade one of these, diosgenin, into the female sex hormone progesterone. By processing some ten tons of Mexican yams in rented and borrowed lab space, Marker finally extracted about four pounds of diosgenin and started a tiny business to produce steroids for the laboratory market. But it was not until 1962, over 23 years later, that Syntex, the company Marker founded, obtained FDA approval for its oral contraceptive.

For both psychological and practical reasons, inventor-entrepreneurs generally avoid early formal plans, proceed step-by-step, and sustain themselves by other income and the momentum of the small advances they achieve as they go along.

Low early costs. Innovators tend to work in homes, basements, warehouses, or low-rent facilities whenever possible. They incur few overhead

1 David McClelland, *The Achieving Society* (New York: Halsted Press, 1976); Gene Bylinsky, *The Innovation Millionaires* (New York: Scribner's, 1976).

2 Eric von Hippel, "Get New Products From Customers," HBR March-April 1982, p. 117.

3 A study at Battelle found an average of 19.2 years between invention and commercial production. Battelle Memorial Laboratories, "Science, Technology, and Innovation," Report to the National Science Foundation, 1973; R.C. Dean, "The Temporal Mismatch: Innovation's Pace vs. Management's Time Horizon," *Research Management*, May 1974, p. 13.

costs; their limited resources go directly into their projects. They pour nights, weekends, and "sweat capital" into their endeavors. They borrow whatever they can. They invent cheap equipment and prototype processes, often improving on what is available in the marketplace. If one approach fails, few people know; little time or money is lost. All this decreases the costs and risks facing a small operation and improves the present value of its potential success.

Multiple approaches. Technology tends to advance through a series of random—often highly intuitive—insights frequently triggered by gratuitous interactions between the discoverer and the outside world. Only highly committed entrepreneurs can tolerate (and even enjoy) this chaos. They adopt solutions wherever they can be found, unencumbered by formal plans or PERT charts that would limit the range of their imaginations. When the odds of success are low, the participation and interaction of many motivated players increase the chance that one will succeed.

A recent study of initial public offerings made in 1962 shows that only 2% survived and still looked like worthwhile investments 20 years later.[4] Small-scale entrepreneurship looks efficient in part because history only records the survivors.

Flexibility and quickness. Undeterred by committees, board approvals, and other bureaucratic delays, the inventor-entrepreneur can experiment, test, recycle, and try again with little time lost. Because technological progress depends largely on the number of successful experiments accomplished per unit of time, fast-moving small entrepreneurs can gain both timing and performance advantages over clumsier competitors. This responsiveness is often crucial in finding early markets for radical innovations where neither innovators, market researchers, nor users can quite visualize a product's real potential. For example, Edison's lights first appeared on ships and in baseball parks; Astroturf was intended to convert the flat roofs and asphalt playgrounds of city schools into more humane environments; and graphite and boron composites designed for aerospace unexpectedly found their largest markets in sporting goods. Entrepreneurs quickly adjusted their entry strategies to market feedback.

Incentives. Inventor-entrepreneurs can foresee tangible personal rewards if they are successful. Individuals often want to achieve a technical contribution, recognition, power, or sheer independence, as much as money. For the original, driven personalities who create significant innovations, few other paths offer such clear opportunities to fulfill all their economic, psychological, and career goals at once. Consequently, they do not panic or quit when others with solely monetary goals might.

Availability of capital. One of America's great competitive advantages is its rich variety of sources to finance small, low-probability ventures. If entrepreneurs are turned down by one source, other sources can be sought in myriads of creative combinations.

Professionals involved in such financings have developed a characteristic approach to deal with the chaos and uncertainty of innovation. First, they evaluate a proposal's conceptual validity: If the technical problems can be solved, is there a real business there for someone and does it have a large upside potential? Next, they concentrate on people: Is the team thoroughly committed and expert? Is it the best available? Only then do these financiers analyze specific financial estimates in depth. Even then, they recognize that actual outcomes generally depend on subjective factors, not numbers.[5]

Timeliness, aggressiveness, commitment, quality of people, and the flexibility to attack opportunities not at first perceived are crucial. Downside risks are minimized, not by detailed controls, but by spreading risks among multiple projects, keeping early costs low, and gauging the tenacity, flexibility, and capability of the founders.

Bureaucratic barriers to innovation

Less innovative companies and, unfortunately, most large corporations operate in a very different fashion. The most notable and common constraints on innovation in larger companies include:

Top management isolation. Many senior executives in big companies have little contact with conditions on the factory floor or with customers who might influence their thinking about technological innovation. Since risk perception is inversely related to familiarity and experience, financially oriented top managers are likely to perceive technological innovations as more problematic than acquisitions that may be just as risky but that will appear more familiar.[6]

4 Business Economics Group, W.R. Grace & Co., 1983.

5 Christina C. Pence, *How Venture Capitalists Make Venture Decisions* (Ann Arbor, Mich.: UMI Research Press, 1982).

6 Robert H. Hayes and David A. Garvin, "Managing as if Tomorrow Mattered," HBR May-June 1982, p. 70; Robert H. Hayes and William J. Abernathy, "Managing Our Way to Economic Decline," HBR July-August 1980, p. 67.

Intolerance of fanatics. Big companies often view entrepreneurial fanatics as embarrassments or troublemakers. Many major cities are now ringed by companies founded by these "nonteam" players—often to the regret of their former employers.

Short time horizons. The perceived corporate need to report a continuous stream of quarterly profits conflicts with the long time spans that major innovations normally require. Such pressures often make publicly owned companies favor quick marketing fixes, cost cutting, and acquisition strategies over process, product, or quality innovations that would yield much more in the long run.

Accounting practices. By assessing all its direct, indirect, overhead, overtime, and service costs against a project, large corporations have much higher development expenses compared with entrepreneurs working in garages. A project in a big company can quickly become an exposed political target, its potential net present value may sink unacceptably, and an entry into small markets may not justify its sunk costs. An otherwise viable project may soon founder and disappear.

Excessive rationalism. Managers in big companies often seek orderly advance through early market research studies or PERT planning. Rather than managing the inevitable chaos of innovation productively, these managers soon drive out the very things that lead to innovation in order to prove their announced plans.

Excessive bureaucracy. In the name of efficiency, bureaucratic structures require many approvals and cause delays at every turn. Experiments that a small company can perform in hours may take days or weeks in large organizations. The interactive feedback that fosters innovation is lost, important time windows can be missed, and real costs and risks rise for the corporation.

Inappropriate incentives. Reward and control systems in most big companies are designed to minimize surprises. Yet innovation, by definition, is full of surprises. It often disrupts well-laid plans, accepted power patterns, and entrenched organizational behavior at high costs to many. Few large companies make millionaires of those who create such disruptions, however profitable the innovations may turn out to be. When control systems neither penalize opportunities missed nor reward risks taken, the results are predictable.

The study

A questionnaire and poll of experts identified several outstanding innovative large companies in Europe, the United States, and Japan for study. These companies had more than $1 billion in sales and programs with at least tens of millions of dollars in initial investment and hundreds of millions of dollars in ultimate annual economic impact. Interviews and secondary sources were used and cross-checked to establish management patterns. Wherever possible, cases on these companies and ventures were written and will be released for public use. Case studies of Sony Corporation, Intel Corporation, Pilkington Brothers, Ltd., and Honda Corporation are already available from the author.

How large innovative companies do it

Yet some big companies are continuously innovative. Although each such enterprise is distinctive, the successful big innovators I studied have developed techniques that emulate or improve on their smaller counterparts' practices. What are the most important patterns?

Atmosphere and vision. Continuous innovation occurs largely because top executives appreciate innovation and manage their company's value system and atmosphere to support it. For example, Sony's founder, Masaru Ibuka, stated in the company's "Purposes of Incorporation" the goal of a "free, dynamic, and pleasant factory...where sincerely motivated personnel can exercise their technological skills to the highest level." Ibuka and Sony's chairman, Akio Morita, inculcated the "Sony spirit" through a series of unusual policies: hiring brilliant people with nontraditional skills (like an opera singer) for high management positions, promoting young people over their elders, designing a new type of living accommodation for workers, and providing visible awards for outstanding technical achievements.

Because familiarity can foster understanding and psychological comfort, engineering and scientific leaders are often those who create atmospheres supportive of innovation, especially in a company's early life. Executive vision is more important than a particular management background—as IBM, Genentech, AT&T, Merck, Elf Aquitaine, Pilkington, and others in my sample illustrate. CEOs of these companies value technology and include technical experts in their highest decision circles.

Innovative managements—whether technical or not—project clear long-term visions for their organizations that go beyond simple economic measures. As Intel's chairman, Gordon Moore, says: "We intend to be the outstandingly successful innovative company in this industry. We intend to continue to be a leader in this revolutionary [semiconductor] technology that is changing the way this world is run." Genentech's original plan expresses a similar vision: "We expect to be the first company to commercialize the [rDNA] technology, and we plan to build a major profitable corporation by manufacturing and marketing needed products that benefit mankind. The future uses of genetic engineering are far reaching and many. Any product produced by a living organism is eventually within the company's reach."

Such visions, vigorously supported, are not "management fluff," but have many practical implications. They attract quality people to the company and give focus to their creative and entrepreneurial drives. When combined with sound internal operations, they help channel growth by concentrating attention on the actions that lead to profitability, rather than on profitability itself. Finally, these visions recognize a realistic time frame for innovation and attract the kind of investors who will support it.

Orientation to the market. Innovative companies tie their visions to the practical realities of the marketplace. Although each company uses techniques adapted to its own style and strategy, two elements are always present: a strong market orientation at the very top of the company and mechanisms to ensure interactions between technical and marketing people at lower levels. At Sony, for example, soon after technical people are hired, the company runs them through weeks of retail selling. Sony engineers become sensitive to the ways retail sales practices, product displays, and nonquantifiable customer preferences affect success. Similarly, before AT&T's recent divestiture, Bell Laboratories had an Operating Company Assignment Program to rotate its researchers through AT&T and Western Electric development and production facilities. And it had a rigorous Engineering Complaint System that collected technical problems from operating companies and required Bell Labs to specify within a few weeks how it would resolve or attack each problem.

From top to bench levels in my sample's most innovative companies, managers focus primarily on seeking to anticipate and solve customers' emerging problems.

Small, flat organizations. The most innovative large companies in my sample try to keep the total organization flat and project teams small. Development teams normally include only six or seven key people. This number seems to constitute a critical mass of skills while fostering maximum communication and commitment among members. According to research done by my colleague, Victor McGee, the number of channels of communication increases as $n[2^{(n-1)} - 1]$. Therefore:

For team size	=	1	2	3	4	5	6	7	8	9	10	11
Channels	=	1	2	9	28	75	186	441	1016	2295	5110	11253

Innovative companies also try to keep their operating divisions and total technical units small—below 400 people. Up to this number, only two layers of management are required to maintain a span of control over 7 people. In units much larger than 400, people quickly lose touch with the concept of their product or process, staffs and bureaucracies tend to grow, and projects may go through too many formal screens to survive. Since it takes a chain of yesses and only one no to kill a project, jeopardy multiplies as management layers increase.

Multiple approaches. At first one cannot be sure which of several technical approaches will dominate a field. The history of technology is replete with accidents, mishaps, and chance meetings that allowed one approach or group to emerge rapidly over others. Leo Baekelund was looking for a synthetic shellac when he found Bakelite and started the modern plastics industry. At Syntex, researchers were not looking for an oral contraceptive when they created 19-norprogesterone, the precursor to the active ingredient in half of all contraceptive pills. And the microcomputer was born because Intel's Ted Hoff "happened" to work on a complex calculator just when Digital Equipment Corporation's PDP8 architecture was fresh in his mind.

Such "accidents" are involved in almost all major technological advances. When theory can predict everything, a company has moved to a new stage, from development to production. Murphy's law works because engineers design for what they can foresee; hence what fails is what theory could not predict. And it is rare that the interactions of components and subsystems can be predicted over the lifetime of operations. For example, despite careful theoretical design work, the first high performance jet engine literally tore itself to pieces on its test stand, while others failed in unanticipated operating conditions (like an Iranian sandstorm).

Recognizing the inadequacies of theory, innovative enterprises seem to move faster from paper studies to physical testing than do noninnovative en-

---

7 In *Managing the Flow of Technology* (Cambridge: MIT Press, 1977), Thomas J. Allen illustrates the enormous leverage provided such technology accessors (called "gatekeepers") in R&D organizations.

terprises. When possible, they encourage several prototype programs to proceed in parallel. Sony pursued 10 major options in developing its videotape recorder technology. Each option had two to three subsystem alternatives. Such redundancy helps the company cope with uncertainties in development, motivates people through competition, and improves the amount and quality of information available for making final choices on scale-ups or introductions.

Developmental shoot-outs.
Many companies structure shoot-outs among competing approaches only after they reach the prototype stages. They find this practice provides more objective information for making decisions, decreases risk by making choices that best reflect marketplace needs, and helps ensure that the winning option will move ahead with a committed team behind it. Although many managers worry that competing approaches may be inefficient, greater effectiveness in choosing the right solution easily outweighs duplication costs when the market rewards higher performance or when large volumes justify increased sophistication. Under these conditions, parallel development may prove less costly because it both improves the probability of success and reduces development time.

Perhaps the most difficult problem in managing competing projects lies in reintegrating the members of the losing team. If the company is expanding rapidly or if the successful project creates a growth opportunity, losing team members can work on another interesting program or sign on with the winning team as the project moves toward the marketplace. For the shoot-out system to work continuously, however, executives must create a climate that honors high-quality performance whether a project wins or loses, reinvolves people quickly in their technical specialties or in other projects, and accepts and expects rotation among tasks and groups.

At Sony, according to its top R&D manager, the research climate does not penalize the losing team: "We constantly have several alternative projects going. Before the competition is over, before there is a complete loss, we try to smell the potential outcome and begin to prepare for that result as early as possible. Even after we have consensus, we may wait for several months to give the others a chance. Then we begin to give important jobs [on other programs] to members of the losing groups. If your team doesn't win, you may still be evaluated as performing well. Such people have often received my 'crystal award' for outstanding work. We never talk badly about these people. Ibuka's principle is that doing something, even if it fails, is better than doing nothing. A strike-out at Sony is OK, but you must not just stand there. You must swing at the ball as best you can."

Skunkworks.
Every highly innovative enterprise in my research sample emulated small company practices by using groups that functioned in a skunkworks style. Small teams of engineers, technicians, designers, and model makers were placed together with no intervening organizational or physical barriers to developing a new product from idea to commercial prototype stages. In innovative Japanese companies, top managers often worked hand-in-hand on projects with young engineers. Surprisingly, *ringi* decision making was not evident in these situations. Soichiro Honda was known for working directly on technical problems and emphasizing his technical points by shouting at his engineers or occasionally even hitting them with wrenches!

The skunkworks approach eliminates bureaucracies, allows fast, unfettered communications, permits rapid turnaround times for experiments, and instills a high level of group identity and loyalty. Interestingly, few successful groups in my research were structured in the classic "venture group" form, with a careful balancing of engineering, production, and marketing talents. Instead they acted on an old truism: introducing a new product or process to the world is like raising a healthy child—it needs a mother (champion) who loves it, a father (authority figure with resources) to support it, and pediatricians (specialists) to get it through difficult times. It may survive solely in the hands of specialists, but its chances of success are remote.

Interactive learning.
Skunkworks are as close as most big companies can come to emulating the highly interactive and motivating learning environment that characterizes successful small ventures. But the best big innovators have gone even farther. Recognizing that the random, chaotic nature of technological change cuts across organizational and even institutional lines, these companies tap into multiple outside sources of technology as well as their customers' capabilities. Enormous external leverages are possible. No company can spend more than a small share of the world's $200 billion devoted to R&D. But like small entrepreneurs, big companies can have much of that total effort cheaply if they try.

In industries such as electronics, customers provide much of the innovation on new products. In other industries, such as textiles, materials or equipment suppliers provide the innovation. In still others, such as biotechnology, universities are dominant, while foreign sources strongly supplement industries such as controlled fusion. Many R&D units have strategies to develop information for trading with outside groups and have teams to cultivate these sources.[7] Large Japanese companies have been notably effective at this. So have U.S. companies as diverse as Du Pont, AT&T, Apple Computer, and Genentech.

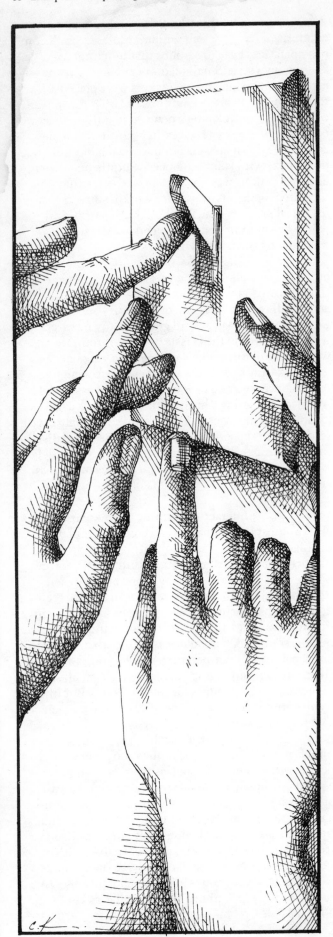

An increasing variety of creative relationships exist in which big companies participate—as joint venturers, consortium members, limited partners, guarantors of first markets, major academic funding sources, venture capitalists, spin-off equity holders, and so on. These rival the variety of inventive financing and networking structures that individual entrepreneurs have created.

Indeed, the innovative practices of small and large companies look ever more alike. This resemblance is especially striking in the interactions between companies and customers during development. Many experienced big companies are relying less on early market research and more on interactive development with lead customers. Hewlett-Packard, 3M, Sony, and Raychem frequently introduce radically new products through small teams that work closely with lead customers. These teams learn from their customers' needs and innovations, and rapidly modify designs and entry strategies based on this information.

Formal market analyses continue to be useful for extending product lines, but they are often misleading when applied to radical innovations. Market studies predicted that Haloid would never sell more than 5,000 xerographic machines, that Intel's microprocessor would never sell more than 10% as many units as there were minicomputers, and that Sony's transistor radios and miniature television sets would fail in the marketplace. At the same time, many eventual failures such as Ford's Edsel, IBM's FS system, and the supersonic transport were studied and planned exhaustively on paper, but lost contact with customers' real needs.

A strategy for innovation

The flexible management practices needed for major innovations often pose problems for established cultures in big companies. Yet there are reasonable steps managers in these companies can take. Innovation can be bred in a surprising variety of organizations, as many examples show. What are its key elements?

An opportunity orientation. In the 1981-1983 recession, many large companies cut back or closed plants as their "only available solution." Yet I repeatedly found that top managers in these companies took these actions without determining firsthand why their customers were buying from competitors, discerning what niches in their markets were growing, or tapping the innovations their own people had to solve problems. These managers foreclosed innumerable options by defining the issue as cost cutting rather than opportunity seeking. As one frustrated division manager in a manufacturing conglomerate put it: "If management doesn't actively seek or welcome technical opportunities, it sure won't hear about them."

By contrast, Intel met the challenge of the last recession with its "20% solution." The professional staff agreed to work one extra day a week to bring innovations to the marketplace earlier than planned. Despite the difficult times, Intel came out of the recession with several important new products ready to go—and it avoided layoffs.

Entrepreneurial companies recognize that they have almost unlimited access to capital and they structure their practices accordingly. They let it be known that if their people come up with good ideas, they can find the necessary capital—just as private venture capitalists or investment bankers find resources for small entrepreneurs.

Structuring for innovation. Managers need to think carefully about how innovation fits into their strategy and structure their technology, skills, resources, and organizational commitments accordingly. A few examples suggest the variety of strategies and alignments possible:

☐ Hewlett-Packard and 3M develop product lines around a series of small, discrete, freestanding products. These companies form units that look like entrepreneurial start-ups. Each has a small team, led by a champion, in low-cost facilities. These companies allow many different proposals to come forward and test them as early as possible in the marketplace. They design control systems to spot significant losses on any single entry quickly. They look for high gains on a few winners and blend less successful, smaller entries into prosperous product lines.

☐ Other companies (like AT&T or the oil majors) have had to make large system investments to last for decades. These companies tend to make long-term needs forecasts. They often start several programs in parallel to be sure of selecting the right technologies. They then extensively test new technologies in use before making systemwide commitments. Often they sacrifice speed of entry for long-term low cost and reliability.

☐ Intel and Dewey & Almy, suppliers of highly technical specialties to OEMs, develop strong technical sales networks to discover and understand customer needs in depth. These companies try to have technical solutions designed into customers' products. Such companies have flexible applied technology groups working close to the marketplace. They also have quickly expandable plant facilities and a cutting-edge technology (not necessarily basic research) group

that allows rapid selection of currently available technologies.

☐ Dominant producers like IBM or Matsushita are often not the first to introduce new technologies. They do not want to disturb their successful product lines any sooner than necessary. As market demands become clear, these companies establish precise price-performance windows and form overlapping project teams to come up with the best answer for the marketplace. To decrease market risks, they use product shoot-outs as close to the market as possible. They develop extreme depth in production technologies to keep unit costs low from the outset. Finally, depending on the scale of the market entry, they have project teams report as close to the top as necessary to secure needed management attention and resources.

☐ Merck and Hoffman-LaRoche, basic research companies, maintain laboratories with better facilities, higher pay, and more freedom than most universities can afford. These companies leverage their internal spending through research grants, clinical grants, and research relationships with universities throughout the world. Before they invest $20 million to $50 million to clear a new drug, they must have reasonable assurance that they will be first in the marketplace. They take elaborate precautions to ensure that the new entry is safe and effective, and that it cannot be easily duplicated by others. Their structures are designed to be on the cutting edge of science, but conservative in animal testing, clinical evaluation, and production control.

These examples suggest some ways of linking innovation to strategy. Many other examples, of course, exist. Within a single company, individual divisions may have different strategic needs and hence different structures and practices. No single approach works well for all situations.

Complex portfolio planning. Perhaps the most difficult task for top managers is to balance the needs of existing lines against the needs of potential lines. This problem requires a portfolio strategy much more complex than the popular four-box Boston Consulting Group matrix found in most strategy texts. To allocate resources for innovation strategically, managers need to define the broad, long-term actions within and across divisions necessary to achieve their visions. They should determine which positions to hold at all costs, where to fall back, and where to expand initially and in the more distant future.

A company's strategy may often require investing most resources in current lines. But sufficient resources should also be invested in patterns that ensure intermediate and long-term growth; provide defenses against possible government, labor, competitive, or activist challenges; and generate needed organizational, technical, and external relations flexibilities to handle unforeseen opportunities or threats. Sophisticated portfolio planning within and among divisions can protect both current returns and future prospects—the two critical bases for that most cherished goal, high price-earnings ratios.

An incrementalist approach

Such managerial techniques can provide a strategic focus for innovation and help solve many of the timing, coordination, and motivation problems that plague large, bureaucratic organizations. Even more detailed planning techniques may help in guiding the development of the many small innovations that characterize any successful business. My research reveals, however, that few, if any, major innovations result from highly structured planning systems. Within the broad framework I have described, major innovations are best managed as incremental, goal-oriented, interactive learning processes.[8]

Several sophisticated companies have labeled this approach "phased program planning." When they see an important opportunity in the marketplace (or when a laboratory champion presses them), top managers outline some broad, challenging goals for the new programs: "to be the first to prove whether rDNA is commercially feasible for this process," or "to create an economical digital switching system for small country telephone systems." These goals have few key timing, cost, or performance numbers attached. As scientists and engineers (usually from different areas) begin to define technical options, the programs' goals become more specific—though managers still allow much latitude in technical approaches.

As options crystallize, managers try to define the most important technical sequences and critical decision points. They may develop "go, no go" performance criteria for major program phases and communicate these as targets for project teams. In systems innovations, for example, performance specifications must be set to coordinate the interactions of subsystems. Successful companies leave open for as long as possible exactly how these targets can be achieved.

While feeding resources to the most promising options, managers frequently keep other paths open. Many of the best concepts and solutions come from projects partly hidden or "bootlegged" by the organization. Most successful managers try to build some slacks or buffers into their plans to hedge their bets, although they hesitate to announce these actions widely. They permit chaos and replication in early investigations, but insist on much more formal planning and controls as expensive development and scale-up proceed. But even at these later stages, these managers have learned to maintain flexibility and to avoid the tyranny of paper plans. They seek inputs from manufacturing, marketing, and customer groups early. Armed with this information, they are prepared to modify their plans even as they enter the marketplace. A European executive describes this process of directing innovation as "a somewhat orderly tumult that can be managed only in an incremental fashion."

Why incrementalism?

The innovative process is inherently incremental. As Thomas Hughes says, "Technological systems evolve through relatively small steps marked by an occasional stubborn obstacle and by constant random breakthroughs interacting across laboratories and borders."[9] A forgotten hypothesis of Einstein's became the laser in Charles Townes's mind as he contemplated azaleas in Franklin Square. The structure of DNA followed a circuitous route through research in biology, organic chemistry, X-ray crystallography, and mathematics toward its Nobel Prize-winning conception as a spiral staircase of matched base pairs. Such rambling trails are characteristic of virtually all major technological advances.

At the outset of the attack on a technical problem, an innovator often does not know whether his problem is tractable, what approach will prove best, and what concrete characteristics the solution will have if achieved. The logical route, therefore, is to follow several paths—though perhaps with varying degrees of intensity—until more information becomes available. Not knowing precisely where the solution will occur, wise managers establish the widest feasible network for finding and assessing alternative solutions. They keep many options open until one of them seems sure to win. Then they back it heavily.

Managing innovation is like a stud poker game, where one can play several hands. A player has some idea of the likely size of the pot at the beginning, knows the general but not the sure route to winning, buys one card (a project) at a time to gain

8 For a further discussion of incrementalism, see James Brian Quinn, "Managing Strategies Incrementally," Omega 10, no. 6 (1982), p. 613; and Strategies for Change: Logical Incrementalism (Homewood, Ill.: Dow Jones-Irwin, 1980).

9 Thomas Hughes, "The Inventive Continuum," Science 84, November 1984, p. 83.

10 Tracy Kidder, The Soul of a New Machine (Boston: Little, Brown, 1981).

information about probabilities and the size of the pot, closes hands as they become discouraging, and risks more only late in the hand as knowledge increases.

Political & psychological support

Incrementalism helps deal with the psychological, political, and motivational factors that are crucial to project success. By keeping goals broad at first, a manager avoids creating undue opposition to a new idea. A few concrete goals may be projected as a challenge. To maintain flexibility, intermediate steps are not developed in detail. Alternate routes can be tried and failures hidden. As early problems are solved, momentum, confidence, and identity build around the new approach. Soon a project develops enough adherents and objective data to withstand its critics' opposition.

As it comes more clearly into competition for resources, its advocates strive to solve problems and maintain its viability. Finally, enough concrete information exists for nontechnical managers to compare the programs fairly with more familiar options. The project now has the legitimacy and political clout to survive—which might never have happened if its totality has been disclosed or planned in detail at the beginning. Many sound technical projects have died because their managers did not deal with the politics of survival.

Chaos within guidelines

Effective managers of innovation channel and control its main directions. Like venture capitalists, they administer primarily by setting goals, selecting key people, and establishing a few critical limits and decision points for intervention rather than by implementing elaborate planning or control systems. As technology leads or market needs emerge, these managers set a few—most crucial—performance targets and limits. They allow their technical units to decide how to achieve these, subject to defined constraints and reviews at critical junctures.

Early bench-scale project managers may pursue various options, making little attempt at first to integrate each into a total program. Only after key variables are understood—and perhaps measured and demonstrated in lab models—can more precise planning be meaningful. Even then, many factors may remain unknown; chaos and competition can continue to thrive in the pursuit of the solution. At defined review points, however, only those options that can clear performance milestones may continue.

Choosing which projects to kill is perhaps the hardest decision in the management of innovation. In the end, the decision is often intuitive, resting primarily on a manager's technical knowledge and familiarity with innovation processes. Repeatedly, successful managers told me, "Anyone who thinks he can quantify this decision is either a liar or a fool....There are too many unknowables, variables....Ultimately, one must use intuition, a complex feeling, calibrated by experience....We'd be foolish not to check everything, touch all the bases. That's what the models are for. But ultimately it's a judgment about people, commitment, and probabilities....You don't dare use milestones too rigidly."

Even after selecting the approaches to emphasize, innovative managers tend to continue a few others as smaller scale "side bets" or options. In a surprising number of cases, these alternatives prove winners when the planned option fails.

Recognizing the many demands entailed by successful programs, innovative companies find special ways to reward innovators. Sony gives "a small but significant" percentage of a new product's sales to its innovating teams. Pilkington, IBM, and 3M's top executives are often chosen from those who have headed successful new product entries. Intel lets its Magnetic Memory Group operate like a small company, with special performance rewards and simulated stock options. GE, Syntex, and United Technologies help internal innovators establish new companies and take equity positions in "nonrelated" product innovations.

Large companies do not have to make their innovators millionaires, but rewards should be visible and significant. Fortunately, most engineers are happy with the incentives that Tracy Kidder calls "playing pinball"—giving widespread recognition to a job well done and the right to play in the next exciting game.[10] Most innovative companies provide both, but increasingly they are supplementing these with financial rewards to keep their most productive innovators from jumping outside.

Match management to the process

Management practices in innovative companies reflect the realities of the innovation process itself. Innovation tends to be individually motivated, opportunistic, customer responsive, tumultuous, nonlinear, and interactive in its development. Managers can plan overall directions and goals, but surprises are likely to abound. Consequently, innovative companies keep their programs flexible for as long as possible and freeze plans only when necessary for strategic purposes such as timing. Even then they keep options open by specifying broad performance goals and allowing different technical approaches to compete for as long as possible.

      Executives need to understand and accept the tumultuous realities of innovation, learn from the experiences of other companies, and adapt the most relevant features of these others to their own management practices and cultures. Many features of small company innovators are also applicable in big companies. With top-level understanding, vision, a commitment to customers and solutions, a genuine portfolio strategy, a flexible entrepreneurial atmosphere, and proper incentives for innovative champions, many more large companies can innovate to meet the severe demands of global competition. ▽

Reprint 85312

Entrepreneurship and Competitiveness

The Revitalization of Everything:
THE LAW
OF THE MICROCOSM

by GEORGE GILDER

rom Ronald Reagan's White House to the centers of French so-
cialism, from the speeches of Democratic liberals to the pages
of Britain's *Economist*, one assumption about U.S. technology
has long held firm: a key American asset is the startup culture
of Silicon Valley and similar centers of entrepreneurship. In the late
1980s, however, the heralds of entrepreneurship as the key to American competitiveness have faced a serious embarrassment. A protest
rang out from the leaders of Silicon Valley itself that far from an asset, the startup culture had become American industry's gravest
weakness in competing with Japan.

Intel Chairman Gordon Moore denounced the venture capital financiers as the "vulture capitalists" of Sand Hill Road, the Palo Alto
promenade of venture funds. Intel President Andrew Grove added
that his company was threatened as much by Wall Street as by Japan.
Not only did American vultures and headhunters prey on his best
people, he said, but also the stock market appraised the fabs and fan-
tasies of Intel defectors at many times the value of the real chips and
achievements of Intel itself.

In a memorable encounter at a Dataquest conference, Jerry Sanders, chairman of Advanced Micro Devices, confronted Pierre Lamond, once a leading figure at National Semiconductor and now a
leading venture capitalist. "You took my best guys to Cypress,"
Sanders charged, "and they made 3 million last year on 14 million in
sales. Fast static RAMs. Big deal. Static RAMs are not exactly a ma-

The system is sick, critics say, and chronic entrepreneurialism is the disease.

George Gilder's 1981 book Wealth and Poverty *became a textbook for the Reagan administration's early attempt to restructure economic policy. Entrepreneurs were the subject of his 1984 book* The Spirit of Enterprise.

jor innovation. [Intel introduced them in 1972.] But so far, so good. The problem is what they'll do next. They succeed by being focused. But all these small firms want to get big, and that means unfocused. After the first 50 million, believe me, it gets much harder. You can't fill large fabs with niche products. So far these companies have just ripped off the big firms without contributing anything significant."[1]

Lamond tried to laugh off the complaints of Sanders and others as merely the maundering of old men who want the world to stop turning as soon as they get on top. That's an understandable response from today's young entrepreneurs. But amid the late 1980s carnage in microchips, with the Japanese sweeping ahead in some measures of market share, the easy answers beg the question.

The leaders of the flagship Silicon Valley companies were bringing a serious message: in the future, success would depend on cooperation and cheap capital, planning and political savvy, lifetime employment and government research. To the entrepreneurs, it was as if Julius Erving had accosted Michael Jordan and solemnly informed him that his basketball career was over unless he learned not to jump. Weakened by "chronic entrepreneurialism" (the coinage of Robert Reich of Harvard), the theory went, many semiconductor companies were headed for catastrophe. "The Japanese are systematically destroying the U.S. industry, piece by piece," Grove claimed. "We are in a demolition derby and some of us are going to die."

For the Silicon Valley patriarchs, the remedy was intervention by the U.S. government to reshape and subsidize the industry. Their ideas bore fruit in Sematech, a chip manufacturing research and development consortium to be funded half by industry and half by government. Although Sematech could help U.S. manufacturers currently damaged by noncommercial Pentagon priorities and personnel demands, the idea of industrial policy seemed to vindicate the leading scholars of the Left. Such figures as Reich, Lester Thurow of MIT, and Chalmers Johnson of Berkeley have long maintained that whether mobilizing for war or for peace, government nearly always plays the leading role in evoking, developing, and financing new technology. Entrepreneurs can best serve as niche suppliers or subcontractors to major corporations.

In the face of Silicon Valley's success, surging forward with ever greater force as government business dwindled, their arguments seemed unconvincing. In the late 1980s, however, a new cadre of more sophisticated analysts has arisen to buttress the argument—most prominently a young scholar at MIT named Charles Ferguson, who emerged as a vocal Cassandra of American microelectronics.[2]

A former consultant at both IBM and LSI Logic, Ferguson shows intimate knowledge of the computer establishment and the semiconductor industry. His case against American entrepreneurs rings with conviction and authority. His conclusion is stark. Echoing Grove, Sanders, and Charles Sporck, president of National Semiconductor, he declares that without urgent and decisive government action, American semiconductor producers cannot compete in global markets. U.S. merchant semiconductor companies will perish, and U.S. production will be reduced to a few specialized plants at IBM, AT&T, and other large enterprises that supply chips solely for their

Have the new startups really 'just ripped off the big firms'?

1. Sanders' complaint is echoed in Alex d'Arbeloff and Frederick Van Veen's HBR article, "Stop Taxing Away Big Companies' Talent," May-June 1986, p. 38.
2. His MIT thesis, *International Competition, Strategic Behavior, and Government Policy in Information Technology Industries*, encompasses his ideas.

own use. Since semiconductors form the heart of all advanced computer, telecom, and defense technologies, the failure of U.S. microelectronics will cripple the American economy and threaten the national defense.

With an eye cynical but shrewd, Ferguson describes the life cycle of a typical startup in America's information industry: It begins with a breakaway from a big company, often an entire team (including engineers, executives, and marketers) lured by prospects of wealth far beyond what their employer can provide. From Sand Hill Road they win an investment of up to $20 million. They lease equipment, office space, and sometimes even a plant. They hire additional engineers and workers from other companies.

With frenzied effort and commitment, they launch a new device—a CAD system, a nonvolatile memory, an application-specific chip, a hard disk drive—mostly based on work at their former employer and competitive with its product line. Weakened by their defection, the large company cannot respond quickly. The new device outperforms all others in the marketplace and sparks massive orders, which the startup cannot fill.

But "help" is on the way. A horde of imitators, also funded by venture capital (54 disk drive manufacturers, 47 gate-array companies, 25 workstation builders, and 11 nonvolatile-memory makers), rush into the market. The startup in question struggles to diversify and escape the stampede. Expenses soar. Mezzanine financing is needed from the venture funds. They are too deeply committed to deny it; the startup gets several millions more. The business teeters but clings to its lead. Finally, if all goes well, the company at last concocts a small quarterly profit and, with the hungry enthusiasm of venture capitalists, underwriters, lawyers, accountants, and consultants, proceeds to a public offering.

Nonetheless, there are already key defections. In part fueled by them, the competition—whether other startups or major players—has become more powerful. The new company dauntlessly forges ahead, expanding its manufacturing capabilities and its marketing effort. The total investment rises toward $200 million.

But the mood has decisively changed. The stock price is slumping and the initial frenzy of work has flagged. Disgruntled shareholders launch a class action suit, alleging they were misled by the prospectus and demanding several million in damages. (They, or at least their lawyers, will get it.) To add injury to insult, Hitachi and Toshiba are threatening to enter the market. The venture funds have found a new fashion; Wall Street is bored by semiconductors or CAD; the top engineers are restive as they gloomily watch their stock option values decline.

Almost overnight, the company begins to age, and the paper millionaires who run it find themselves suddenly poorer. They are deep in debt and the IRS is attacking some of their tax shelters, used years earlier. They are slipping behind on their deadlines for the next product generation, the mortgages on their Los Altos houses, even the next payments on their platinum credit cards.

Desperate for further funds, denied in the United States, they turn abroad. Another way of putting it is to say they decide to sell out. They resolve to put their company—chiefly the new technologies it

Many American startups have sold out to Asia when the crunch came. So what?

The old Silicon Valley stars are now telling the youngsters they can no longer jump and slam-dunk on Wall Street.

owns—on the market. In the last several years many American start-ups have indeed sold out to Asia when the going got tough.

The American system says, "So what." But Ferguson says this is disastrous. In selling where the buyers are, Japan or Korea, the entrepreneurs are not selling just their own assets; they are selling the public assets of America.

Embodied in the business are not only the owners' work and ingenuity but also the value of their experience at a large company, the value of the damage inflicted on it after they broke away, and the value of subsidized research conducted at U.S. universities. In addition, there is the value of the licenses, patents, standards, and architectures embodied in the product and a vantage point in the U.S. marketplace. Finally, there is the value of tax code subsidies favoring small and growing enterprises that can show rapidly rising capital gains, R&D expenditures, tax-loss carryforwards, and investment tax credits. And although large corporations exploit tax benefits more massively and resourcefully than small ones do, most of Ferguson's claims are plausible, if overwrought. The capital gains "subsidy," for example, is now a penalty in proportion to inflation.

In any case, the tax advantages of venture capital do somewhat inflate the costs of established companies of all sizes that have to bid for land, labor, equipment, and capital against the startups. Trained people become less valuable (if they learn anything special they may leave) and also more expensive (they can threaten to leave). While the entire industry must share the costs of the startup sector, according to Ferguson, the U.S. economy wins few compensating benefits.

Ferguson is not content merely to criticize U.S. entrepreneurs; he has a far larger argument to make. It is not the fault of the entrepreneurs that they betray their country and their industry. It is the fault of the crippling limits of laissez-faire economics. Personal optimization is suboptimal for the country and the industry. Entrepreneurial self-interest leads, as by an invisible hand, both to the wealth of persons and to the poverty of nations.

This was not always true, Ferguson acknowledges. There was a time when the players could jump and slam-dunk on Wall Street without hurting the industry. But regardless of historical successes, American entrepreneurialism now conflicts with the most profound and powerful trends in information technology. In the past, the semiconductor, computer, telecommunications, and defense industries could proceed separately, spearheaded by small enterprises. But with the rise of chip densities to millions of transistors, integrated circuits now embrace entire systems. Bringing together the once separate worlds of computers, factory automation, and telecommunications, these systems require technical, financial, and even political resources that small companies cannot muster.

According to Ferguson, these changes spring from a basic law of information technology. In design, assembly, training, testing, networking, or marketing, costs rise with complexity and complexity rises with the number of objects to be managed. For example, the number of connections between nodes of a network increases by the square of the number of nodes. This rule applies remorselessly, whether to the proliferation of transistors on high-density chips, of components in complex computer systems, of lines in software code, of terminals in a data processing network, or of human interaction on a factory floor. Complexity swamps all systems made of large numbers of simple components, such as the American semiconductor industry produced in its heyday.

Moreover, as Ferguson might add, the same law applies to semiconductor *companies*, which themselves comprise an industrial system of uncoordinated and narrow-based components. This system will suddenly be swamped by a tsunamic wave of complexity.

The only answer, Ferguson maintains, is hierarchy: competitive rules, modular interfaces, and industry standards imposed from the top. This theme is familiar to followers of design pioneers Carver Mead and Lynn Conway, as well as industry observers who have also urged top-down approaches as the answer to the problem of electronics design complexity. Ferguson, though, is not speaking merely of designing a chip or a computer but of designing an industry or even an economy. Modularity and hierarchy must be forced from the top. They require rules and standards to guide the producers of future modules and connectable systems. They require control by large corporations and governments.

The heavy cost of developing standards inflicts big penalties on the industry leader. It must make the technical effort to determine the standards and the political effort to impose them. These efforts expand markets and lower prices for the entire industry. But in a fragmented marketplace, the costs cannot be recovered. Unless government or oligopoly power disciplines the industry, the companies that pay for these standards and architectures become sitting ducks for rivals that can avoid these costs.

In information technology, Uncle Sam has been the sitting duck. Nearly all standards and architectures in hardware, software, and network interfaces have originated in the United States, largely with IBM and AT&T (or under their sponsorship). These standards collectively cost scores of billions of dollars to develop and propagate. But because of antitrust laws, lax enforcement of intellectual property rights, and MITI's prohibition of auctions for licenses in Japan, this huge endowment has become available at far below its cost. Between 1956 and 1978, when most of the key innovations arose, Japan is estimated to have paid some $9 billion for U.S. technologies that required—depending on assignment of costs—between $500 billion and $1 trillion to develop.

The real cost may have been even higher, however, because by setting critical design targets, standards shift the focus of competition from the invention of products to their manufacture on a global scale. Because manufacturing is itself a complex system, power again flows upward. A globally competitive plant for high-volume commodity production costs some $250 million. Requiring integration of an array of technologies—sophisticated computer controls and design systems, advanced magnetics and vacuum equipment, materials science and photonics, automation and robotics—manufacturing imposes huge economies of technical scope.

At the same time, whether in integrated circuits, integrated CPUs, networked terminals, computers on-line thousands of miles apart, or telecom networks around the globe, communications, rather than components, increasingly define the systems. Intercon-

Semiconductor companies will be swamped by a tsunamic wave of complexity.

nections dictate the structure of the solution. These constraints necessarily push the power out of small companies into companies large enough to define the entire system.

As Ferguson concludes, the technologically optimal form for the global information industry might well consist of IBM, AT&T, and a few companies in Japan. Oligopoly is optimal, not only for the competitive advantage of particular nations but also for the welfare of the world. Yet the United States remains afflicted with an extraordinarily fragmented information arena: a chaos of companies, architectures, operating systems, network protocols, semiconductor processes, design systems, and software languages, all controlled by entrepreneurs avid for personal wealth or by sophisticated employees poised to flee to the highest bidder, whether a venture capitalist or a foreign conglomerate. Except at IBM and possibly AT&T, American electronics defines or defends no larger interests.

And as Ferguson and the Silicon Valley patriarchs insist, the law of complexity pushes decisions ever higher up the hierarchy and dictates ever larger organizations. The system is sick, and chronic entrepreneurialism is the disease. The remedy, Ferguson, Reich, and others agree, is an onslaught of government subsidies and guidance favoring established businesses and counteracting the bias toward new companies.

In essence, these industrial policy scholars want the United States to copy Japan as it is popularly viewed – boasting a powerful combination of MITI and favored industries. But they fail to see that in every one of the manufacturing industries that the Japanese have dominated, they have generated far more companies and more intense domestic rivalry than the United States. The Japanese created, for example, at least four times as many companies in steel, autos, motorcycles, and consumer electronics, and six times as many companies in robotics as the United States. It was such established American oligopolies as GE and RCA, General Motors and Ford that succumbed to the more fragmented and entrepreneurial Japanese.

Indeed, the only key industries in which the United States launched appreciably more companies than Japan were computers and semiconductors. Despite Japan's early lead in transistor radios and in mass production of consumer chips, Uncle Sam still prevails in computer and semiconductor hardware and software. What needs to be explained is not Japan's success in microelectronics but America's success.

For the critics, the answer is the Pentagon, the initial big customer for computers and integrated circuits. But in fact, during the post-World War II decade when defense dominated technology and confiscatory U.S. tax rates stifled entrepreneurship, American manufacturers lost the lead to Japan in transistor mass production and to the Soviet Union in missiles. The semiconductor industry did not burst into its upward spiral until the 1960s, when tax rates were slashed and the military share of industry sales dropped some 80%.

The secret of the U.S. success was the very venture system that the critics condemn. It counteracted high capital costs by efficiently targeting funds, released energies that were often stagnant in large companies, attracted a crucial flow of inventive immigrants, and fostered a wildfire diffusion of technology that compensated for the

The American strength is not in the law of complexity.

lack of national coordination. The American strength derives not from the law of complexity but from the law of the microcosm.

This law, discovered by Carver Mead of Cal Tech in 1968, says that complexity grows exponentially only beyond the chip. In the microcosm, on particular slivers of silicon, efficacy grows far faster than complexity. Therefore, power must move down, not up.

In volume, anything on a chip is cheap. But as you move out of the microcosm, prices rise exponentially. A connection on a chip costs a few millionths of a cent, while the cost of a lead from a plastic package is about a cent, a wire on a printed circuit board is ten cents, backplane links between boards are on the order of a dollar apiece, and links between computers, whether on copper cables or through fiber-optic threads or off satellites, cost between a few thousand and millions of dollars to make. As a result, efforts to centralize the overall system drastically reduce the efficiency of computing.

When Ferguson says that complexity increases by the square of the number of nodes, he actually makes a case not for centralized authority but for its impossibility. Beyond a certain point comes the combinatorial explosion: large software programs tend to break down faster than they can be repaired. For communications, connections may multiply. But coordination and command impose impossible burdens on centralized systems.

These principles remain obscure to many observers because they conflict with a powerful tendency in the economics of data storage and transfer. When John von Neumann invented the architecture still dominant in computers today, the industry operated in the macrocosm of electromechanics. In the macrocosm, active elements (switches) tended to be more expensive than storage devices. The data processors or switching elements were fragile, complex, and expensive vacuum tubes with tungsten filaments. The storage devices were either throwaway paper punch cards or magnetized plastic. Most important of all, interconnections were made of virtually costless copper wire.

Von Neumann's computer architecture reflected these relative costs of paper, plastic, wire, and complex tubes. He economized on vacuum tube switches for processing and was lavish with wires and storage. Made of different materials, moreover, these components had to be kept separate. Although communication by wire between them was easy, the interfaces among the separate functions – converting data from the processor to the punch card, tape, or magnetic device, and back again – required complex and expensive peripheral driver, sensor, controller, and converter systems.

As a fixed cost of a computer, such electromechanical peripherals enhanced the economies of scale for centralized processors, with large storage facilities attached. For example, the vacuum tube drivers, sense amplifiers, and other support for early magnetic core memories at IBM weighed several thousand pounds and were hundreds of times heavier than the memory core planes themselves. Since the cost of the peripherals was quite independent of the size of the memory, small amounts of storage cost hugely more per bit than large amounts.

All these conditions of a still essentially electromechanical computer industry favored the mystique of IBM and its von Neumann mainframes. A famous market survey estimated a total world de-

Efficacy in the microcosm grows far faster than complexity.

mand for about 50 computers. The machine sat on a pedestal in the central processing room, guarded by a credentialed guild of data processing gurus.

These conditions led experts to see the computer as a leviathan instrument of Big Brother and to prophesy the emergence of huge organizations to manage its powers. Predictions of a totalitarian 1984 gained credibility from the image of Big Blue in suits of gray. Gravitating to the hands of the state as well as other large bureaucracies, the computer would give the state new powers to manage the economy and manipulate individuals. Students in the late 1960s wore badges parodying the familiar punch card warning: "I am a human being. Do not spindle, fold, or mutilate." At Berkeley and other university campuses, Luddite rebellions broke out against this soulless new machine.

South in Pasadena, however, Carver Mead's exploration of the physics of solid-state computation had led him to completely contrary conclusions. He contended that there were no limits to the miniaturization of switches except spontaneous quantum tunneling. Features on a chip could be reduced from the 20-micron dimensions of the day all the way down to a quarter of a micron. In other words, Mead was predicting millions of transistors on one chip. When that happened, he reasoned, switches would be nearly free—merely an infinitesimal transistor on a silicon substrate. Working memory could be made of the same switches on the same material. Wire would become expensive, clogging the silicon surface with alien metals hard to lay down and prone to electromigration from heat or high currents. Leads to the outside world from the tiny chip would be a serious problem.

These developments capsized every key assumption of the von Neumann paradigm. It was prodigal with wire and remote memory, and focused all processing in one supremely fast central unit. It favored giant computers. In concept totally obsolete, it survives today, only slightly modified, as the dominant computer architecture.

In the new regime, however, the von Neumann components—storage, interconnect, and processor—all are made of the same materials by the same process. The entire computer has become increasingly solid state. Working memory is imprinted on silicon. Even the controllers to mass storage disk media are solid-state integrated circuits and monolithic analog-to-digital and digital-to-analog converters.

The macrocosm of electromechanics still dominates the computer industry.

Unlike the electromechanical peripherals of magnetic cores, these silicon peripherals cost radically less the greater the volume of production. In other words, the more computers built and sold, the cheaper the memory access. Controllers have plunged down the learning curve and now cost just a few dollars, an amount suitable for personal computing. The premium for separation of functions and for scale of operation and storage has given way to a still greater premium for integration and miniaturization in a world of widely distributed processing power.

Provided that complexity is concentrated on single chips rather than spread across massive networks, efficacy in the microcosm does indeed grow far faster than complexity. The power of the chip grows much faster than the power of a host processor running a vast system of many computer terminals. The power of the individual commanding a single workstation – or small network of specialized terminals – grows far faster than the power of an overall bureaucratic system. The power of entrepreneurs using distributed information technology grows far faster than the power of vast institutions attempting to bring information technology to heel.

Rather than pushing decisions up through the hierarchy, microelectronics pulls them remorselessly down to the individual. This is the law of the microcosm. This is the secret of the new American challenge in the global economy. The new law of the microcosm has emerged, leaving Orwell, von Neumann, and even Charles Ferguson in its wake. With the microprocessor and related chip technologies, the computing industry has replaced its previous economies of scale with new economies of microscale.

Nonetheless, the new rules are not well understood. In the last five years, IBM, Digital Equipment, Hewlett-Packard, and most of the remnants of the once awesome BUNCH (Burroughs, Univac, NCR, Control Data, and Honeywell), as well as the entire Japanese computer industry, time and time again have foundered unwittingly on these new microelectronic facts of life. While multibillion dollar industries emerged in networked workstations, led by Sun and Apollo, and in minisupercomputers, led by Convex, Alliant, N-Cube, Multiflow, and many others, the leading companies still upheld the von Neumann principle that computing should be centralized and serial rather than parallel and distributed. Even DEC allowed a $3 billion workstation industry to erupt in the midst of its market rather than give up its concept of the time-shared VAX-run network.

But the force of change has been inexorable. By 1987, measured in millions of instructions per second per dollar, the new Intel 386 microprocessor-based desktop computers were 90 times more cost effective than mainframes. Mainframes remained valuable for rapid and repeated disk access and transaction processing for banks and airlines. But small computers were barging in everywhere else. Distributed peer networks of specialized machines and servers were becoming ever more efficient than hierarchical networks run by mainframe or minicomputer hosts. In many special applications, like graphics and signal processing, embedded microprocessors outperform large computer systems. The computer on a chip costs only a few dollars and far excels the computer on a pedestal.

The law of the microcosm even invaded the inner sanctum of the von Neumann legacy: the organization of individual computers themselves. The need for change was manifest in the famous Cray supercomputer, still functioning powerfully in laboratories around the globe. Judging from its sleek surfaces and stunning gigaflop specifications (billions of floating point operations per second), the Cray appears to be high technology. But it hides the scandal of the "mat": remove the back panel and you will see a madman's pasta of tangled wires. The capacity of these wires – electrons can travel just nine inches a nanosecond – is the basic limit of the technology.

The Mead mandate to economize on wire while proliferating switches led inexorably to parallel architectures, in which computing jobs were distributed among increasingly large numbers of processors interconnected on single chips or boards and closely coupled to fast solid-state memories. Such machines sometimes outperformed von Neumann supercomputers in specialized applications.

Rather than pushing decisions up through the hierarchy, microelectronics pulls them down to the individual.

A symbolic victory came when HiTech, a parallel machine made of $100,000 worth of application-specific chips, challenged and generally outperformed the $15 million Cray Blitz supercomputer in the world chess championships for computers.

As circuits become denser, costs decline exponentially. The very physics of computing dictates that complexity and interconnections – and thus computational power – be pushed down from the system into single chips where they cost a few dollars and are available to entrepreneurs. This rule constrains the future of even IBM. Ralph Gomory, IBM's chief scientist, predicted in 1987 that within a decade the central processing units of supercomputers will have to be concentrated within a space of three cubic inches. The supercomputer core of the 1990s will be suitable for a laptop.

Following microcosmic principles in pursuing this goal, IBM last December joined the venture capitalists and sponsored a new company founded by Steve Chen, a computer designer who had split from Cray. Chen plans to use massive parallelism to achieve a hundredfold rise in supercomputer power.

Projecting conservatively from current trends, James Meindl, the magisterial former head of Stanford Electronics Laboratories, has predicted that by the year 2000 a billion components will be packed on a single chip. That will mean a drop in feature sizes to the one-quarter of a micron prophesied by Carver Mead in 1968. A billion transistors will offer the computing power of 20 Cray 2 CPUs on one chip, or 20 VAX minicomputers together with all their memory.

This kind of projection, however, assumes little change in the von Neumann architecture. That architecture will be abandoned for many purposes, yielding a far greater enhancement of computer power than even Meindl's estimates suggest. But there will be one key limit: stay on one chip or a small set of chips. As soon as you leave the microcosm, you run into dire problems. The physics dictate that when feature sizes drop, the voltages needed drop proportionately, the speed rises proportionately, the area needed for a computing element drops geometrically, and the switching energy and heat dissipation drop exponentially. Everything improves but the wires. Even for on-chip connections, the resistance and capacitance and delay rise in accordance with the resistance-capacitance product. For off-chip communications, the delay rises by a catastrophic exponential of the reduction in feature size.

Restriction of the computing power to one or a very few chips will enable the promise of the new technology to be fulfilled. With fiber-optic networks and even with superconducting interconnects (recently demonstrated at IBM and several other laboratories to outperform fiber-optic threads by a factor of 100), we can confidently expect mastery of such challenges as continuous speech recognition, interactive three-dimensional graphics, complex expert systems, and real-time modeling of many natural processes.

What we cannot expect is centralized command and control. Networks will function chiefly for communication of results; only at the cost of huge inefficiencies will they function for centralization and coordination of computing power. This constraint probably prohibits a centralized strategic defense system, for example, but permits very cheap and effective local networks of interceptors.

The computer on a chip outperforms the computer on a pedestal.

Above all, the law of the microcosm means that the computer will remain chiefly a personal appliance, not a governmental or bureaucratic apparatus. Integration will be downward onto the chip, not upward from the chip. Small companies, entrepreneurs, inventors, and creators will benefit greatly. But large, centralized organizations will tend to lose relative efficiency and power.

Predicting a continuing convergence of the computer world with the telecommunications industry, Ferguson implies that the oligopolistic tendencies of telecom will prevail in computers. But the flow of influence is in the other direction: the same law of the microcosm that is transforming the computer industry is already shaking the telephone network. Though afflicted by obtuse regulators fearful of monopoly, the telecom establishment is actually under serious attack from microelectronic entrepreneurs.

Once a pyramid controlled from the top, where the switching power was concentrated, the telephone system is becoming what Peter Huber of the Manhattan Institute calls a "geodesic network." Under the same pressure Carver Mead describes in the computer industry, the telecommunications world has undertaken a massive effort to use cheap switches to economize on wire. Packet switching systems, private branch exchanges, local area networks, smart buildings, and a variety of intelligent switching nodes all are ways of funneling increasing communications traffic onto ever fewer wires.

As Huber explains, the pyramidal structure of the Bell system was optimal only as long as switches were expensive and wires were cheap. When switches became far cheaper than wires, a horizontal ring emerged as the optimal network. By the end of 1987, the effects of this trend were increasingly evident. The public telephone network commanded some 115 million lines, while private branch exchanges held 30 million lines. But the public system was essentially stagnant, while PBXs were multiplying at a pace of nearly 20% a year. Moreover, increasingly equipped with circuit cards offering modem, facsimile, and even PBX powers, the 33 million personal computers in use in the United States can potentially function as telecom switches.

Personal computers are not terminals, in the usual sense, but seminals, sprouting an ever-expanding network of microcosmic devices. AT&T and the regional Bell companies will continue to play a central role in telecommunications (if they are released from archaic national and state webs of regulation). But the fastest growth will continue to occur on the entrepreneurial frontiers at the fringes of the network. And inverted by the powers of the microcosm, the fringes will increasingly become central as time passes.

One of the leaders of the assault on the Bell pyramid is Jerry Sanders of Advanced Micro Devices, who is focusing his company on providing chips for the telecom markets. Sanders once famously declared that semiconductors would be the "oil of the eighties." Ferguson, Reich, and others now fear or favor giant corporations conspiring to monopolize chip production as OPEC once cartelized oil production. They predict that by dominating advanced manufacturing technology and supplies, a few companies will gain the keys to the dominant technologies of the information age.

Unlike oil, however, which is a material extracted from sand, semiconductor circuitry is written on sand and its substance is

The computer will remain not a bureaucratic tool, but a personal appliance.

Semiconductor circuitry is written on sand and its substance is ideas.

ideas. The chip is a medium for ideas, much like a floppy disk, a CD-ROM (compact disk-read only memory), a 35-millimeter film, a phonograph record, or a videocassette. All these devices cost a few dollars to make in volume and all ultimately sell for the value of their contents – the images and ideas they bear. A memory chip sells for a couple of dollars; a microprocessor that costs about the same amount to make may sell for as much as an ounce of gold. A blank CD-ROM also costs a couple of dollars, but if it contains the operating system for a new IBM mainframe, Fujitsu may have to pay $700 million for it. In the microcosm, the message remains far more important than the medium.

To say that huge conglomerates will take over the world information industry because they have the most efficient chip factories or the purest silicon is like saying Canadians will dominate world literature because they have the tallest trees.

In appraising the predictions of the prophets of oligopoly, we have a powerful test. Most of the recent spate of predictions originated in 1985. Since then, we have seen three years of change and turmoil in the industry. Between 1982 and 1987, a record 97 semiconductor companies emerged. If the prophets were correct, these companies would be in trouble today. But the vast majority are already profitable, their total revenues now approach $2 billion, and their success ratio far exceeds the performance of the startups in the supposed heyday of the industry between 1966 and 1976. By most standards, the average productivity of the newcomers is far higher than the output of established companies.

If the doomsayers were correct, few of these companies could afford to build semiconductor factories. But in 1986 and 1987, some 200 minifabs were constructed for making leading-edge, custom semiconductors. Some of these facilities offer the most efficient, advanced submicron processes in the industry. Contrary to widespread contentions that the industry is growing ever more capital intensive, the efficiency of the new production gear far exceeds its incremental costs.

The appropriate measure of production in information technologies is not output of "chips" or even "computers." Chips double in capacity every two or three years and computers gain power at a similar pace, retarded only slightly by the slower advance of software. Nor is the best measure the total output of transistors; although this index is an improvement over unit sales of chips, it misses the advances in design. The appropriate standard is not output in dollars either, for the cost per unit is plummeting while the real value of the output soars. The correct measure is functionality or utility to the customer.

In delivering functions cheaply to the customer, the new semiconductor production gear every year advances decisively over its predecessors. For example, Chips & Technologies, founded in 1985, is the fastest growing company in the history of the industry. Its sales per employee are some $650,000, or four times the level of most established companies. Its product is a series of chip-sets for cloning IBM AT and 386-based computers with a small fraction of the number of chips used by IBM. This innovation allowed Tandy, PCs Limited, and other U.S. companies to regain dominant market share with clones of IBM standard computers. Together with another startup called Weitek (providing fast math coprocessors), Chips & Technologies also helped Compaq keep the lead against both IBM and the Japanese. Compaq is now a $1.2 billion business.

Chips & Technologies and Weitek have avoided direct fabrication of chips, farming out their production to Japanese and American companies that have excess fab space. But other startups, like Cypress, Performance Semiconductor, and Integrated Device Technology, have created some of the most advanced fabs in the industry. Lamond's Cypress—attacked by Sanders—has decisively swept by the $50 million barrier. Xicor has mastered a nonvolatile memory production process that has so far defied the best efforts of Intel and the Japanese. And Micron Technology, a 1980s startup nearly destroyed in the DRAM glut of 1985 and 1986, has made several key process innovations (reducing the size and number of layers on a DRAM to some 40% below most of its rivals) and maintains production costs below its Japanese competitors.

The first successful billion-component chip will be designed, simulated, and tested on a massively parallel desktop supercomputer that will yield functionality far beyond its cost. Those 20 Crays of computing power will make the chip incomparably more potent than current microprocessors that take scores of designers to create and are built in a $150 million factory. It will be manufactured on a laser direct-write system or an X-ray stepper that, dollar for dollar, will far outproduce its predecessors.

Doubtless all the business magazines will still be speaking of the incredible expense in building and equipping a semiconductor plant—the X-ray stepper, for instance, will cost three or four times what today's lithographic stepper costs. But in functional output per dollar of investment, the fab of the year 2000 will be immensely more efficient than the Goliath fab making DRAMs today. By the law of the microcosm, the industry will continue to become more productive in its use of capital, more intensive in its mastery of the promise of information technology.

Finally, if the doomsayers were correct, the United States would still be losing global market share in electronics. But since 1985, U.S. companies have been steadily gaining market share in most parts of the computer industry and more than holding their own in semiconductors. In mid-1987, the U.S. semiconductor open market (excluding IBM and other captive producers that consume a third of U.S. output) again exceeded the total Japanese market in size (the Japanese have no companies categorized as captive). A year of Japanese leadership in that index had led to many prophecies of doom for the U.S. merchant companies.

The drive to predict the demise of chronic entrepreneurialism continues strong in intellectual circles. Many critics of capitalism resent its defiance of academic or social standards of meritocracy. William Gates, the founder of Microsoft, left Harvard for good during his sophomore year. The system often gives economic dominance to people who came to our shores as immigrants with little knowledge of English, to all the nerds and wonks disdained at the senior prom or the Ivied cotillion. Some academics maintain a mind-set still haunted by the ghost of Marxism. But the entrepreneur remains the driving force of economic growth in all vibrant economies, including the U.S. economy, the most vibrant of all. ▽

Beyond entrepreneurialism to U.S. competitiveness

FROM THE PEOPLE WHO BROUGHT YOU VOODOO ECONOMICS

by CHARLES H. FERGUSON

Many economic writers—including some of the most outspoken in recent years—have argued for the superiority of small, entrepreneurial companies over large, established institutions in furthering U.S. competitiveness. They've argued that, given the efficiency of competitive markets, it is futile for government to intervene in industrial activities. Some claimed that recent U.S. business reverses, especially in manufacturing, represent a beneficial shift—from mass production for commodity markets toward higher value-added, specialized markets and services. The "spirit of enterprise," to use author George Gilder's nice phrase, guarantees that U.S. industry remains robust because the market's action is inherently healing.

The argument is highly appealing, but the facts do not sustain it. In the wake of voodoo economics, U.S. corporate executives must now defend themselves against an equally dangerous successor—voodoo competitive doctrine. In fact, this country faces serious problems that cannot be solved by the unaided

Editor's note: This article joins the debate begun in HBR by George Gilder's "The Revitalization of Everything: The Law of the Microcosm" (March-April 1988). Bound copies of both articles are available from HBR Reprints, Operations Dept., Boston, Mass. 02163. Tel. 617-495-6192. Fax 617-495-6985. Reprint number 88355.

Charles H. Ferguson, a former analyst at IBM and consultant to LSI Logic and Intel, is a research associate at the Center for Technology, Policy, and Industrial Development at the Massachusetts Institute of Technology.

efforts of individual entrepreneurs, however ingenious. Nor does the decline of vital U.S. industries—financial services, automobiles, steel, advanced electronics—reflect the immanent advantages of small companies over large companies. Rather it reflects the failure of the current terms of competition to provide established corporations the incentives and resources they need for long-term investment, growth, and competitiveness.

And is there anyone who can do that voodoo as well as Gilder himself, whose recent HBR article

> **Nimble, small companies can't survive against stable, concentrated, and protected industrial alliances.**

argues—with drama and wrong-headedness—that one of the country's most vital industries, the U.S. semiconductor industry, is flourishing?

Gilder contends that the U.S. semiconductor industry is vigorous because of the entrepreneurial energy of small design companies and "minifabs." He tells us that Japan's industry has succeeded by being even more entrepreneurial than America's. He argues that the rise of personal computers over mainframes and local PBXs over centralized switching both con-

Semiconductor Market Share Data

Shipments in Billions of Dollars

	1978	1979	1980	1981	1982	1983	1984	1985	1986
U.S.-Based	$ 4.78	$ 6.62	$ 8.44	$ 8.00	$ 8.03	$ 9.73	$14.00	$10.65	$11.38
Japan-Based	2.49	2.93	3.84	4.17	4.68	6.63	9.80	8.76	11.86
Europe-Based	1.41	1.65	1.62	1.54	1.35	1.41	2.10	2.07	2.86
All Others	0.23	0.30	0.32	0.36	0.10	0.14	0.20	0.18	0.25
World Market	8.91	11.49	14.22	14.07	14.16	17.91	26.10	21.66	26.35

Percent Share of World Market

	1978	1979	1980	1981	1982	1983	1984	1985	1986
United States	53.61%	57.55%	59.35%	56.86%	56.71%	54.33%	53.64%	49.15%	43.19%
Japan	27.94	25.49	27.00	29.64	33.05	37.02	37.55	40.46	45.01
Europe	15.86	14.36	11.39	10.95	9.53	7.87	8.05	9.56	10.85
All Others	2.59	2.60	2.25	2.56	0.71	0.78	0.77	0.83	0.95

Sources: 1978-1981: ICE Corporation; 1982-1986: Semiconductor Industry Association (SIA). All tables found in a book by Thomas R. Howell, Janet H. MacLaughlin, William A. Noellert, and Alan W. Wolff, *The Microelectronics Race* (Boulder, Colo., and London, England: Westview Press, Inc., 1988). Reprinted with permission.

Note: ICE data adjusted by (1) deleting estimate for U.S. integrated circuit captive production, and (2) adjusting 1978 and 1979 data for "all others" to exclude Council of Mutual Economic Aid estimates.

tributes to and exemplifies a large-scale technological shift that favors industrial fragmentation. Thus the proper way to keep U.S. industry competitive is to keep the entrepreneurial impulse strong—and, at all cost, to avoid government intervention. In my view—but not only mine—these claims represent a serious case of wishful thinking.

The United States is now a worldwide net importer of high-technology products. It was a $27 billion net exporter in 1981.[1] To Japan, the United States is a net exporter of soybeans, wheat, corn, lumber, and aircraft; the United States, in contrast, is a net importer from Japan of computers, robots, advanced materials, numerically controlled machine tools, telecommunications equipment, consumer electronics—and semiconductors, amounting to more than $500 million a year. A wide spectrum of evidence, ranging from world market-shares to patent statistics, suggests a fundamental technological decline.

Moreover, some of America's most successful industries, like the aircraft and chemical industries, owe their vitality to the strength and foresight of a few large companies. High-technology industries appear to require increasingly capital-intensive cost structures dominated by R&D, computer networks,

1. See William Finan et al., *The U.S. Trade Position in High Technology: 1980-1986*, a report prepared for the Joint Economic Committee of Congress, 1986.
2. See Gordon E. Forward, "Wide-Open Management at Chaparral Steel," HBR May-June 1986, p. 96.

highly flexible production systems, and worldwide organizations for marketing and customer support. Indeed, patterns of industrial conduct suggest that large companies usually lead technology-intensive sectors and will even more frequently dominate the mature global markets of established sectors.

Consider the U.S. integrated steel industry. For decades it displayed behavior normally associated with cartels, extreme inefficiency, inertia in adoption of technological innovations, and it was dogged by labor-management friction. It was eventually defeated by foreign industries (first in Japan, more recently in Korea and elsewhere) and also by the rise of entrepreneurial U.S. minimills that used a low initial-cost technology based on scrap and electric arc furnaces.[2] But the growth of minimills is limited technologically (to markets insensitive to scrap impurities) and also by financial and institutional constraints. The growth of minimills has not even come close to compensating for the decline of the integrated industry, and the United States remains a net importer.

The Japanese and Korean steel industries, in contrast, are concentrated, strategically coordinated, government-protected oligopolies. They are dominated by a few large producers linked to even larger industrial groups. Average integrated mill capacity is much higher than in even the largest U.S. facilities, and the minimill sector is entirely absent; these large, coordinated, and protected producers are efficient, technologically progressive, and flexible.

Most Korean manufacturing, moreover, is controlled by four huge industrial groups (Hyundai, Samsung, Daewoo, and Goldstar). The Japanese financial services industries, now beginning to penetrate U.S. securities and banking markets, are far more concentrated than America's and also far more protected and regulated. The world's seven largest banks are all Japanese; in 1987, the five largest U.S. banks had average assets of $88 billion, while Japan's seventh largest, the Industrial Bank of Japan, had assets of $161 billion. In 1982, the Japanese commercial banking sector contained 86 companies versus 182 for Germany and 14,960 for the United States. The Japanese nonresidential construction industry, which now holds about 4% of the U.S. market, is yet another government-protected oligopoly dominated by large companies like Shimizu, Kajima, and Ohbayashi. I will show that the Japanese semiconductor, computer, and telecommunications equipment sectors are, if anything, even more concentrated.

Thus we have a puzzling situation. Japanese, Korean, and even German competitors seem not to share America's passion for fragmentation and entrepreneurial zeal. U.S. industry falls victim not to nimble, small companies but to huge, industrial complexes embedded in stable, strategically coordinated alliances often supported by protectionist governments—exactly by the kind of political and economic structures that, according to the free-market entrepreneurship argument, give rise to stagnant cartels.

Since 1980, the U.S. semiconductor industry's share of the world market has declined from 60% to 40%, while Japan's share has nearly doubled to almost 50%. This is no cyclical aberration. For more than a decade, the Japanese industry has systematically imported U.S. technology, invested enormous resources into mastering it, and then grown more quickly than America's. Between 1974 and 1984, U.S. semiconductor production grew an average of 14% annually, while Japanese production grew 21% annually. And in complementary metal oxide semiconductor (CMOS) integrated circuits, an advanced technology that will soon dominate the industry, Japanese production grew 63% annually, versus 32% for the U.S. industry.[3]

Japan thus became a net exporter of semiconductors by 1980, while the United States is now a large net importer, even of design-intensive products like microprocessors. In the industry recession of 1985,

the U.S. industry's revenues declined more than Japan's; 60,000 workers were laid off, and U.S. companies lost over $1 billion. Six of the world's ten largest semiconductor producers are now Japanese; two were Japanese a decade ago. The U.S. semiconductor capital equipment industry has suffered correspondingly, while Japanese capital equipment producers have tripled their world market share to 40% in the last decade.

Finally, the Japanese industry has surpassed the United States in manufacturing technology, in critical areas of capital equipment, in some categories of device design, and in emerging process technologies like gallium arsenide. In several important areas no viable U.S. producers remain, so U.S. buyers must depend on Japanese suppliers who are often also their direct competitors (a point to which I shall return).

Of 25 microelectronics technologies surveyed by the Defense Science Board in 1987, the United States led in only three and was gaining in only one.[4] More than 40% of the papers accepted for the Institute of Electrical and Electronics Engineers Solid State Circuits Conference now come from Japan.[5] And, according to the National Science Foundation's 1985 report, "Science Indicators," Japan now accounts for twice as much of world integrated-circuit patenting activity as the United States, versus half the U.S. level ten years ago. A senior executive at a major U.S.

Semiconductor Market Share Trends

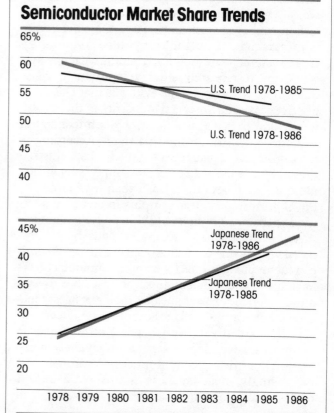

3. Dataquest Inc., Semiconductor Industry Service, 1986.
4. See the *Augustine Report* of the Defense Science Board Task Force on Foreign Semiconductor Dependency, 1987.
5. Damien Saccocio, "Publish or Perish?" unpublished manuscript, MIT Department of Political Science, 1986.

computer manufacturer told me in 1987 that, by contrast, U.S. semiconductor producers represent only 4% of his company's memory supply but 25% of its quality problems.

Most experts believe that without deep changes in both industry behavior and government policy, U.S. microelectronics will be reduced to permanent, deci-

Six of the world's ten largest semiconductor producers are now Japanese.

sive inferiority within ten years. Already we find that only one U.S. company (IBM, that well-known entrepreneurial company) is mass-producing one-megabit memories, while at least four Japanese companies are doing so. In several advanced technologies (X-ray lithography, advanced packaging, gallium arsenide, 3-D devices), IBM and AT&T are the only U.S. companies with world-class R&D efforts as opposed to at least half a dozen major Japanese producers. And in some areas, even IBM is falling behind. World-class semiconductor technology now requires enormous investment; rejuvenating U.S. industry will cost billions of dollars.

Of course, further U.S. decline will ultimately prove even more expensive. By the year 2000, the world semiconductor market alone will exceed $100 billion; and even more important, microelectronics is increasingly critical to computers, communications systems, automobiles, aircraft, weapons systems, and to research and development in many fields. Indeed, there is some evidence that U.S. competitiveness in downstream industries is already suffering, and that the decline of U.S. semiconductor technology contributes to this trend. According to the Commerce Department's annual "U.S. Industrial Outlook," the United States now imports $4 billion more in computers from Japan than it exports, and the U.S. worldwide trade surplus in computers has declined from $7 billion in 1981 to $3 billion now.

And because Japan's computer industry is dominated by the same companies that dominate its semiconductor production, U.S. computer manufacturers have become dependent, in some cases heavily so, on semiconductors supplied by their strongest Japanese competitors. All U.S. computer producers except IBM are already very dependent on Japanese memories; several now depend on Japanese competitors for critical central processor components. Increasingly, these Japanese companies use their newest technology internally before marketing it to competitors.

Thus as the U.S. decline continues, U.S. computer producers are being forced to choose between inferior technology and subordination to Japanese companies. A growing number of U.S. and European companies (including Honeywell, Amdahl, National Advanced Systems, BASF, ICL, and Siemens), seeing the handwriting on the wall, are turning themselves into distributors of Japanese computers, and the Japanese computer industry's share of the world market has doubled to 20% in the past decade.

As for Gilder's elitist "doomsayers," these include a wide number of university researchers and senior personnel of my acquaintance in the U.S. Defense Department, the CIA, the National Security Agency, the National Science Foundation, and most major U.S. semiconductor, computer, and electronic capital equipment producers. My conclusion, after meetings with groups in the U.S. Defense Science Board, the White House Science Council, and others, is that only economists moved by the invisible hand have failed to apprehend the problem.

All of which brings us to Gilder's "law of the microcosm." This seems to have two components. First, the increasing use of computers, advanced information systems, and microelectronics-based products leads to declining costs and a rise in the productivity of capital equipment. Second, important technology trends—like increasing system complexity and interconnection costs—force a decentralization of information processing and favor proliferation of small systems over massive, centralized processors. Complexity is increasingly embedded in the chip, obviating the need for a big and complex organization.

But improving productivity and widening use of personal systems do not imply that, on balance, technology trends favor small, entrepreneurial companies or fragmented industry structures. Personal computing does, of course, lower the initial cost of obtaining systems technology. As small computers, flexible manufacturing systems, and electronic control systems get better and cheaper, the barriers to entry in certain industries do seem to be falling, for example in sectors based on machining. But the reason that powerful personal computers (and PBXs, and many other things as well) are becoming inexpensive is that semiconductors, personal computers, and most supporting software are mass-produced, mass-market goods. The supplying industries have huge initial and fixed costs—which is precisely why they have low unit-production costs.

Indeed, since the information technology sector continues to both grow and progress technologically, companies unable to sustain large, continuing expenditures for R&D and capital investment are unlikely to survive more than one or two product generations –which is precisely the problem that has plagued the U.S. semiconductor industry.

Granted, progress in information technology does continue to open market opportunities, some of which are seized by brilliant entrepreneurs and small companies. But these new companies either grow to become mass marketers or fall victim to irresistible forces. Hence, for instance, the personal computer industry is only a decade old, but already its initial fragmentation has given way to a concentrated structure in which three companies–IBM, NEC, and Apple–account for half of world production. Other large companies, particularly Japanese and Korean

> **Why do powerful computers get cheaper? Because huge corporations, not small ones, mass-produce them.**

industrial complexes, hold most of the remaining market. At most, U.S. entrepreneurs control one-fourth of the world market–even including Apple, which by most definitions is no longer a startup. In the context of global markets, then, U.S. entrepreneurs are of minor and declining importance.

Moreover, there are a few technology trends Gilder overlooks. One is the enormous demand, created by the rise of personal computing and flexible automation, for large-scale networking infrastructure and for systems architectures capable of accommodating them. Companies able to develop and manage such systems, and to establish their own protocols for the network as a whole, are favored over those that cannot. Moreover, the increasing power of digital communications networks favors global operations, and globalization generally requires large, capital-rich companies.

But perhaps most important for the semiconductor industry is the need of advanced microelectronics for phenomenally complex technologies and close coordination of capital equipment, semiconductor, and systems production. Development of submicron technology requires huge investment in fundamental technology and capital equipment. Concomitantly, the increasing complexity of circuits necessitates use of capital-intensive, computerized design systems.

The long-term viability of small-scale entrepreneurship in semiconductor production ended with the advent of Very Large Scale Integration (VLSI) in the late 1970s. In 1974, capital expenditures equaled

6% of revenue in both the Japanese and the U.S. semiconductor industries; by 1984, the Japanese industry's capital expenditures had risen to 28% of revenues, compared with 20% for the U.S. industry.[6] Several studies concluded that the major U.S. producers were seriously undercapitalized. During this period, minimum efficient plant scale escalated from perhaps $25 million to at least $200 million, and capital equipment costs rose steeply.

Developing each new generation of process technology costs about $100 million, and product design costs sometimes exceed $50 million. Dataquest Corporation statistics show that between 1980 and 1985, R&D spending by the five largest Japanese semiconductor producers averaged 16% of revenues versus 12% for the five largest U.S. producers.

Similar trends are evident in the computer industry as well. Once again, U.S. capital expenditures are increasing, but Japanese expenditures are growing faster. It now appears that the entire information technology sector is headed toward a single, wide technology base dominated by microelectronics, systems architecture, software, and flexible mass manufacturing. Cost structures will be dominated by the initial and fixed costs of R&D, capital investment, and marketing. Marginal and direct labor costs will decline to negligible levels. Hence, while U.S. startups may continue to colonize small, new markets, the overwhelming majority of semiconductor and computer markets will be dominated by diversified, vertically integrated companies with wide technology bases and global operations.

So much for trends that favor decentralization. Let's look at Japanese and U.S. industrial structures. That Gilder attributes Japanese success to competition among many entrepreneurial companies is extraordinary. As I implied earlier, the Japanese semiconductor industry is–like Japanese steel–a stable, concentrated, government-protected, vertically integrated oligopoly that built its success not on new companies and novel ideas but on imported U.S. technology and high-quality mass manufacturing. The United States prototyped and patented innovative technologies. Japanese companies then licensed, imitated, or sometimes stole them, ultimately overpowering smaller U.S. companies in maturing world markets.

Six companies–Hitachi, Fujitsu, NEC, Toshiba, Mitsubishi, and Matsushita–have consistently controlled 80% of Japanese semiconductor production. (They also account for 60% of Japanese semiconductor consumption.) Not counting unconsolidated af-

---

6. Dataquest Inc., Semiconductor Industry Service, 1985.

filiates, of which each company has many, the smallest of these companies now has annual revenues exceeding $15 billion. These same companies also control 80% of Japanese computer production, 80% of telecommunications equipment production, and about half of Japanese consumer electronics production. All have close linkages, including equity cross-ownership, with suppliers and affiliated industrial groups, banks, insurance companies, and trading houses. They have a long history of cooperation with MITI, Nippon Telephone & Telegraph (NTT), and each other. And though Gilder does not take up this point, they have an equally long history of infringements on the intellectual property rights of U.S. companies that often remain unpunished.

A Dataquest annual report shows that NEC is Japan's—now also the world's—largest open-market semiconductor producer, with semiconductor revenues of $2 billion and corporate revenues of $16 billion in 1986. Two-thirds of NEC's semiconductor production occurs in a single factory complex on Kyūshū; it does not resemble Gilder's minifabs. NEC's semiconductor operations are coordinated with its other businesses; NEC circuits are designed into its other electronic products, its semiconductor design systems use NEC mainframes and supercomputers, personnel are transferred between divisions, and NEC manufactures a number of semiconductor products exclusively for its own computers.

NEC entered the microprocessor market by licensing Intel's designs, then by designing Intel-compatible products, allegedly by illegal copying of Intel's microcode. Intel has sued, but NEC legal tactics have repeatedly delayed the trial; at one point NEC halted proceedings by charging that the judge was biased because he belonged to a small investment club that owned two shares of Intel stock worth $80! Meanwhile the NEC products continue to be marketed.

Like the other producers, NEC is embedded in Japan's industrial system through structures that stabilize the industry, insulate it from foreign penetration, and subsidize its long-term growth. At least one-third of NEC's equity and much of its debt is held by other companies in the Sumitomo group, which comprises 130 companies, including the world's third and sixteenth largest banks, a huge trading company, and two of Japan's largest insurance companies. Linkages unthinkable in the United States are routinely found in the Japanese industry. In 1986, for example, Sumitomo Bank and Sumitomo Life Insurance together held not only 12.1% of NEC (the major semiconductor producer in the Sumitomo group) but also 3.7% of Sharp and 9.2% of Matsu-

Capital Spending in U.S. vs. Japanese Semiconductor Companies
(in millions of dollars)

	Japanese Companies		U.S. Companies	
	Capital Spending	Percent of Sales	Capital Spending	Percent of Sales
1976	$ 238.6	21.3%	$ 306.0	9.0%
1977	179.4	14.1	413.4	10.6
1978	453.2	18.2	650.1	13.6
1979	656.3	22.4	887.1	13.4
1980	956.2	24.9	1,299.8	15.4
1981	1,046.7	25.1	1,424.0	17.8
1982	1,301.0	27.8	1,188.4	14.8
1983	2,234.3	33.7	1,323.3	13.6
1984	3,508.4	35.8	3,010.0	21.5
1985	2,960.9	33.8	1,789.2	16.8
1986	2,585.5	21.8	990.1	8.7

Sources: U.S. companies 1976-1986: SIA; Japanese companies 1976-1984: MITI as reported in *Japanese Semiconductor Industry Yearbook 1985*, and in *The Japanese Semiconductor Industry 1981-1982*, BA ASIA, Limited (1985-1986); ICE Corporation.

Note: Percentage levels based on local currency.

Methodology: R&D as a percent of sales taken from indicated sources. Absolute R&D spending derived from World Semiconductor Trade Statistics (WSTS) sales data, using percentage shown.

shita. (Matsushita, Japan's fifth largest semiconductor producer, is a diversified electronics firm with revenues of more than $35 billion.) In 1986, another financial institution, Dai-Ichi Mutual Life, held 2.9% of NEC, 2.8% of Hitachi, 4.9% of Toshiba, 2% of Mitsubishi, and 6% of Oki.[7]

These companies and their banks also hold equity in many electronic capital equipment, materials, and services companies. Fujitsu is Japan's fourth largest semiconductor producer, whose revenues of $15 billion derive primarily from sales of IBM compatible computers. (IBM has been litigating against Fujitsu since 1976 for copying of system software totaling several billion dollars.) Fujitsu also owns 22% of Advantest, one of Japan's two major producers of semiconductor test equipment.[8] The other major producer is Ando, which is 51% owned by NEC; together they account for 90% of Japanese semiconductor test equipment production. Fujitsu also owns 40% of Fanuc, a $2 billion company that is Japan's largest producer of industrial robots, and 46% of Amdahl, a $1.5 billion U.S. vendor of IBM compatible computers that markets Fujitsu machines.

7. *Japan Company Handbook* (Tokyo, Japan: Toyo Keizai Shinposha, Ltd., 1986).
8. Ibid.

Japanese producers and their major suppliers also send personnel to each others' plants, engage in cooperative R&D, and have close R&D and/or procurement relationships with NTT. These activities are furthered by government subsidies and coordinated with protectionist policies. They contribute to the closure of the domestic market, and allow the Japanese industry to behave cohesively in global competition. Until recently, for example, U.S. companies were essentially precluded from operating in Japan. In 1974, when U.S. industry still held technical superiority and dominated world markets, U.S. companies operated 45 factories in Europe but only 6 in Japan—despite the fact that Japan's market was already larger than Europe's. Both government policy and the Japanese economic system inhibited the formation of independent Japanese companies. No organized venture capital market existed, stringent controls limited public offerings by small companies, and Japanese employment practices sharply limited personnel mobility.

If this is entrepreneurship, then the Soviet Union is a democracy. Yet this combination of oligopoly, strategic coordination, and national protectionism did not impede Japanese industry. On the contrary, stability, long time-horizons, and low investment costs permitted Japanese producers to make long-term investments and to overpower and outmaneuver U.S. industry in strategic confrontations—whether in technology licensing, price competition, or Japanese market access.

By contrast, the U.S. semiconductor industry has displayed extreme entrepreneurialism. Half of U.S. semiconductor and related capital equipment production occurs in companies that did not even exist 25 years ago, and industry leadership rises and falls with technological generations. Only the two largest merchant (that is, open-market) producers, Texas Instruments and Motorola, have consistently remained

Big Japanese companies license—or steal—the intellectual property of little U.S. ones.

leaders in the semiconductor industry. Many others rose rapidly as young startups, only to collapse later on. Mostek's revenues rose from $210 million in 1981 to $467 million in 1984—only to decline to $125 million in 1985, when the company was sold to Thomson CSF. And in 1985, the U.S. industry's worst year in history, nearly 100 new semiconductor and capital equipment startups raised $300 million in venture capital.

R&D Spending in U.S. vs. Japanese Semiconductor Companies
(in millions of dollars)

	Japanese Companies		U.S. Companies	
	R&D Spending	Percent of Sales	R&D Spending	Percent of Sales
1976	$ 164.7	14.7%	$ 227.8	6.7%
1977	199.8	15.7	300.3	7.7
1978	375.9	15.1	384.3	8.0
1979	427.8	14.6	470.0	7.1
1980	483.8	12.6	624.6	7.4
1981	621.3	14.9	776.0	9.7
1982	725.4	15.5	875.3	10.9
1983	941.5	14.2	943.8	9.7
1984	1,078.0	11.0	1,414.0	10.1
1985	1,314.0	15.0	1,597.5	15.0
1986	N.A.	N.A.	1,581.8	13.9

Sources: U.S. companies 1976-1986: SIA; Japanese companies 1976-1984: MITI as reported in *Japanese Semiconductor Industry Yearbook 1985*; Japanese 1985 R&D% based on estimate from all electronics R&D spending. See Thomas M. Chesser, "The Electronics Industry Combats a Stronger Yen," *Smith Barney International*, September 8, 1986.

Note: Percentage levels based on local currency.

Methodology: R&D as a percent of sales taken from indicated sources. Absolute R&D spending derived from WSTS sales data, using percentage shown.

This fragmentation, instability, and entrepreneurialism are not signs of well-being. In fact, they are symptoms of the larger structural problems that afflict U.S. industry. In semiconductors, a combination of personnel mobility, ineffective intellectual property protection, risk aversion in large companies, and tax subsidies for the formation of new companies contribute to a fragmented, "chronically entrepreneurial" industry. U.S. semiconductor companies are unable to sustain the large, long-term investments required for continued U.S. competitiveness.

Companies avoid long-term R&D, personnel training, and long-term cooperative relationships because these are presumed, often correctly, to yield no benefit to the original investors. Economies of scale are not sufficiently developed. An elaborate infrastructure of small subcontractors has sprung up in Silicon Valley. Personnel turnover in the American merchant semiconductor industry has risen to 20% compared with less than 5% in IBM and Japanese corporations. Since few U.S. merchant producers invest in the future, successive generations of new technology-driven markets are naturally colonized by new entrepreneurs.

Thus the U.S. semiconductor industry's instability doomed it. Fragmentation discouraged badly needed coordinated action – to develop process technology and also to demand better public education and government support. Indeed, a high proportion of the social returns to semiconductor technology were consumed or wasted rather than reinvested.

In fact, the U.S. semiconductor industry often functions as a public service organization for its foreign competitors. Many companies have licensed technologies to the Japanese giants, disinvested, and exited. Then, downstream industries switched to Japanese suppliers while the U.S. semiconductor industry lobbied for protectionism. Only a deep crisis, in combination with IBM's remarkable efforts on behalf of Sematech – the industry's process technology consortium – produced the first signs of productive cooperation in U.S. microelectronics.

What can be done? We have to be clear about the forces that have acted to reduce the investment levels, time horizons, and strategic coordination of U.S. industry relative to Japanese competitors. Capital costs have been higher, and linkages between the financial and real sectors weaker, in the United States. Japan has graduated more than twice as many engineers per capita as the United States, and until recently, U.S. professional labor costs have been far higher than Japan's.

In industries heavily dependent on R&D, capital investment, systems infrastructure, and process engineering – i.e., all high technology industries – higher capital and skilled labor costs have substantially increased the hurdle rate for investments and made investors less patient. In entrepreneurial U.S. industries, these problems have been exacerbated by the need to pay risk premiums for capital and by the need to raise salaries in order to retain critical personnel.

Moreover, the U.S. government has consistently failed to enforce intellectual property rights, open access to Japanese markets, obtain reciprocal access to Japanese technology and education, or represent U.S. industries. Government inaction has reduced the appropriability of returns to investments, opened the way to large-scale intellectual property theft by Japanese firms, and made it more attractive for U.S. companies to sell licenses to Japanese companies rather than concentrate on developing new products or penetrating Japanese markets. The openness of the U.S. university system has tended to benefit entrepreneurs and foreign competitors. Finally, throughout the postwar period, the U.S. tax system has in varying degrees favored new ventures over established ones by its treatment of stock options, capital gains, R&D expenditures, and loss carryforwards.

There is a cautionary tale here. When U.S. industry could live off the accumulated superiority of its technology, it could temporarily avoid necessary investments in fundamental R&D. Now, however, it can neither avoid them nor afford them. The United

> **The U.S. semiconductor industry will doom itself without coordinated development of process technology.**

States can no longer assume that its technology leads the world or that its economic health is guaranteed. Only long-term collective action and large domestic investments – in education, in reforming government procurement and tax policies, in R&D and capital formation – will ensure that the United States participates fully in the information revolution.

Correspondingly, faith in the market must give way to a more sophisticated view of strategic behavior, of the incentive effects of government action, and of relationships among technology, management, and industry performance. The witch doctors have had their say. One hopes that more effective medicine can be developed and administered before the patient collapses.

Reprint 88304

In Question
Perspectives on business debates-in-progress.

Small business is: a) inherently dynamic, b) too small to survive, c) insignificant to manufacturing, d) none of the above.

Can Small Business Help Countries Compete?

by Robert Howard

Robert Howard is an associate editor of HBR, where he covers human resource management and industrial organization. His book Brave New Workplace *was published by Viking Penguin in 1985.*

For most of this century, it was a common sense of business that success came with size. Then came the 1980s, and this bit of managerial wisdom – like most others – was turned on its head. While bloated corporations were downsizing, small ones were proliferating. According to a much-publicized finding by MIT researcher David Birch, small companies of fewer than 100 employees were responsible for as many as eight out of ten new jobs. When many big companies were slow to respond to shifts in technology and markets, small companies were on the cutting edge of innovation – a trend symbolized by the high-tech startup in California's Silicon Valley and Boston's Route 128.

So what was once a truism – that big is necessarily better – has become the focus of a hotly contested debate. Depending on which side you're on, either small business is inherently dynamic, innovative, and entrepreneurial – in contrast to sluggish corporate bureaucracies – or small business is backward, isolated, starved for R&D, and doomed to extinction in the marketplace or acquisition by powerful global giants.

The problem with this debate is that its images of small and big business are static at a time when both are changing. Neither set of stereotypes is adequate to characterize the diversity and complexity of economic relationships in business today. The question remains: What is the place of small business in a global economy? Put simply: *Can small business help countries compete?*

The books, reports, and other texts discussed here represent a major step forward in the argument about small business. Together, they serve to reframe the debate by making three important – and intriguingly counterintuitive – claims:

1. Small business is most important where it is least predominant.

The very term "small business" evokes images of the service or retail sectors, where small companies are most common. If the issue is international competitiveness, however, the place to look is manufacturing, which, at least for the time being, dominates international trade. Small companies make up a small portion of the U.S. manufacturing sector. But on the scales of international competition, the performance of a small tool-and-die manufacturer or metal-cutting shop weighs more heavily than that of the local shoe store, catering company, or 7-Eleven.

The roughly 355,000 U.S. manufacturers with fewer than 500 employees are responsible for approximately 46% of the value added in U.S. manufactured products. They make up what *TechnEcon*, the newsletter of Michigan's Industrial Technology Institute, calls the "base" of the manufacturing economy. To an important extent, the competitiveness of major U.S. manufacturing corporations depends on these small suppliers. Even highly integrated companies such as General Motors spend more than half of each sales dollar on purchases from suppliers. Cutting in half the in-house production costs at large companies would reduce overall product costs by around 15%. Doing the same at small and midsize companies would double that percentage.

2. The real issue isn't size; it's industrial organization.

According to the traditional view, large size brings efficiency at the price of a certain rigidity, and small size brings flexibility at the price of instability. But technological and economic developments are making possible a new kind of organization that combines the virtues of both. In this new organizational model, it's not the size of a company that matters so much as the quality of the business relationships tying companies to each other. The key unit of production is no longer the individual company but a decentralized network of companies. Sometimes, these networks consist of vertical links tying small suppliers to large final assemblers. In other cases, the links are horizontal–binding together a number of more or less equal small companies. In both cases, these networks make possible continual innovation through a delicate balance of competition and cooperation, demands and support.

Some examples described in the publications cited here:

□ Japan's supplier-group system, which ties large final assemblers to small suppliers in long-term relationships of collaboration.

□ Europe's industrial districts, where networks of highly specialized small companies combine state-of-the-art technology and skilled labor to produce high value-added products.

□ California's Silicon Valley, where a new generation of semiconductor companies has remained innovative and competitive by constructing complex alliances and cooperative relationships.

3. A country's capacity to build strong production networks constitutes a new kind of competitive advantage.

These new business relationships do not develop automatically. It takes managers willing to redefine how they interact with suppliers, customers, and competitors. And it requires government, trade associations, unions, and other social groups to create an institutional context–think of it as a new kind of infrastructure, as important as highways or a telecommunications system–in which networks can flourish. Countries that successfully establish such an infrastructure will have an advantage in the international marketplace that others will not.

TechnEcon: Research Newsletter of Automation and American Manufacturing
Ann Arbor, Michigan: Industrial Technology Institute
Published three times per year.

The Re-emergence of Small Enterprise: Industrial Restructuring in Industrialized Economies
edited by Werner Sengenberger, Gary Loveman, and Michael Piore
Geneva, Switzerland: International Labour Organization, 1990
312 pages.

"Skills Without a Place: The Reorganization of the Corporation and the Experience of Work"
by Charles Sabel
An address to the plenary session of the British Sociological Association
April 2, 1990.

Making Things Better: Competing in Manufacturing
A report of the Office of Technology Assessment, U.S. Congress
Washington, D.C.: Government Printing Office, 1990
244 pages.

The Machine That Changed the World
by James P. Womack, Daniel T. Jones, and Daniel Roos
New York: Rawson Associates, 1990
323 pages.

Flexible Manufacturing Networks: Cooperation for Competitiveness in a Global Economy
by C. Richard Hatch
Washington, D.C.: Corporation for Enterprise Development, 1988
27 pages.

"Regional Networks and the Resurgence of Silicon Valley"
by AnnaLee Saxenian
California Management Review 33, No. 1, Fall 1990.

Employers Large and Small
by Charles Brown, James Hamilton, and James Medoff
Cambridge: Harvard University Press, 1990
109 pages.

These three claims offer a fresh way to think about small business and the competitiveness debate. The relative lack in the United States of small-business networks and the infrastructure to support them goes a long way toward explaining why, with a few exceptions, the small-manufacturing sector in the United States lags behind that of other major industrial nations. Ironically, while many in the United States have been celebrating small busi-

> After declining for decades, small business's share of employment is growing.

ness, other countries–in particular, Japan and West Germany–have been using public policy to make small manufacturing a powerful asset of international competition.

The rediscovery of small business in the 1980s quite rightly emphasized the creative energies of individual entrepreneurs and the benefits of relatively unconstrained competition. Building a competitive small-business manufacturing sector in the 1990s may require something else again: an understanding of the economic benefits of cooperation and the importance of public policy to reshape business relationships to the ends of competitive success.

The Business Logic of Small-Scale Production

To understand the new role of small business in manufacturing, begin with a dramatic empirical finding: for most of this century, the size of the small-business sector (measured by the share of overall employment in companies with fewer than 100 employees) was shrinking throughout the industrialized world. But starting around 1970, that trend began to reverse. Small business's employment share began to grow slightly. When small units of large businesses are added to the calculation, the trend toward small-scale production is even more pronounced.

This is the central conclusion of *The Re-emergence of Small Enterprise*, a major international study of small business funded by the International Labour Organization (ILO). The study analyzes the role of small business and its share of employment in nine countries, including the United States, West Germany, and Japan. According to the volume's editors—economists Werner Sengenberger of the ILO, Gary Loveman of the Harvard Business School, and Michael Piore of MIT—growth in industries like services, where small companies are in the large majority, explains only part of the increase. The employment shift is also happening within specific sectors. For example, between 1980 and 1986, manufacturing employment at large U.S. companies of 500 employees or more declined by 10.8%—nearly 1.8 million jobs. During the same period, small manufacturers employing less than 100 workers added 326,000 jobs —an increase of 7.5%.

For Sengenberger, Loveman, and Piore, what's important about this trend is not the size of the shift—in most cases, it is small, a matter of a few percentage points. The fact that it is occurring so uniformly throughout the industrialized world—at more or less the same time and in many different countries with widely varying economic structures—suggests that something fundamental is going on. Employment growth in both small companies and small units of big companies reflects basic economic and technological changes. In the early part of this century, standardized mass markets and rigid mass-production technologies gave rise to the large, vertically integrated corporation. Today, increased demand for more specialized products, nonstop technological innovation, and cheaper and more flexible computer-based production technologies are inaugurating a decentralization of production.

In their 1984 book, *The Second Industrial Divide,* Piore and MIT political scientist Charles Sabel coined the term "flexible specialization" to describe this phenomenon. In a recent address to the British Sociological Association, Sabel described the new kind of organization that is emerging in the era of innovation-based flexible competition. His suggestive term for it is the "metacorporation"—a work organization "designed to be easily redesigned."

Managers hardly need to be reminded of the imperatives driving this trend. In a volatile business environment in which a company's competitive advantage can disappear almost overnight, the chief managerial challenge is to reduce the costs and—even more important—the time of product development. The faster a company can conceive, design, and bring new products to market, the more successfully it will incorporate innovations and shift rapidly from declining market segments to more prosperous ones.

The precondition of this competitive strategy is a radical increase in organizational flexibility. To speed the development process, companies must link the conception of a product more closely to its actual manufacture in a process of "simultaneous engineering," which blurs the hierarchical distinctions within a company. Traditional divisions between R&D, engineering, manufacturing, and sales give way to product-development teams.

But Sabel goes on to argue that this blurring of boundaries takes place not only inside the corporation but outside it as well in its relations with

CARTOON BY GEORGE DOLE

other companies. In the traditional mass-production organization, for example, supplier relations are at arm's length and adversarial. Customers maintain a large vendor base, frequently shift orders among vendors in a search for the cheapest price, and favor short-term contracts, rarely longer than a year. But to take advantage of the latest innovations and speed the design and production of components, relations with subcontractors must become much more collaborative. Large corporations jointly design new components with their suppliers, enter into joint ventures to exploit a new technology, or spin off technologies difficult to commercialize in-house to new startups. As a result, "the corporation becomes more a federation of companies than a single organizational entity," tied together in a system that Sabel terms "collaborative manufacturing."

What's more, the loosening of boundaries extends to the relationships between business and other social institutions. As decentralized collaborative manufacturing spreads, dense regional clusters of highly specialized small units flourish. Too small to do their own R&D, worker training, and the like, these small companies come to depend on outside institutions—universities and community colleges, trade associations, governments—to provide these services collectively. Thus the meta-corporation is woven into the social fabric far more tightly than the vertically integrated corporation of the past.

These trends create a new economic space for a particular kind of small company that is close to the market, technologically dynamic, and linked to other companies in complex networks of production. The ILO study identifies two types of networks: "kingdoms" tie small suppliers to a large corporate customer in a vertical supplier chain, under the strategic direction of the big company; "republics" join small, highly specialized companies to each other in a horizontal network where no one company dominates. These two models are not mutually exclusive. As befits the logic of flexibility,

they are highly fluid. The same company can shift from one to another over a period of time or even belong to both simultaneously.

What do these networks look like? Consider three examples: a classic kingdom, the Japanese supplier-group system; a classic republic, Europe's industrial districts; and a hybrid that seems to transcend both, second-generation semiconductor companies of Silicon Valley.

Kingdoms and Republics

The predominance of small business in the Japanese economy is well known. About 75% of manufacturing employment in Japan is in small and midsize companies, in contrast to about 35% in the United States. Less well known is the central role these small suppliers play in providing the flexibility and high quality that makes Japan's large corporations such formidable international competitors.

Both *Making Things Better*, a report of the U.S. Congress's Office of Technology Assessment (OTA), and *The Machine That Changed the World*, the product of a five-year study by the International Motor Vehicle Program at MIT, describe this role in admirable detail. In auto, electronics, and other key manufacturing industries in Japan, production is organized according to the supplier-group system—a network of large and small companies arranged in a pyramid. At the top, a large "parent" company is responsible for final assembly. It deals with a first tier of smaller companies who make major components and subassemblies. These first-tier suppliers then manage relations with a more numerous second tier of manufacturing specialists. These companies in turn work with a third and sometimes even fourth tier of smaller and smaller companies specializing in increasingly narrow tasks.

Unlike traditional customer-supplier relations in the United States, Japanese suppliers have long-term relationships with their customers, sometimes lasting over decades. According to one recent survey of Japanese subcontractors, 68% of the respondents had never

changed their parent, and 53% had been doing business with the same parent for 15 years or more. Even more important, Japanese suppliers and customers constantly share detailed information about production costs and techniques. And joint agreements about how to share savings from cost reductions and productivity improvements are made before a particular job is undertaken.

Most descriptions of the supplier-group system present it as little more than a way for powerful, big companies to take advantage of weaker, smaller ones—for example, by forcing suppliers to bear the costs of downturns. As both the OTA report and the MIT study rightly emphasize, this is much too simplistic a view.

Lead companies do put great pressure on their suppliers. They insist on high quality and continual price reductions. And since they typically

> Japanese companies both pressure and support their suppliers.

have more than one source for a particular component or part, they can punish a supplier who fails to meet these demands by cutting its share of sales in favor of a more compliant competitor. What's more, wages at subcontractors, especially in the lower tiers, are at least 25% below those at the lead companies, and workers do not enjoy the employment security that the core workers at big companies do. But lead companies also provide a great deal of support, primarily financial and technical, that allows the small suppliers to continually upgrade their technology and production techniques.

It is precisely this combination of competition and cooperation that makes for a responsive, high-quality, and increasingly dynamic industrial system. The supplier-group system allows the lead company to stay lean and focused. The responsibility for designing and manufacturing whole subassemblies is delegated to first-tier suppliers. Nissan, for example, has only one seating supplier for its new Infiniti Q45 model. General Motors, in many cases, is still dealing with 25 suppliers providing the 25 needed parts to the seat-building department of its assembly plants. The strong ties and frequent informal contacts between customers and

> **Nissan has one seating supplier for its new Infiniti Q45; GM has as many as 25.**

suppliers also make simultaneous engineering of new products easier. Japanese suppliers often take part in the joint engineering and analysis of new components up to two years before a new product is manufactured. In 1988, Nisshin Kogyo, a leading Japanese brake manufacturer, had a product-development team of seven engineers, two cost analysts, and a liaison person located at Honda's R&D center to work daily with Honda's development engineers on the design of a new car.

Small companies also benefit. They get reliable long-term markets. Even more important, the mix of competition and cooperation is a constant spur to innovation. In automobiles and electronics, parent companies lend state-of-the-art equipment to suppliers and sometimes even provide the financial help to buy it. They also assign engineers or technicians to teach small companies how to use new equipment or organize work more efficiently. In this way, new technologies cascade through the system. And as small companies become more adept at the use of these technologies, the flow of assistance and innovation begins to move up as well as down – spreading the risks of innovation throughout the system and creating a huge outside source of product and process improvements for the parent company.

But close ties between big and small companies are not the only

source of the competitiveness of Japan's small manufacturing companies. Government policies and aid have also been decisive. The OTA estimates that the Japanese government provides about *20 times* more financial aid to small business than the U.S. government does. In 1988 alone, low-cost direct loans to smaller companies from government financial institutions in Japan amounted to more than $27 billion – with loan guarantees providing an additional $56 billion.

The Japanese government also provides half the $470 million annual budget for a national system of 185 testing and research centers. For a small fee, companies can use equipment at the center that they can't afford to purchase on their own and consult staff engineers about special problems. This "dense, nationwide network of free, public technology extension services for small and medium-sized firms," argues the OTA, is a second crucial source of support for small Japanese companies.

In contrast to kingdoms, republics feature horizontal connections between specialty producers that work together to produce complete components and finished goods. Strategic direction is provided not by one big company but by a "broker" – usually a public institution or private-membership organization – that delivers the services and coordination individual companies cannot provide on their own.

The classic example of the republic model is the industrial districts of Europe. In Italy, West Germany, and Denmark, entire regions have developed thriving manufacturing sectors based on this network model. C. Richard Hatch's *Flexible Manufacturing Networks* is a good introduction to the phenomenon.

Consider, for example, the region of Emilia-Romagna in north central Italy. With a population of only 4 million, Emilia-Romagna has some 90,000 small manufacturing companies, the vast majority with 50 employees or less. These companies account for about 40% of the region's employment and span a variety of industries, including machine tools,

automatic machinery, motorcycles, automobiles, electronic controls, and apparel.

Although manufacturing businesses in Emilia-Romagna are tiny, through networks they can compete globally in state-of-the-art technology niches. Take the Modena-based robotics manufacturer FSM. With only 16 workers, it is at the center of a small network that produces globally competitive robotics for the diesel engine industry. FSM handles the systems design, assembly and testing, and global marketing. Meanwhile, five other local companies supply the electronic controls, machining, hydraulic components, welding, and fabrication. None of these companies has more than 20 employees. Only one big company is involved in the network: the German electronics giant Siemens provides the motor.

Like the Japanese supplier-group system, the horizontal networks of Emilia-Romagna maintain a creative tension between cooperation and competition. Small companies compete to join the most successful and most profitable networks. And

> **FSM is a globally competitive robotics manufacturer; it has only 16 employees.**

companies frequently belong to many different networks at the same time – for example, serving as suppliers to large companies even as they pursue joint development and production with other small partners. The republic structure also allows them to cope with rapid changes in technology and markets. According to Hatch, one reason FSM does not simply buy out its partners is that given the uncertainties of technological development in robotics, a certain measure of independence is preferable to integration.

SEVEN KEY PHRASES FOR SUCCESS IN SELLING

CARTOON BY H. MARTIN

Government assistance has been crucial to the development of the European industrial districts as well – although in a different way than in Japan. The networks in Emilia-Romagna are largely the creation of the regional government, in collaboration with entrepreneurs organized in trade associations and workers in unions. For example, the Emilia-Romagna government has helped fund ten applied R&D centers for networks throughout the region. One, known as CITER, does market forecasting, performs design research, and provides access to new technologies for some 600 small knitwear companies in the city of Carpi, the center of Emilia-Romagna's high-fashion knitwear industry. Through CITER, these companies have access to advanced technologies and global markets they could never afford to develop on their own. While CITER's government funding was temporary – today the organization subsists entirely on membership dues – the funding was a crucial catalyst in forming the network.

In both Japan and Italy, these new business relationships linking companies more closely to each other and to other social institutions have transformed what traditionally has been a relatively backward sector of the economy. Today Japanese small manufacturing companies increasingly keep pace with big ones in the purchase of advanced technology. As they improve their technological capability, some first-tier suppliers are able to take on more complex tasks, including the assembly of entire products, and pass on their previous tasks to second- and third-tier suppliers, allowing them to move up the supplier chain as well. And while, for the most part, wages in Japanese small manufacturing still lag behind those at big companies, the best small companies pay even more than the large corporations do.

In some cases, small companies are even breaking the exclusive bonds that have traditionally tied them to a single parent. For example, in the Tokyo industrial district of Ota-ku, famous for its thousands of innovative small factories and where some 95% of the roughly 9,000 plants have 30 or fewer employees, there are now about 1,000 companies with no strong links to major corporations. The government is encouraging such companies to form cooperative associations that replace the vertical ties to big companies with horizontal ties to other similar small companies. These networks of small companies work together on R&D and share technical, management, and marketing information. In this respect, at least, it would appear that some Japanese kingdoms are turning into republics.

In Emilia-Romagna, collaborative manufacturing has been an engine of economic development. In 1970, Emilia-Romagna was the fourth poorest of Italy's 21 regions, its industries buffeted by growing international competition. By 1985, it was the second wealthiest, and wage rates were 25% above the Italian average. In fact, some networks have become so successful that they have become the target of takeovers by large corporations. According to the OTA report, large companies are coming to play a more dominant role in some Italian industrial districts. In some cases, decentralized production continues, but under the growing financial and strategic control of locally dominant companies or outside corporations. If kingdoms can turn into republics, republics may also be turning into kingdoms.

And as a third example of a manufacturing network suggests, new hybrids are growing that seem to explode the distinction between kingdom and republic altogether.

Revisiting Silicon Valley

Silicon Valley's high-tech startups were the prime symbol of small-business dynamism in the 1980s—

that is, until the Valley's commodity semiconductor manufacturers ran into the wall of Japanese competition. According to an article by AnnaLee Saxenian in a recent issue of the *California Management Review*, a second generation of small semiconductor companies in Silicon Valley has so far avoided the mistakes of its forebears by creating a third version of the network model.

Companies like Cypress Semiconductor, Weitek, and Altera are small specialty chip designers and manufacturers. By focusing on short runs of high-performance components

> In Silicon Valley, small companies cooperate with big companies— without losing their room to maneuver.

and custom products targeted at niche markets, these companies are consistently able to stay at the forefront of the innovation process and introduce new products far more quickly than traditional semiconductor companies. They do so by establishing strong horizontal ties to each other—much like republics. Since 1979, new semiconductor startups in the region have forged more than 350 alliances with each other and with other companies. Most involve technology sharing, subcontracting of chip fabrication, or joint product development. Like kingdoms, the ties between these companies also extend to large corporations—both first-generation semiconductor manufacturers and computer systems makers. But in no sense do these big companies dominate the network. Indeed, in many respects, exactly the opposite is the case.

Take, for example, two small companies: Weitek designs high-performance chips for math-intensive operations. It has 230 employees and did $49 million in sales in 1989 with a net income of

about $7 million. Altera makes programmable logic devices. With 300 employees, it had around $60 million in sales and a net of $11 million.

Neither Weitek nor Altera has any chip-production facilities. Instead, they have formed strong cooperative relationships with a variety of small and large chip and computer systems manufacturers. For example, Altera has a $7.4 million equity stake in Cypress and has agreed to go as high as $15 million. In exchange, the company receives a guaranteed fraction of Cypress's output at cost plus, and early access to the company's next-generation manufacturing technology. Meanwhile, Cypress gets an infusion of cash, the opportunity to produce at capacity, and a right to Altera's state-of-the-art products. Weitek has formed similar tight relationships with suppliers and customers—most visibly, an agreement with systems maker Hewlett-Packard to manufacturer Weitek chips in HP's own state-of-the-art fabrication facility.

Weitek is a small company and HP a large one. But in no sense is HP Weitek's "parent." Even in their relationships with big corporations, the small Silicon Valley companies' technological expertise gives them far more room to maneuver than suppliers typically have. Part of the agreement is that the Weitek chips manufactured at HP can be sold to anyone—including HP competitors like Sun Microsystems. And in exchange for giving Texas Instruments a license to some of Altera's second-generation products, the company has won the right to use some of TI's manufacturing processes at other semiconductor manufacturers.

As these last examples suggest, cooperation among Silicon Valley semiconductor companies does not lead to the kind of tight integration that hinders innovation. Much like the Japanese supplier groups and European industrial districts, cooperation is always spiced by intense competition. Both customers and suppliers make an explicit effort to avoid dependence on any one company and to preserve their own autonomy. For example, most Silicon Valley companies prefer that no single customer account for more than 20% of a supplier's output.

The result is a system that allows companies to share the costs and the risks of innovation. Relationships leverage a company's presence in the marketplace, minimize fixed costs, and get products to market faster. According to Saxenian, product-introduction times have shrunk from more than two years to as little as nine months. The success of these companies, she writes, "demonstrates that neither scale nor vertical integration is necessary to survive in the increasingly capital-intensive semiconductor industry."

Government doesn't play the role in Silicon Valley that it does in either the Japanese or Italian examples. Indeed, Silicon Valley entrepreneurs are among the most antigovernment businesspeople around. And yet, Saxenian emphasizes the importance of regional institutions – Stanford University, trade associations, local business organizations, and specialized consulting, market research, PR, and venture capital firms – to the small semiconductor companies' success. These institutions are the glue that holds Valley networks together, providing a variety of services that allow companies to focus on their distinctive competence.

> # U.S. small manufacturing companies consistently lag in implementing new technologies.

Saxenian argues that the reason first-generation semiconductor companies like Advanced Micro Devices or National Semiconductor have had such problems competing in the global economy is that they abandoned this cooperative infrastructure. As these companies grew, they became increasingly integrated manufacturers of commodity products. And following traditional American mass production, their relationships with suppliers and customers became more adversarial.

The second-generation companies are a response to this organizational choice by the commodity producers. But to succeed in the long term, Saxenian argues, they will have to institutionalize their cooperation by creating their own version of the Italian service centers to supply the worker training, long-term R&D, and strategic planning that no one company can supply on its own.

The New Rules of Small-Business Competition

These three diverse examples offer some common lessons. Call them the new rules of small-business competition: Forge close relationships with customers, suppliers, and other partners. Maintain a creative tension between competition and cooperation. Focus on continual innovation. And create the kind of social infrastructure that both pushes and helps small companies to achieve these goals. How does U.S. small manufacturing stack up to these criteria? Despite the Silicon Valley case, not very well.

Certainly, the best U.S. manufacturers – companies like Motorola or Xerox come to mind – have made enormous strides in recent years toward improving the quality of their supplier networks. They have realized that, just as a company's human resources help define its distinctive core competence, so does the quality of its relationships with small suppliers. They have reduced the number of suppliers, lengthened contracts, collaborated more closely in product design, and redefined the customer-supplier relationship as a partnership. And, of course, many small companies cooperate informally with each other, even though they don't think of themselves as belonging to a formal network.

Still, the evidence marshaled in these studies suggests that many U.S. small manufacturing companies suffer from some weaknesses. They consistently lag far behind big companies in implementing the new technologies on which increased productivity depends. Just to give one example: in the largest survey to date on the rate at which U.S. companies are adopting new production

technologies (conducted by the U.S. Department of Commerce), large plants with more than 500 employees were as much as 16 times more likely to use certain technologies than small plants with fewer than 100 workers.

What's more, even as supplier relations are changing, the legacy of the traditional adversarial model looms large. In some cases, large companies use longer term relationships with suppliers merely as a way to shift costs and competition to smaller companies – in effect, exerting pressure without offering support. Often the only change has been to shift the adversarial relationship from the traditional criterion – low price – to new criteria such as quality or on-time delivery. And large customers still rarely influence small-company decisions to use new technologies – let alone provide the kind of financial and technical assistance that is common in Japan. The authors of *The Machine That Changed the World*, for example, argue that in the U.S. auto industry, "the reforms made to date have involved pushing the traditional mass-supply system to its limits under pressure, rather than fundamentally changing the way the system works."

But the greatest weakness of U.S. small manufacturing may not be in management but in politics. In the all-important area of small-business economic policy that shapes the institutional framework in which small companies operate, outdated assumptions hamper effective action.

To the degree that small businesses in this country have a political agenda, it is to exempt themselves from government regulations such as plant-closing legislation, mandated health benefits, or increases in the minimum wage. John Motley, chief lobbyist for the National Federation of Independent Business, recently expressed the typical view: "The vast majority of our members don't want anything from government except to be left alone."

Predictably, such attitudes have ensured that federal small-business policy is both minimal and misdirected. Aside from some small programs for businesses owned by minorities, women, and people with disabilities, the U.S. Small Business Administration makes no direct loans to small business. The United States has nothing to compare to Japan's nationwide network of technical assistance to small companies.

In the absence of coordinated federal action, some state governments are actively encouraging small-business economic development. Although Birch's claim that small business creates the vast majority of new jobs has been largely discredited, most of these programs still focus more on generating employment

> **In West Germany, government policies that don't favor small business actually help it to compete.**

than on improving the competitiveness of existing companies. By 1988, 43 states were providing some $700 million in startup financing to new small businesses. In contrast, total funding of state *and* federal programs for the technological modernization of already existing manufacturing companies was less than a tenth as much—roughly $40 million to $50 million per year.

The problem is that in the absence of a coherent small-business competitiveness policy, it is too easy for small companies to compete on low wages rather than high quality and productivity, thus dooming the small-manufacturing sector to second-class status. As economists Charles Brown, James Hamilton, and James Medoff point out in *Employers Large and Small*, not only do small companies not create anywhere near as many jobs as their advocates have

claimed, they also pay lower wages (by as much as 30%), provide fewer benefits, and in many cases offer poorer working conditions.

Given the new rules of global competition, this makes neither social nor economic sense. Consider, by contrast, the approach in West Germany, where small and midsize companies—known as the *Mittelständ*—combine state-of-the-art technology and skilled labor to produce high value-added products. Mittelständ businesses dominate the machinery and machine-tools sector, the most powerful in the German economy, and play a central role in others as well. In chemicals, for example, corporate giants BASF, Bayer, and Hoechst produce only one-quarter of the industry's output. Another 1,600 companies—most with fewer than 500 employees—account for the rest.

In West Germany, unlike the United States and Japan, there is almost no gap in wages and working conditions between Mittelständ companies and large corporations. The reason is the institutional factors that shape the environment in which the Mittelständ companies operate. Government policies place stringent demands on companies, then offer them effective support in meeting the demands. For example, German labor law mandates sector-wide collective bargaining and a high minimum wage. This substantially narrows the wage gap between small and large companies. At the same time, West Germany's excellent national vocational-education system ensures that small companies have access to highly skilled labor. The result is a system that forces small business to compete on high quality rather than low wages.

This and other foreign examples suggest a new direction for U.S. small business. Call it "public entrepreneurship," in which the most important "startups" are organizations

that help small manufacturing companies adjust to the new competitive environment.

Some interesting initiatives move in that direction:

☐ The Michigan Modernization Service is a state office that provides assistance with technology, marketing, and worker training to small manufacturers in Michigan. The state government has also helped fund the Industrial Technology Institute, an applied research and consulting organization for local companies. One of its programs works to strengthen the traditionally weak ties between auto-industry suppliers by identifying local companies with complementary production capacities and encouraging collaboration.

☐ The state of Pennsylvania's new Manufacturing Innovation Networks program (MAIN) provides money for small companies, trade associations, unions, and other groups engaged in cooperative efforts to solve shared business problems.

☐ The U.S. National Institute of Standards and Technologies (NIST) has established three regional national manufacturing technology centers. With an annual budget of $9 million, their mission is to work with small and midsize companies to improve their ability to assimilate new technologies. Through NIST programs, some companies are experimenting with the network models that have proved so successful in other countries.

Such initiatives are only a beginning, and it remains to be seen what combination of new business relationships and public support will best suit U.S. small manufacturing. But at least one thing is clear: small business can help countries compete only if countries create the conditions that make for a dynamic small-business sector. In the end, a society gets the kind of small business it wants. ⎔

Reprint 90604

Entrepreneurship reconsidered: the team as hero

Robert B. Reich

" 'Wake up there, youngster,' said a rough voice.

"Ragged Dick opened his eyes slowly and stared stupidly in the face of the speaker, but did not offer to get up.

" 'Wake up, you young vagabond!' said the man a little impatiently; 'I suppose you'd lay there all day, if I hadn't called you.' "

So begins the story of *Ragged Dick, or Street Life in New York*, Horatio Alger's first book – the first of 135 tales written in the late 1800s that together sold close to 20 million copies. Like all the books that followed, *Ragged Dick* told the story of a young man who, by pluck and luck, rises from his lowly station to earn a respectable job and the promise of a better life.

Nearly a century later, another best-selling American business story offered a different concept of heroism and a different description of the route to success. This story begins:

"All the way to the horizon in the last light, the sea was just degrees of gray, rolling and frothy on the surface. From the cockpit of a small white sloop – she was 35 feet long – the waves looked like hills coming up from behind, and most of the crew preferred not to glance at them....Running under shortened sails in front of the northeaster, the boat rocked one way, gave a thump, and then it rolled the other. The pots and pans in the galley clanged. A six-pack of beer, which someone had forgotten to stow away, slid back and forth across the cabin floor, over and over again. Sometime late that night, one of the crew raised a voice against the wind and asked, 'What are we trying to prove?' "

The book is Tracy Kidder's *The Soul of a New Machine*, a 1981 tale of how a team – a crew – of hardworking inventors built a computer by pooling their efforts. The opening scene is a metaphor for the team's treacherous journey.

Separated by 100 years, totally different in their explanations of what propels the American economy, these two stories symbolize the choice that Americans will face in the 1990s; each celebrates a fundamentally different version of American entrepreneurship. Which version we choose to embrace will help determine how quickly and how well the United States adapts to the challenge of global competition.

Which will we celebrate: individual heroes or teams?

Horatio Alger's notion of success is the traditional one: the familiar tale of triumphant individuals, of enterprising heroes who win riches and rewards through a combination of Dale Carnegie-esque self-improvement, Norman Vincent Peale-esque faith, Sylvester Stallone-esque assertiveness, and plain, old-fashioned good luck. Tracy Kidder's story, by contrast, teaches that economic success comes through the talent, energy, and commitment of a team – through *collective* entrepreneurship.

Stories like these do more than merely entertain or divert us. Like ancient myths that captured and contained an essential truth, they shape how we see and understand our lives, how we make sense of our experience. Stories can mobilize us to action and affect our behavior – more powerfully than simple and straightforward information ever can.

Robert B. Reich teaches political economy and management at the John F. Kennedy School of Government, Harvard University. His most recent book is Tales of a New America *(Times Books, 1987), which explores in greater depth the issues discussed in this article.*

To the extent that we continue to cele-brate the traditional myth of the entrepreneurial hero, we will slow the progress of change and adaptation that is essential to our economic success. If we are to compete effectively in today's world, we must begin to celebrate collective entrepreneurship, endeavors in which the whole of the effort is greater than the sum of individual contributions. We need to honor our teams more, our aggressive leaders and maverick geniuses less.

Heroes & drones

The older and still dominant American myth involves two kinds of actors: entrepreneurial heroes and industrial drones – the inspired and the perspired.

In this myth, entrepreneurial heroes personify freedom and creativity. They come up with the Big Ideas and build the organizations – the Big Machines – that turn them into reality. They take the initiative, come up with technological and organiza-tional innovations, devise new solutions to old prob-lems. They are the men and women who start vibrant new companies, turn around failing companies, and shake up staid ones. To all endeavors they apply daring and imagination.

The myth of the entrepreneurial hero is as old as America and has served us well in a number of ways. We like to see ourselves as born mavericks and fixers. Our entrepreneurial drive has long been our distinguishing trait. Generations of inventors and in-vestors have kept us on the technological frontier. In a world of naysayers and traditionalists, the American character has always stood out – cheerfully optimistic, willing to run risks, ready to try anything. During World War II, it was the rough-and-ready American GI who could fix the stalled jeep in Normandy while the French regiment only looked on.

Horatio Alger captured this spirit in hundreds of stories. With titles like *Bound to Rise*, *Luck and Pluck*, and *Sink or Swim*, they inspired mil-lions of readers with a gloriously simple message: in America you can go from rags to riches. The plots were essentially the same; like any successful entrepreneur, Alger knew when he was onto a good thing. A father-less, penniless boy – possessed of great determination, faith, and courage – seeks his fortune. All manner of villain tries to tempt him, divert him, or separate him from his small savings. But in the end, our hero pre-vails – not just through pluck; luck plays a part too – and by the end of the story he is launched on his way to fame and fortune.

At the turn of the century, Americans saw fiction and reality sometimes converging. Edward Harriman began as a $5-a-week office boy and came to head a mighty railroad empire. John D. Rockefeller rose from a clerk in a commission merchant's house to be-come one of the world's richest men. Andrew Carnegie started as a $1.20-a-week bobbin boy in a Pittsburgh cotton mill and became the nation's foremost steel magnate. In the early 1900s, when boys were still read-ing the Alger tales, Henry Ford made his fortune mass-producing the Model T, and in the process became both a national folk hero and a potential presidential candidate.

Alger's stories gave the country a noble ideal – a society in which imagination and effort summoned their just reward. The key virtue was self-reliance; the admirable man was the self-made man; the goal was to be your own boss. Andrew Carnegie ar-ticulated the prevailing view:

"Is any would-be businessman…content in forecasting his future, to figure himself as labouring all his life for a fixed salary? Not one, I am sure. In this you have the dividing line between business and non-business; the one is master and depends on profits, the other is servant and depends on salary."[1]

The entrepreneurial hero still captures the American imagination. Inspired by the words of his immigrant father, who told him, "You could be any-thing you want to be, if you wanted it bad enough and were willing to work for it," Lido Iacocca worked his way up to the presidency of Ford Motor Company, from which he was abruptly fired by Henry Ford II, only to go on to rescue Chrysler from bankruptcy, thumb his nose at Ford in a best-selling autobiography, renovate the Statue of Liberty, and gain mention as a possible presi-dential candidate.[2] Could Horatio Alger's heroes have done any better?

Peter Ueberroth, son of a traveling alu-minum salesman, worked his way through college, single-handedly built a $300 million business, went on to organize the 1984 Olympics, became *Time* maga-zine's Man of the Year and the commissioner of base-ball. Steven Jobs built his own computer company from scratch and became a multimillionaire before his thirtieth birthday. Stories of entrepreneurial heroism come from across the economy and across the country: professors who create whole new industries and be-come instant millionaires when their inventions go from the laboratory to the marketplace; youthful engi-

1 Andrew Carnegie,
The Business of Empire
(New York:
Doubleday, Page, 1902), p. 192.

2 See Lee Iacocca and William Novak,
Iacocca: An Autobiography
(New York:
Bantam Books, 1984).

3 George Gilder,
The Spirit of Enterprise
(New York:
Simon and Schuster, 1984), p. 213.

4 Ibid., p. 147.

neers who quit their jobs, strike out on their own, and strike it rich.

In the American economic mythology, these heroes occupy center stage: "Fighters, fanatics, men with a lust for contest, a gleam of creation, and a drive to justify their break from the mother company."[3] Prosperity for all depends on the entrepreneurial vision of a few rugged individuals.

If the entrepreneurial heroes hold center stage in this drama, the rest of the vast work force plays a supporting role—supporting and unheralded. Average workers in this myth are drones—cogs in the Big Machines, so many interchangeable parts, unable to perform without direction from above. They are put to work for their hands, not for their minds or imaginations. Their jobs typically appear by the dozens in the help-wanted sections of daily newspapers. Their routines are unvaried. They have little opportunity to use judgment or creativity. To the entrepreneurial hero belongs all the inspiration; the drones are governed by the rules and valued for their reliability and pliability.

Our Big Ideas travel quickly to foreign competitors.

These average workers are no villains—but they are certainly no heroes. Uninteresting and uninterested, goes the myth, they lack creative spark and entrepreneurial vision. These are, for example, the nameless and faceless workers who lined up for work in response to Henry Ford's visionary offer of a $5-per-day paycheck. At best, they put in a decent effort in executing the entrepreneurial hero's grand design. At worst, they demand more wages and benefits for less work, do the minimum expected of them, or function as bland bureaucrats mired in standard operating procedures.

The entrepreneurial hero and the worker drone together personify the mythic version of how the American economic system works. The system needs both types. But rewards and treatment for the two are as different as the roles themselves: the entrepreneurs should be rewarded with fame and fortune; drones should be disciplined through clear rules and punishments. Considering the overwhelming importance attached to the entrepreneur in this paradigm, the difference seems appropriate. For, as George Gilder has written, "All of us are dependent for our livelihood and progress not on a vast and predictable machine, but on the creativity and courage of the particular men who accept the risks which generate our riches."[4]

Why Horatio Alger can't help us anymore

There is just one fatal problem with this dominant myth: it is obsolete. The economy that it describes no longer exists. By clinging to the myth, we subscribe to an outmoded view of how to win economic success—a view that, on a number of counts, endangers our economic future:

☐ In today's global economy, the Big Ideas pioneered by American entrepreneurs travel quickly to foreign lands. In the hands of global competitors, these ideas can undergo continuous adaptation and improvement and reemerge as new Big Ideas or as a series of incrementally improved small ideas.

☐ The machines that American entrepreneurs have always set up so efficiently to execute their Big Ideas are equally footloose. Process technology moves around the globe to find the cheapest labor and the friendliest markets. As ideas migrate overseas, the economic and technological resources needed to implement the ideas migrate too.

☐ Workers in other parts of the world are apt to be cheaper or more productive—or both—than workers in the United States. Around the globe, millions of potential workers are ready to underbid American labor.

☐ Some competitor nations—Japan, in particular—have created relationships among engineers, managers, production workers, and marketing and sales people that do away with the old distinction between entrepreneurs and drones. The dynamic result is yet another basis for challenging American assumptions about what leads to competitive success.

Because of these global changes, the United States is now susceptible to competitive challenge on two grounds. First, by borrowing the Big Ideas and process technology that come from the United States and providing the hardworking, low-paid workers, developing nations can achieve competitive advantage. Second, by embracing collective entrepreneurship, the Japanese especially have found a different way to achieve competitive advantage while maintaining high real wages.

Americans continue to lead the world in breakthroughs and cutting-edge scientific discoveries. But the Big Ideas that start in this country now quickly travel abroad, where they not only get produced at high speed, at low cost, and with great efficiency, but also undergo continuous development and improvement. And all too often, American companies get bogged down somewhere between invention and production.

Several product histories make the point. Americans invented the solid-state transistor in 1947. Then in 1953, Western Electric licensed the technology to Sony for $25,000 — and the rest is history. A few years later, RCA licensed several Japanese companies to make color televisions — and that was the beginning of the end of color television production in the United States. Routine assembly of color televisions eventually shifted to Taiwan and Mexico. At the same time, Sony and other Japanese companies pushed the technology in new directions, continuously refining it into a stream of consumer products.

In 1968, Unimation licensed Kawasaki Heavy Industries to make industrial robots. The Japanese took the initial technology and kept moving it forward. The pattern has been the same for one Big Idea after another. Americans came up with the Big Ideas for videocassette recorders, basic oxygen furnaces, and continuous casters for making steel, microwave ovens, automobile stamping machines, computerized machine tools, integrated circuits. But these Big Ideas — and many, many others — quickly found their way into production in foreign countries: routine, standardized production in developing nations or continuous refinement and complex applications in Japan. Either way, the United States has lost ground.

Older industrial economies, like our own, have two options: they can try to match the low wages and discipline under which workers elsewhere in the world are willing to labor, or they can compete on the basis of how quickly and how well they transform ideas into incrementally better products. The second option is, in fact, the only one that offers the possibility of high real incomes in America. But here's the catch: a handful of lone entrepreneurs producing a few industry-making Big Ideas can't execute this second option. Innovation must become both continuous and collective. And that requires embracing a new ideal: collective entrepreneurship.

The new economic paradigm

If America is to win in the new global competition, we need to begin telling one another a new story in which companies compete by drawing on the talent and creativity of all their employees, not just a few maverick inventors and dynamic CEOs. Competitive advantage today comes from continuous, incremental innovation and refinement of a variety of ideas that spread throughout the organization. The entrepreneurial organization is both experience-based and decentralized, so that every advance builds on every pre-

"We've decided to tell individuals we treat them like institutions, and tell institutions we treat them like individuals."

vious advance, and everyone in the company has the opportunity and capacity to participate.

While this story represents a departure from tradition, it already exists, in fact, to a greater or lesser extent in every well-run American and Japanese corporation. The difference is that we don't recognize and celebrate this story — and the Japanese do.

Consider just a few of the evolutionary paths that collective entrepreneurship can take: vacuum-tube radios become transistorized radios, then stereo pocket radios audible through earphones, then compact discs and compact disc players, and then optical-disc computer memories. Color televisions evolve into digital televisions capable of showing several pictures simultaneously; videocassette recorders into camcorders. A single strand of technological evolution connects electronic sewing machines, electronic typewriters, and flexible electronic workstations. Basic steels give way to high-strength and corrosion-resistant steels, then to new materials composed of steel mixed with silicon and custom-made polymers. Basic chemicals evolve into high-performance ceramics, to single-crystal silicon and high-grade crystal glass. Copper wire gives way to copper cables, then to fiber-optic cables.

These patterns reveal no clear life cycles with beginnings, middles, and ends. Unlike Big Ideas that beget standardized commodities, these products undergo a continuous process of incremental change and adaptation. Workers at all levels add value not solely or even mostly by tending machines and carrying out routines, but by continuously discovering opportunities for improvement in product and process.

In this context, it makes no sense to speak of an "industry" like steel or automobiles or televisions or even banking. There are no clear borders around any of these clusters of goods or services. When products and processes are so protean, companies grow or decline not with the market for some specific good, but with the creative and adaptive capacity of their workers.

Workers in such organizations constantly reinvent the company; one idea leads to another. Producing the latest generation of automobiles involves making electronic circuits that govern fuel consumption and monitor engine performance; developments in these devices lead to improved sensing equipment and software for monitoring heartbeats and moisture in the air. Producing cars also involves making flexible robots for assembling parts and linking them by computer; steady improvements in these technologies, in turn, lead to expert production systems that can be applied anywhere. What is considered the "automobile industry" thus becomes a wide variety of technologies evolving toward all sorts of applications that flow from the same strand of technological development toward different markets.

In this paradigm, entrepreneurship isn't the sole province of the company's founder or its top managers. Rather, it is a capability and attitude that is diffused throughout the company. Experimentation and development go on all the time as the company searches for new ways to capture and build on the knowledge already accumulated by its workers.

Distinctions between innovation and production, between top managers and production workers blur. Because production is a continuous process of reinvention, entrepreneurial efforts are focused on many thousands of small ideas rather than on just a few big ones. And because valuable information and expertise are dispersed throughout the organization, top management does not solve problems; it creates an environment in which people can identify and solve problems themselves.

Most of the training for working in this fashion takes place on the job. Formal education may prepare people to absorb and integrate experience, but it does not supply the experience. No one can anticipate the precise skills that workers will need to succeed on the job when information processing, know-how, and creativity are the value added. Any job that could be fully prepared for in advance is, by definition, a job that could be exported to a low-wage country or programmed into robots and computers; a routine job is a job destined to disappear.

In collective entrepreneurship, individual skills are integrated into a group; this collective capacity to innovate becomes something greater than the sum of its parts. Over time, as group members work through various problems and approaches, they learn about each others' abilities. They learn how they can help one another perform better, what each can contribute to a particular project, how they can best take advantage of one another's experience. Each participant is constantly on the lookout for small adjustments that will speed and smooth the evolution of the whole. The net result of many such small-scale adaptations, effected throughout the organization, is to propel the enterprise forward.

You have to constantly reinvent the company.

Collective entrepreneurship thus entails close working relationships among people at all stages of the process. If customers' needs are to be recognized and met, designers and engineers must be familiar with sales and marketing. Salespeople must also have a complete understanding of the enterprise's capacity to design and deliver specialized products. The company's ability to adapt to new opportunities and capitalize on them depends on its capacity to share information and involve everyone in the organization in a systemwide search for ways to improve, adjust, adapt, and upgrade.

Collective entrepreneurship also entails a different organizational structure. Under the old paradigm, companies are organized into a series of hierarchical tiers so that supervisors at each level can make sure that subordinates act according to plan. It is a structure designed to control. But enterprises designed for continuous innovation and incremental improvement use a structure designed to spur innovation at all levels. Gaining insight into improvement of products and processes is more important than rigidly following rules. Coordination and communication replace command and control. Consequently, there are few middle-level managers and only modest differences in the status and income of senior managers and junior employees.

Simple accounting systems are no longer adequate or appropriate for monitoring and evaluating job performance: tasks are intertwined and interdependent, and the quality of work is often more important than the quantity of work. In a system where each worker depends on many others—and where the success of the company depends on all—the only appropriate measurement of accomplishment is a collective one. At the same time, the reward system reflects this new approach: profit sharing, gain sharing, and performance bonuses all demonstrate that the success of the company comes from the broadest contribution of all the company's employees, not just those at the top.

Finally, under collective entrepreneurship, workers do not fear technology and automation as a threat to their jobs. When workers add value through judgment and knowledge, computers become tools that expand their discretion. Computer-generated information can give workers rich feedback about their own efforts, how they affect others in the production process, and how the entire process can be improved. One of the key lessons to come out of the General Motors-Toyota joint venture in California is that the Japanese automaker does not rely on automation and technology to replace workers in the plant. In fact, human workers still occupy the most critical jobs – those where judgment and evaluation are essential. Instead, Toyota uses technology to allow workers to focus on those important tasks where choices have to be made. Under this approach, technology gives workers the chance to use their imagination and their insight on behalf of the company.

The team as hero

In 1986, one of America's largest and oldest enterprises announced that it was changing the way it assigned its personnel: the U.S. Army discarded a system that assigned soldiers to their units individually in favor of a system that keeps teams of soldiers together for their entire tours of duty. An Army spokesperson explained, "We discovered that individuals perform better when they are part of a stable group. They are more reliable. They also take responsibility for the success of the overall operation."

In one of its recent advertisements, BellSouth captures the new story. "BellSouth is not a bunch of individuals out for themselves," the ad proclaimed. "We're a team."

Collective entrepreneurship is already here. It shows up in the way our best run companies now organize their work, regard their workers, design their enterprises. Yet the old myth of the entrepreneurial hero remains powerful. Many Americans would prefer to think that Lee Iacocca single-handedly saved Chrysler from bankruptcy than to accept the real story: a large team of people with diverse backgrounds and interests joined together to rescue the ailing company.

Bookstores bulge with new volumes paying homage to American CEOs. It is a familiar story; it is an engaging story. And no doubt, when seen through the eyes of the CEO, it accurately portrays how that individual experienced the company's success. But what gets left out time after time are the experiences of the rest of the team – the men and women at every level of the company whose contributions to the company created the success that the CEO so eagerly claims. Where are the books that celebrate their stories?

Most people would rather think that Lee Iacocca saved Chrysler than know the truth.

You can also find inspirational management texts designed to tell top executives how to be kinder to employees, treat them with respect, listen to them, and make them feel appreciated. By reading these books, executives can learn how to search for excellence, create excellence, achieve excellence, or become impassioned about excellence – preferably within one minute. Managers are supposed to walk around, touch employees, get directly involved, effervesce with praise and encouragement, stage celebrations, and indulge in hoopla.

Some of this is sound; some of it is hogwash. But most of it, even the best, is superficial. Lacking any real context, unattached to any larger understanding of why relationships between managers and workers matter, the prescriptions often remain shallow and are treated as such. The effervescent executive is likely to be gone in a few years, many of the employees will be gone, and the owners may be different as well. Too often the company is assumed to be a collection of assets, available to the highest bidder. When times require it, employees will be sacked. Everybody responds accordingly. Underneath the veneer of participatory management, it is business as usual – and business as usual represents a threat to America's long-term capacity to compete.

If the United States is to compete effectively in the world in a way designed to enhance the real incomes of Americans, we must bring collective entrepreneurship to the forefront of the economy. That will require us to change our attitudes, to downplay the myth of the entrepreneurial hero, and to celebrate our creative teams.

First, we will need to look for and promote new kinds of stories. In modern-day America, stories of collective entrepreneurship typically appear in the sports pages of the daily newspaper; time after time, in accounts of winning efforts we learn that the team with the best blend of talent won – the team that emphasized teamwork—not the team with the best individual athlete. The cultural challenge is to move these stories from the sports page to the business page. We need to shift the limelight from maverick founders and shake-'em-up CEOs to groups of engineers, production workers, and marketers who successfully innovate new products and services. We need to look for opportunities to tell stories about American business from the perspective of all the workers who make up the team, rather than solely from the perspective of top managers. The stories are there—we need only change our focus, alter our frame of reference, in order to find them.

Second, we will need to understand that the most powerful stories get told, not in books and newspapers, but in the everyday world of work. Whether managers know it or not, every decision they make suggests a story to the rest of the enterprise. Decisions to award generous executive bonuses or to provide plush executive dining rooms and executive parking places tell the old story of entrepreneurial heroism. A decision to lay off 10% of the work force tells the old story of the drone worker. Several years ago, when General Motors reached agreement on a contract with the United Auto Workers that called for a new relationship based on cooperation and shared sacrifice, and then, on the same day, announced a new formula for generous executive bonuses, long-time union members simply nodded to themselves. The actions told the whole story. It is not enough to acknowledge the importance of collective entrepreneurship; clear and consistent signals must reinforce the new story.

Collective entrepreneurship represents the path toward an economic future that is promising for both managers and workers. For managers, this path means continually retraining employees for more complex tasks; automating in ways that cut routine tasks and enhance worker flexibility and creativity; diffusing responsibility for innovation; taking seriously labor's concern for job security; and giving workers a stake in improved productivity through profit-linked bonuses and stock plans.

For workers, this path means accepting flexible job classifications and work rules; agreeing to wage rates linked to profits and productivity improvements; and generally taking greater responsibility for the soundness and efficiency of the enterprise. This path also involves a closer and more permanent relationship with other parties that have a stake in the company's performance—suppliers, dealers, creditors, even the towns and cities in which the company resides.

Under collective entrepreneurship, all those associated with the company become partners in its future. The distinction between entrepreneurs and drones breaks down. Each member of the enterprise participates in its evolution. All have a commitment to the company's continued success. It is the one approach that can maintain and improve America's competitive performance—and America's standard of living—over the long haul. ▽

Reprint 87309

Our entrepreneurial economy

From the front lines of economic activity comes an unexpected bit of happy news: Americans are at last learning how to manage entrepreneurship

Peter F. Drucker

Wrenching structural changes in the nation's industrial base have largely obscured an important new reality: small, new businesses have formed the main driving force for the nation's economic growth. More important, these businesses are by no means limited to high-tech industries. In field after field, especially in the service sector, technological advances, demographic shifts, and the availability of capital have encouraged start-up ventures to challenge conventional wisdom and experiment with new approaches to the market. Out of his broad familiarity with historical patterns of business development, the author sees this burst of entrepreneurial activity to be distinctive in its systematic application of good management practice.

Mr. Drucker is Clarke Professor of Social Science and Management at the Claremont Graduate School and professor emeritus of management at the Graduate Business School of New York University. He is the widely respected author of numerous books and articles, including more than 20 contributions to HBR, and has for many years studied, written about, and consulted with entrepreneurial companies.

Illustrations by Robert Pryor.

It is no longer news that small and new businesses provided most of the 20-odd million new jobs generated from 1970 to 1980 by the American economy. What is not generally known, however, is that this trend has continued, has even accelerated, during the recent recession. Indeed, over the last three years, *Fortune* "500" companies have lost some three million jobs, but businesses less than ten years old have *added* at least 750,000 jobs and slightly more than a million new employees.

This trend is almost the exact opposite of the typical post-World War II pattern. Between 1950 and 1970, either big businesses or governments created three out of every four new domestic jobs. In any downturn, job losses centered in new and small enterprises. From 1950 to 1970, then, the growth dynamics of the American economy lay in established institutions, but since 1970 — and especially since 1979 — these dynamics have moved to the entrepreneurial sector.

Life after high tech

Contrary to "what everybody knows," high-tech activities — that is, computers, gene splicing, and so on — account for only a small portion of this entrepreneurial sector. True, of the *Inc.* "100" (the 100 fastest growing, publicly owned companies that are not less than 5 or more than 15 years old), one-quarter are computer-related. But the *Inc.* sample consists of publicly owned new companies and is hardly representative of the whole entrepreneurial group: it has a quite heavy bias in the direction of high tech. Even so, last year there were five restaurant chains in the group, two women's wear manufacturers, and several health care providers.

High-tech companies get more than their share of attention because they are fashionable and fairly easy to finance through public stock offerings. By contrast, such equally fast growing operations as leasing companies, specialized hand tool makers, barbershop chains, and providers of continuing education are far less glamorous and so, far less in the public eye. Somewhat more visible are the transportation services like Federal Express and Emery Air Freight, whose success has forced our stodgiest bureaucracy, the U.S. Post Office, into inaugurating Express Mail — its first real innovation since it was pushed, kicking and screaming, into parcel post all of 70 years ago.

Altogether, a good deal less than one-third of the new entrepreneurship is in high tech. The rest divides fairly evenly into what people usually mean when they say "services" (restaurants, money market funds, and the like) and so-called primary activities that create wealth-producing capacity (education and training, health care, and information). Nor is this flurry of entrepreneurship confined to the Sunbelt. To be sure, 20 of the *Inc.* "100" are in California, but the same number are in the supposedly stagnant Mid-Atlantic region: New York, New Jersey, and Pennsylvania. Minnesota has 7, Colorado 5.

Remember, too, that the *Inc.* "100" and similar lists contain only businesses, although the new entrepreneurship is by no means confined to businesses. It is going strong in what we are beginning to call the "Third Sector" — nonprofit but nongovernmental activities. While the government conducts one study after another of the crises in health care, the Third Sector is busily creating new health care institutions — some founded by hospitals, some in competition with them, but each designed to turn the crisis into an entrepreneurial opportunity. There are, for example, independent clinics for diagnosis and primary care; ambulatory surgical centers; centers for psychiatric diagnosis and treatment; and freestanding maternity "motels."

Public schools may be closing, but entrepreneurship flourishes in private nonprofit education. In the suburban area in which I live, a neighborhood baby-sitting cooperative, founded by a few mothers some six years ago, has grown into a school with 200 children. A "Christian" school established a few years ago by the local Baptists is taking over from the city of Claremont a 15-year-old junior high school, which has stood vacant for lack of pupils for the last five years. Continuing education of all kinds — executive management programs for mid-career managers and refresher courses for doctors, engineers, lawyers, and physical therapists — is growing again after a temporary setback in 1981 and 1982.

The most important area of entrepreneurship, however, may well be an emerging "Fourth Sector" of public-private partnerships, in which governmental units, usually municipalities, determine performance standards and contract out for services — like fire protection, garbage collection, and bus transportation — to private companies on the basis of competitive bids. The city of Lincoln, Nebraska has since 1975 pioneered in efforts to couple better service with lower costs. This is, of course, the same Lincoln, Nebraska where the Populists and William Jennings Bryan first led the way toward municipal ownership of public services a hundred years ago. In Minneapolis, Control Data Corporation is building innovative public-private partnerships in education and even in the management and rehabilitation of prisoners.

The entrepreneurial surge is not entirely confined to the United States. Britain now has a booming Unlisted Securities Market (comparable to our over-the-counter market), which allows young and growing companies to raise capital without the great expense of a stock market underwriting. In Japan the fastest growing company during the last ten years has not been a transistor maker or an automobile company but a retail chain that acquired licenses from the United States for 7-Eleven food stores and Denny's restaurants. Italy, too, has a thriving entrepreneurial sector, but it is largely part of the "gray" economy and so does not appear in the figures of tax collectors or government statisticians. In France, however, the Mitterrand government has snuffed out much entrepreneurial activity by its move toward centralized planning and government control of credit.

On balance, however, the wave of entrepreneurial activity is primarily an American phenomenon. With respect to the steel, automobile, and consumer electronics industries, America shares equally in the crisis that afflicts all developed countries, Japan included. But in entrepreneurship — in creating the different and the new — the United States is way out in front.

The sources of entrepreneurialism

By any reasonable measure, then, the entrepreneurial economy in America is a fact. But how can we explain its emergence? Four major developments suggest themselves:

1   The rapid evolution of knowledge and technology made it possible, even 15 years ago, to see that the last decades of the twentieth century would more closely resemble the last decades of the nineteenth (when a new major technology leading almost at once to the emergence of a new industry appeared

on average every 18 months) than they would the 50 years following World War I. And we can say with high confidence that we are no more than midway into this period of renewed technology-based entrepreneurship.

Within the next 15 years, for example, we will surely see the most profound changes in the way we teach and learn since the printed book was introduced 500 years ago. The computer has, of course, a highly visible part to play here, but the real agent for educational change is the new scientific knowledge we have gained since Wilhelm Wundt in Germany and William James in this country first asked, 100 years ago, "How do we learn?"

2   Demographic trends explain a good deal of what is happening in service industries. The rapid growth of restaurant chains is a response to the emergence of the two-earner family; entrepreneurial ventures in the continuing education of adults reflect the post-World War II emergence of very large numbers of well-schooled adults. Indeed, recent entrepreneurial ventures based primarily on demographics have proven more successful than those based on new scientific technologies.

3   During the last 15 years, the United States has developed a unique and fairly effective system for supplying venture capital. No longer must small businesses suffer from a lack of access to capital. Today, in fact, there may well be more venture capital available than ventures deserving investment.

This system, by and large, supplies financing only to enterprises that are well past their babyhood, have a good track record, and are capable of absorbing fairly large sums—say, $250,000 and up. But who nurtures the true start-up enterprise? And how? We really do not know, yet the money clearly is there. Nothing like this invisible, private, unorganized but effective funding mechanism existed 20 or 30 years ago. Even though the published figures on capital formation and investment give no clue, what must have happened—apparently only in the United States—is a massive shift of individual investors toward private, local start-up ventures.

4   Finally, and perhaps most important, American industry has begun to learn how to manage entrepreneurship. Even established companies like IBM have done remarkably well as entrepreneurs, as have several of the larger pharmaceutical companies and financial institutions. The vigor shown these past few years by our largest and most traditionbound private business, AT&T, is surely worthy of note. More extraordinary still is the entrepreneurial spirit and competence of the one industry that everyone, 30 years ago, had given up for dead—the American railroad.

One railroad company, CSX, which grew out of the merger of the old Chesapeake & Ohio with the equally old Atlantic Coast Line, is now integrating railroads, barge lines, pipelines, slurry lines, and trucking lines into the world's first total land-transportation system. Another railroad, the Southern, has single-handedly changed transportation pricing and rate-making. A third, Union Pacific, is leading in developing the natural resources along its lines and in its territory.

Developing managerial skill

Many of the new entrepreneurs have learned what almost none of their predecessors knew: why and how to manage. Indeed, the very businesses they are in often involve the application of systematic management.

In the past, for example, barbershops were rarely profitable; at most they provided a working-class wage to a few people, including the owner, who was a working barber himself. Not one of these shops could have afforded a paid "manager," nor were there any chains of shops under common ownership. Today, however, one of the fastest growing and most profitable new ventures is a chain of barbershops in the Southwest, in which each unit is run by a manager earning an above-average middle-class salary.

Neither of the two young men who conceived, designed, and now manage the chain had worked in a barbershop before. What they did was ask the simple question, "What are the key elements in the performance of a barbershop?" The answer: store location; full utilization of barbers and barber chairs (that is, minimum "downtime"); standardized, high-quality work done at scheduled times; and no waiting on the part of customers.

Accordingly, they studied the location of successful barbershops and found that what everybody in the trade "knew" was wrong. They also discovered that 30-second spots on local TV were their most effective selling tool. This discovery led to their decision to open simultaneously ten or more shops in one metropolitan area—a decision that enabled them to go immediately on local TV and to break even within three months instead of the customary three years. Finally, they developed a three-month training program for managers, applied routine time-and-motion analysis to barbering, standardized the seemingly endless diversity of hairstyles and haircuts, and reduced the time needed for a good haircut by almost 60%. They were, as a result, able to eliminate waiting time.

Indeed, their ads say, "If you don't sit in a barber chair within twelve and a half minutes after you enter our shop, your haircut is on us."

Consider, too, a quite different type of fast-growing chain in the Midwest: psychiatric centers. This venture grew out of an analysis of the demands on a psychiatric-psychological practice. To the surprise of the chain's founder, it turned out that the segmentation of demands, their frequency, their seriousness, and the resources needed to meet them were predictable within margins of plus or minus 7.5%.

By constructing a diagnostic profile for the initial examination, the founders made it possible for a paramedic, usually a social worker with little or no formal psychiatric training, to do new patients' workups and determine the appropriate referral: to a psychiatrist, to a clinical psychologist, to a family counselor, to a social worker, or whatever. The profile also helps identify the few true exceptions when a senior professional should examine a new patient immediately. A group of seniors, one of whom has actually seen each patient, then reviews these conclusions once a week.

The whole process represents an MBO program of textbook purity: each staff member, patient, and patient category (e.g., alcoholics) has objectives for both diagnosis and treatment, which are reviewed against actual results every three months. A follow-up service, headed up by a woman whose former experience was as a dealer-service representative for one of the major Japanese automobile companies, keeps in contact with former patients on a systematic schedule.

Birth of a profession

What these and other new "service" entrepreneurs are doing is to apply to their businesses the analysis that Frederick Taylor first applied 100 years ago to the tasks of manual workers and that Georges Doriot of the Harvard Business School applied 50 years ago to manufacturing. These systematic management practices also distinguish today's successful high-tech entrepreneurs. Entrepreneurs of an earlier generation neither had nor wanted to acquire the weight of accumulated knowledge on managing people, communications, team formation, marketing, cash flow, and even innovation itself.

The new entrepreneurs, however, tend to have management training and attend management seminars and programs in massive numbers. Many— maybe most—become entrepreneurs only after they develop managerial experience in large organizations. Indeed, management students—even those at the prestigious business schools—increasingly see entrepreneurship as their ultimate aim and as the career for which their education best prepares them. Although it has become fashionable to contrast a supposedly obsolete "managerial" era of the past with a triumphantly emerging "entrepreneurial" era, it makes better sense to see in this flowering of an entrepreneurial economy the triumph of systematic management.

But also, clearly something important has happened to fairly large numbers of young Americans—to their attitudes, their values, their aspirations. Where are all the "hedonists," the "status seekers," the "me-tooers," and the "conformists" of the recent past? They are not turning out as David Riesman in *The Lonely Crowd,* or William H. Whyte in *The Organization Man,* or even Charles Reich in *The Greening of America* predicted. Without doubt, the emergence of the entrepreneurial economy is as much a cultural and psychological, as it is an economic or technological, event.

Implications for policy

These developments argue quite strongly that most "scientific" diagnoses of the nation's present economic ills are highly suspect. We are, for example, very likely *not* to be, as Jay W. Forrester and his group at MIT claim we are, in a long-term Kondratieff trough, but in the first stages of a long-term Kondratieff expansion.[1]

The Russian Nikolai Kondratieff, one of the founders of mathematical economics, 60 years ago identified a 50-year business cycle based on the inherent logic of technology. Typically, in the last decades of one of these cycles, old and mature industries seem to do exceptionally well, earning record profits and providing record employment. Actually, they are already in decline, for what looks like record profits is in fact underinvestment and the distribution of no-longer-needed capital.

When fast decline becomes manifest, there follows a 20-year trough, a long period of stagnation, low profits, and unemployment. Although the next generation of technologies may already exist, those technologies do not yet absorb enough capital or generate enough employment to fuel the economic growth needed to initiate another period of expansion.

There is, however, an atypical Kondratieff cycle. Industries based on old and mature technol-

---

1 For an example,
   see Jay W. Forrester,
   "A Longer View of
   Current Economic Conditions,"
   Systems Dynamic Group

Working Paper No. D-3405
(Cambridge: MIT,
Sloan School Of Management,
March 24, 1983).

ogies do indeed quickly decline, as is the case today in all developed countries. But industries based on new technologies and market opportunities grow so rapidly that they generate the requisite investment demand and employment to produce overall economic growth. As Joseph Schumpeter and others have shown, the Kondratieff trough experienced by Great Britain and France in the late nineteenth century simply did not happen in the United States or Germany. True, old and mature industries did decline; overall, however, there was rapid economic growth, not stagnation. Industries based on new technologies and market opportunities grew fast enough to provide investment demand and employment.

The surest indication of such an atypical cycle—and precisely what we see about us today in the United States—is the emergence of entrepreneurs across a spectrum of activities that extends far beyond what at the time is considered high tech. It is, to be sure, a period of high risk, rapid change, considerable turbulence, and severe anxiety. Real dangers abound that have nothing to do with business cycles—the threat of war, for example, or of the collapse of raw material producers. Nevertheless, it is a period of great opportunity, of fast-growing employment in certain areas, and of rapid overall growth. And as Schumpeter understood, what distinguishes such an atypical cycle from a more conventional trough is not the play of abstract economic forces. It is entrepreneurial energy.

What role for government?

As another national election approaches, discussion grows ever more heated about what government should do during this time of industrial transition. One line of argument, best represented by Robert Reich's *The Next American Frontier*, presses for government *not* to support employment in the old smokestack industries but to hasten their automation while subsidizing their redundant blue-collar workers. The key assumption here—that we will more quickly regain industrial leadership the sooner we decrease blue-collar manual employment in traditional mass-production industries—has good historical precedent. During the past 40 years, the faster we reduced blue-collar manual employment on the land, the more regularly we boosted agricultural production.

Reich's advice to his fellow Democrats that they put more distance between themselves and their traditional base of support among blue-collar unions, though novel, is surely shrewd and well taken. But his complementary suggestion to call on big government for central planning of the new high technologies—even if good politics—is wretched economics and bound to fail.

This questionable suggestion assumes that high tech is by itself where most future economic growth will happen. It clearly is not. It comprises only a part of the arena for growth, and by no means the main part. The biggest areas with the largest high-paying employment opportunities are elsewhere: in health care, for instance, and in continuing education. Government planning centered on high-tech industries will inevitably miss major growth areas.

Furthermore, can government really plan for the unknown? Whether planning is done Russian-style, Japanese-style, or French-style, it aims, by definition, at "catching up"—that is, at doing what some other country has already done but doing it better, more quickly, and with fewer mistakes, false starts, and failures. Hence, efforts to plan for the unknown have always ended up, like French high-tech planning under Mitterrand in the last three years, in misallocation of resources, frustration, and bad guesses about true growth areas. No one can plan for what does not yet exist; all one can do is encourage or discourage it.

How then do we encourage entrepreneurial growth in the American economy? Of course, we must guard against sacrificing tomorrow on the altar of yesterday, as the British have done so consistently for the past 30 years. Of course, we must cushion the impact of falling employment in the old smokestack industries. Doing all this without hurting the capacity of new employers to generate new jobs is going to be excruciatingly difficult and will require political decisions as hard as any ever made in this country.

Beyond trying not to stunt this new economic growth, the only thing government can effectively do is to remove obstacles. Indeed, the greatest help government can provide the entrepreneurial economy is to assuage the most crippling ailment of infant enterprises: their chronic cash shortage. Exempting new enterprises for five to seven years from taxes on profits retained in the business would not cost the Treasury much. But it might well be the most effective industrial policy of all. ▽

Reprint 84105

READ THE FINE PRINT

REPRINTS
Telephone: 617-495-6192
Fax: 617-495-6985

Current and past articles
are available, as is an
annually updated index.
Discounts apply to
large-quantity purchases.

Please send orders to
HBR Reprints
Harvard Business School
Publishing Division
Boston, MA 02163.

HOW CAN *HARVARD BUSINESS REVIEW* ARTICLES WORK FOR YOU?

For years, we've printed a microscopically small notice on the editorial credits page of the *Harvard Business Review* alerting our readers to the availability of *HBR* articles.

Now we invite you to take a closer look at some of the many ways you can put this hard-working business tool to work for you.

IN THE CORPORATE CLASSROOM.

There's no more effective, or cost-effective, way to supplement your corporate training programs than in-depth, incisive *HBR* articles.

Affordable and accessible, it's no wonder hundreds of companies and consulting organizations use *HBR* articles as a centerpiece for management training.

IN-BOX INNOVATION.

Where do your company's movers and shakers get their big ideas? Many find the inspiration for innovation in the pages of *HBR*. They then share the wealth and spread the word by distributing *HBR* articles to company colleagues.

IN MARKETING AND SALES SUPPORT.

HBR articles are a substantive leave-behind to your sales calls. And they can add credibility to your direct mail campaigns. They demonstrate that your company is on the leading edge of business thinking.

CREATE CUSTOM ARTICLES.

If you want to pack even greater power in your punch, personalize *HBR* articles with your company's name or logo. And get the added benefit of putting your organization's name before your customers.

AND THERE ARE 500 MORE REASONS IN THE *HBR CATALOG.*

In all, the *Harvard Business Review Catalog* lists articles on over 500 different subjects. Plus, you'll find books and videos on subjects you need to know.

The catalog is yours for just $8.00. To order *HBR* articles or the *HBR Catalog* (No. 21019), call 617-495-6192. Please mention telephone order code 025A when placing your order. Or FAX us at 617-495-6985.

And start putting *HBR* articles to work for you.

**Harvard Business School
Publications**

Call 617-495-6192 to order the *HBR Catalog.*

(Prices and terms subject to change.)